# CBSE Term II 2022

# Social Science

## Class X

# CBSE Term II 2022

# Social Science

## Class X

Complete Theory Covering NCERT

Case Based Questions

Short/Long Answer Questions

3 Practice Papers with Explanations


*Authors*
Aditya Raj
Nandini Sharma



arihant
**ARIHANT PRAKASHAN** (School Division Series)

CBSE Term II
2022

**ARIHANT PRAKASHAN** (School Division Series)



卐 **Administrative & Production Offices**

**Regd. Office**
'Ramchhaya' 4577/15, Agarwal Road, Darya Ganj, New Delhi -110002
Tele: 011- 47630600, 43518550

卐 **Head Office**
Kalindi, TP Nagar, Meerut (UP) - 250002, Tel: 0121-7156203, 7156204

卐 **Sales & Support Offices**
Agra, Ahmedabad, Bengaluru, Bareilly, Chennai, Delhi, Guwahati, Hyderabad, Jaipur, Jhansi, Kolkata, Lucknow, Nagpur & Pune.

卐 **ISBN:** 978-93-25796-63-8

卐 **PRICE:** ₹150.00

**PO No:** TXT-XX-XXXXXXX-X-XX

Published by Arihant Publications (India) Ltd.

For further information about the books published by Arihant, log on to www.arihantbooks.com or e-mail at info@arihantbooks.com

Follow us on   

# Contents

**Unit 1 India and the Contemporary World - II**

| | | |
|---|---|---|
| *CHAPTER 01* | Nationalism in India | ***1-17*** |
| *CHAPTER 02* | The Making of a Global World* | ***18-33*** |
| *CHAPTER 03* | The Age of Industrialisation* | ***34-47*** |

**Unit 2 Contemporary India – II**

| | | |
|---|---|---|
| *CHAPTER 01* | Minerals and Energy Resources** | ***48-63*** |
| *CHAPTER 02* | Manufacturing Industries | ***64-80*** |
| *CHAPTER 03* | Lifelines of National Economy | ***81-95*** |

**Unit 3 Democratic Politics – II**

| | | |
|---|---|---|
| *CHAPTER 01* | Political Parties | ***96-109*** |
| *CHAPTER 02* | Outcomes of Democracy | ***110-122*** |

**Unit 4 Economics**

| | | |
|---|---|---|
| *CHAPTER 01* | Money and Credit | ***123-134*** |
| *CHAPTER 02* | Globalisation and the Indian Economy | ***135-146*** |

**Practice Papers (1-3)** ***149-160***

* *These chapters should be assessed in the periodic test only and will not be evaluated in the board examination.*

** *The theoretical aspect of this chapter should be assessed in the Periodic Tests only and will not be evaluated in board examination. However, the map items of this chapter as given in the Map List will be evaluated in board examination.*

# Syllabus CBSE Term II Class X

| Themes | Learning Objectives |
|---|---|
| **Unit 1: India and the Contemporary World – II** | |
| **Section 1: Events and Processes** | |
| **2. Nationalism in India**<br>• The First World War, Khilafat and Non - Cooperation<br>• Differing Strands within the Movement<br>• Towards Civil Disobedience<br>• The Sense of Collective Belonging | • Recognize the characteristics of Indian nationalism through a case study of Non-Cooperation and Civil Disobedience Movement.<br>• Analyze the nature of the diverse social movements of the time.<br>• Familiarize with the writings and ideals of different political groups and individuals.<br>• Appreciate the ideas promoting Pan Indian belongingness. |
| **Section 2: Livelihoods, Economies and Societies**<br>*Note: Any one theme of the following. The theme selected should be assessed in the periodic test only and will not be evaluated in the board examination:* | |
| **3. The Making of a Global World**<br>• The Pre-modern world<br>• The Nineteenth Century (1815-1914)<br>• The Inter war Economy<br>• Rebuilding a World Economy: The Post-War Era | • Show that globalization has a long history and point to the shifts within the process.<br>• Analyze the implication of globalization for local economies.<br>• Discuss how globalization is experienced differently by different social groups. |
| **4. The Age of Industrialization**<br>• Before the Industrial Revolution<br>• Hand Labour and Steam Power<br>• Industrialization in the colonies<br>• Factories Come Up<br>• The Peculiarities of Industrial Growth<br>• Market for Goods | • Familiarize with the Pro- to-Industrial phase and Early – factory system.<br>• Familiarize with the process of industrialization and its impact on labour class.<br>• Enable them to understand industrialization in the colonies with reference to Textile industries. |
| **Unit 2: Contemporary India – II** | |
| **3. Minerals and Energy Resources**<br>• What is a mineral?<br>• Mode of occurrence of Minerals<br>• Ferrous and Non-Ferrous Minerals | • Identify different types of minerals and energy resources and places of their availability<br>• Feel the need for their judicious utilization |

Cont.

- Non-Metallic Minerals
- Rock Minerals
- Conservation of Minerals
- Energy Resources
  - Conventional and Non- Conventional
- Conservation of Energy Resources

*Note: The theoretical aspect of chapter 'Minerals and Energy Resources' to be assessed in the Periodic Tests only and will not be evaluated in Board Examination. However, the map items of this chapter as given in the Map List will be evaluated in Board Examination*

**6. Manufacturing Industries**

- Manufacturing Industries
- Importance of manufacturing
- Contribution of Industry to National Economy
- Industrial Location
- Classification of Industries
- Spatial distribution
- Industrial pollution and environmental degradation
- Control of Environmental Degradation

- Bring out the importance of industries in the national economy as well as understand the regional disparities which resulted due to concentration of industries in some areas.
- Discuss the need for a planned industrial development and debate over the role of government towards sustainable development.

**7. Lifelines of National Economy**

- Transport – Roadways, Railways, Pipelines, Waterways, Airways
- Communication
- International Trade
- Tourism as a Trade

- Explain the importance of transport and communication in the ever-shrinking world.
- Understand the role of trade and tourism in the economic development of a country.

## Unit 3: Democratic Politics – II

**6. Political Parties**

- Why do we need Political Parties?
- How many Parties should we have?
- National Political Parties
- State Parties
- Challenges to Political Parties
- How can Parties be reformed?

- Analyze party systems in democracies.
- Introduction to major political parties, challenges faced by them and reforms in the country.

**7. Outcomes of Democracy**

- How do we assess democracy's outcomes?
- Accountable, responsive and legitimate government
- Economic growth and development
- Reduction of inequality and poverty
- Accommodation of social diversity
- Dignity and freedom of the citizens

- Evaluate the functioning of democracies in comparison to alternative forms of governments.
- Understand the causes for continuation of democracy in India.
- Distinguish between sources of strengths and weaknesses of Indian democracy.

## Unit 4: Economics

| | |
|---|---|
| **3. Money and Credit**<br>• Money as a medium of exchange<br>• Modern forms of money<br>• Loan activities of Banks<br>• Two different credit situations<br>• Terms of credit<br>• Formal sector credit in India<br>• Self Help Groups for the Poor | • Understand poverty as a challenge.<br>• Identify vulnerable group and interstate disparities.<br>• Appreciate the initiatives of the government to alleviate poverty. |
| **4. Globalization and the Indian Economy**<br>• Production across countries<br>• Interlinking production across countries<br>• Foreign Trade and integration of markets<br>• What is globalization?<br>• Factors that have enabled Globalization<br>• World Trade Organization<br>• Impact of Globalization on India<br>• The Struggle for a fair Globalization | • Explain the working of the Global Economic phenomenon. |

# List of Map

## CBSE Term II Class X

### A. HISTORY (Outline Political Map of India)

**Chapter - 2 Nationalism in India** – (1918 – 1930) for Locating and Labelling / Identification

1. **Indian National Congress Sessions:**
   a. Calcutta (Sep. 1920) b. Nagpur (Dec. 1920) c. Madras (1927)

2. **Important Centres of Indian National Movement**
   a. Champaran (Bihar) - Movement of Indigo Planters
   b. Kheda (Gujarat) - Peasant Satyagrah
   c. Ahmedabad (Gujarat) - Cotton Mill Workers Satyagraha
   d. Amritsar (Punjab) - Jallianwala Bagh Incident
   e. Chauri Chaura (U.P.) - Calling off the Non-Cooperation Movement
   f. Dandi (Gujarat) - Civil Disobedience Movement

### B. GEOGRAPHY (Outline Political Map of India)

**Chapter 5: Minerals and Energy Resources**

**Power Plants**- (Locating and Labelling only)

a. **Thermal**
- Namrup
- Singrauli
- Ramagundam

b. **Nuclear**
- Narora
- Kakrapara
- Tarapur
- Kalpakkam

**Chapter 6: Manufacturing Industries** (Locating and Labelling Only)

**Cotton Textile Industries:**

a. Mumbai b. Indore c. Surat
d. Kanpur e. Coimbatore

**Iron and Steel Plants:**

a. Durgapur b. Bokaro c. Jamshedpur
d. Bhilai e. Vijaynagar f. Salem

**Software Technology Parks:**

a. Noida b. Gandhinagar c. Mumbai
d. Pune e. Hyderabad f. Bengaluru
g. Chennai h. Thiruvananthapuram

**Chapter 7: Lifelines of National Economy**

**Major Ports:** (Locating and Labelling)

a. Kandla b. Mumbai c. Marmagao
d. New Mangalore e. Kochi f. Tuticorin
g. Chennai h. Vishakhapatnam i. Paradip
j. Haldia

**International Airports:**

a. Amritsar (Raja Sansi) b. Delhi (Indira Gandhi International)
c. Mumbai (Chhatrapati Shivaji) d. Chennai (Meenam Bakkam)
e. Kolkata (Netaji Subhash Chandra Bose) f. Hyderabad (Rajiv Gandhi)

# CBSE Circular

**Acad - 51/2021, 05 July 2021**

## Exam Scheme Term I & II

**केन्द्रीय माध्यमिक शिक्षा बोर्ड**

(शिक्षा मंत्रालय, भारत सरकार के अधीन एक स्वायत संगठन)

**CENTRAL BOARD OF SECONDARY EDUCATION**

(An Autonomous Organisation under the Ministryof Education, Govt. of India)

**CBSE/DIR (ACAD)/2021** **Date: July 05, 2021**
**Circular No: Acad-51/2021**

**All the Heads of Schools affiliated to CBSE**

**Subject: Special Scheme of Assessment for Board Examination Classes X and XII for the Session 2021-22**

COVID 19 pandemic caused almost all CBSE schools to function in a virtual mode for most part of the academic session of 2020-21. Due to the extreme risk associated with the conduct of Board examinations during the second wave in April 2021, CBSE had to cancel both its class X and XII Board examinations of the year 2021 and results are to be declared on the basis of a credible, reliable, flexible and valid alternative assessment policy. This, in turn, also necessitated deliberations over alternative ways to look at the learning objectives as well as the conduct of the Board Examinations for the academic session 2021-22 in case the situation remains unfeasible.

CBSE has also held stake holder consultations with Government schools as well as private independent schools from across the country especially schools from the remote rural areas and a majority of them have requested for the rationalization of the syllabus, similar to last year in view of reduced time permitted for organizing online classes. The Board has also considered the concerns regarding differential availability of electronic gadgets, connectivity and effectiveness of online teaching and other socio-economic issues specially with respect to students from economically weaker section and those residing in far flung areas of the country. In a survey conducted by CBSE, it was revealed that the rationalized syllabus notified for the session 2020-21 was effective for schools in covering the syllabus and helped learners in achieving learning objectives in a less stressful manner.

In the above backdrop and in line with the Board's continued focus on assessing stipulated learning outcomes by making the examinations competencies and core concepts based, student-centric, transparent, technology-driven, and having advance provision of alternatives for different future scenarios, the following schemes are introduced for the Academic Session for Class X and Class XII 2021-22.

# केन्द्रीय माध्यमिक शिक्षा बोर्ड

(शिक्षा मंत्रालय, भारत सरकार के अधीन एक स्वायत संगठन)

# CENTRAL BOARD OF SECONDARY EDUCATION

(An Autonomous Organisation under the Ministryof Education, Govt. of India)

## Special Scheme for 2021-22

A. **Academic session to be divided into 2 Terms with approximately 50% syllabus in each term:**

The syllabus for the Academic session 2021-22 will be divided into 2 terms by following a systematic approach by looking into the interconnectivity of concepts and topics by the Subject Experts and the Board will conduct examinations at the end of each term on the basis of the bifurcated syllabus. This is done to increase the probability of having a Board conducted classes X and XII examinations at the end of the academic session.

B. **The syllabus for the Board examination 2021-22 will be rationalized** similar to that of the last academic session to be notified in July 2021. For academic transactions, however, schools will follow the curriculum and syllabus released by the Board vide Circular no. F.1001/CBSE-Acad/Curriculum/2021 dated 31 March 2021. Schools will also use alternative academic calendar and inputs from the NCERT on transacting the curriculum.

C. **Efforts will be made to make Internal Assessment/ Practical/ Project work more credible and valid** as per the guidelines and Moderation Policy to be announced by the Board to ensure fair distribution of marks.

## Details of Curriculum Transaction

- Schools will continue teaching in distance mode till the authorities permit in-person mode of teaching in schools.
- **Classes IX-X: Internal Assessment** (throughout the year-irrespective of Term I and II) would include the *3 periodic tests, student enrichment, portfolio and practical work/ speaking listening activities/ project.*
- **Classes XI-XII: Internal Assessment** (throughout the year-irrespective of Term I and II) would include end of topic or unit tests/ exploratory activities/ practicals/ projects.
- Schools would create a student profile for all assessment undertaken over the year and retain the evidences in digital format.
- CBSE will facilitate schools to upload marks of Internal Assessment on the CBSE IT platform.
- Guidelines for Internal Assessment for all subjects will also be released along with the rationalized term wise divided syllabus for the session 2021-22.The Board would also provide additional resources like sample assessments, question banks, teacher training etc. for more reliable and valid internal assessments.

# केन्द्रीय माध्यमिक शिक्षा बोर्ड

(शिक्षा मंत्रालय, भारत सरकार के अधीन एक स्वायत संगठन)

# CENTRAL BOARD OF SECONDARY EDUCATION

(An Autonomous Organisation under the Ministryof Education, Govt. of India)

## Term I Examinations:

- At the end of the first term, the Board will organize **Term I Examination** in a flexible schedule to be conducted between November-December 2021 with a window period of 4-8 weeks for schools situated in different parts of country and abroad. Dates for conduct of examinations will be notified subsequently.
- The Question Paper will have Multiple Choice Questions (MCQ) including case-based MCQs and MCQs on assertion-reasoning type. Duration of test will be **90 minutes** and it will cover only the rationalized syllabus of **Term I only** (i.e. approx. 50% of the entire syllabus).
- Question Papers will be sent by the CBSE to schools along with marking scheme.
- The exams will be conducted under the supervision of the External Center Superintendents and Observers appointed by CBSE.
- The responses of students will be captured on OMR sheets which, after scanning may be directly uploaded at CBSE portal or alternatively may be evaluated and marks obtained will be uploaded by the school on the very same day. The final direction in this regard will be conveyed to schools by the Examination Unit of the Board.
- Marks of the **Term I** Examination will contribute to the final overall score of students.

## Term II Examination/ Year-end Examination:

- At the end of the second term, the Board would organize **Term II or Year-end Examination** based on the rationalized syllabus of Term II only (i.e. approximately 50% of the entire syllabus).
- This examination would be held around **March-April 2022** at the examination centres fixed by the Board.
- The paper will be of **2 hours duration** and have questions of different formats (case-based/ situation based, open ended- short answer/ long answer type).
- In case the situation is not conducive for normal descriptive examination a **90 minute MCQ based exam** will be conducted at the end of the Term II also.
- Marks of the Term II Examination would contribute to the final overall score.

***To cover this situation, we have given both MCQs and Subjective Questions in each Chapter.***

# केन्द्रीय माध्यमिक शिक्षा बोर्ड

(शिक्षा मंत्रालय, भारत सरकार के अधीन एक स्वायत संगठन)

# CENTRAL BOARD OF SECONDARY EDUCATION

(An Autonomous Organisation under the Ministryof Education, Govt. of India)

## Assessment / Examination as per different situations

**A. In case the situation of the pandemic improves and students are able to come to schools or centres for taking the exams.**

Board would conduct Term I and Term II examinations at schools/centres and the theory marks will be distributed equally between the two exams.

**B. In case the situation of the pandemic forces complete closure of schools during November-December 2021, but Term II exams are held at schools or centres.**

Term I MCQ based examination would be done by students online/offline from home - in this case, the weightage of this exam for the final score would be reduced, and weightage of Term II exams will be increased for declaration of final result.

**C. In case the situation of the pandemic forces complete closure of schools during March-April 2022, but Term I exams are held at schools or centres.**

Results would be based on the performance of students on Term I MCQ based examination and internal assessments. The weightage of marks of Term I examination conducted by the Board will be increased to provide year end results of candidates.

**D. In case the situation of the pandemic forces complete closure of schools and Board conducted Term I and II exams are taken by the candidates from home in the session 2021-22.**

Results would be computed on the basis of the Internal Assessment/Practical/Project Work and Theory marks of Term-I and II exams taken by the candidate from home in Class X / XII subject to the moderation or other measures to ensure validity and reliability of the assessment.

In all the above cases, data analysis of marks of students will be undertaken to ensure the integrity of internal assessments and home based exams.

**Dr. Joseph Emmanuel**
**Director (Academics)**

CHAPTER 01

# Nationalism in India

### In this Chapter...


- The First World War, Khilafat and Non-Cooperation Movement
- Differing Strands within the Movement
- Towards Civil Disobedience
- The Sense of Collective Belonging


In India, the growth of modern nationalism is connected to the anti-colonial movement. People began discovering their unity in the process of their struggle with colonialism. The Congress under the leadership of Mahatma Gandhi tried to unite each class and group together within one movement.

## The First World War, Khilafat and Non-Cooperation Movement

The First World War (1914) created a new economic and political situation worldwide. India faced various problem during the war period. For example

- Defence expenditure increased.
- Custom duties were raised and income tax was introduced.
- Prices of food grains were increased and doubled between 1913 and 1918.
- Villagers were recruited forcefully in army.

After the war in 1918-19 and 1920-21, Indian industries faced heavy loses, people suffered from acute shortage of food, influenza epidemic, etc. In such a critical situation, a new leader **Mahatma Gandhi** came to India from South Africa in January, 1915.

### The Idea of Satyagraha

Gandhiji's method of movement and protest based on **truth** and **non-violence** was known as **Satyagraha.** The idea of Satyagraha emphasised on the power of truth. As per Gandhiji without being aggressive a Satyagrahi could win the battle through non-violence.

In 1917, Gandhiji travelled to **Champaran** in Bihar to inspire the peasants to struggle against oppressive plantation system. In the same year Gandhiji also organised a Satyagraha to support the peasants in **Kheda** district of Gujarat who were suffering from shortage of food due to crop failure and a plague epidemic.

In 1918, Gandhiji went to **Ahmedabad** to organise a Satyagraha movement amongst cotton mill workers.

### The Rowlatt Act

The Rowlatt Act was passed through the **Imperial Legislative Council in 1919** but Indian members opposed the Act. According to this act, the political prisoners could be detained in prison for two years without any trial. Gandhiji decided to oppose this Act with Satyagraha.

On 6th April, 1919 Gandhiji launched a nation wide **Satyagraha** with a *hartal*. Rallies were organised in various cities, workers went on strike in railway workshop and shops were closed down. Several local leaders were arrested. Gandhiji was barred (restricted) from entering Delhi.

On 10th April, 1919 the police in Amritsar opened fired on peaceful procession. **Martial Law**[1] was imposed in Amritsar and the command of the area was given to **General Dyer**.

### Jallianwala Bagh Massacre

On **13th April, 1919**, a large crowd gathered in the enclosed ground of Jallianwala Bagh in Amritsar, Punjab. Some people gathered there to protest against government's repressive measures, while some came to attend the annual **Baisakhi fair**. Many of them unaware of the martial law that was imposed.

General Dyer blocked the exit points of the ground and gave order to open fire on the crowd. Hundreds of people were killed in this incident. As the news spread, strikes, clashes with the police and attacks on government buildings started.

The government responded with force to end the movement by humiliating people. Satyagrahis were forced to rub their noses on the ground, crawl on the streets and do salaam (salute) to all sahibs. **Rabindranath Tagore** returned his title, **Knighthood** during this incident. Mahatma Gandhi called off the Satyagraha Movement when he saw spread of violence.

## Khilafat Movement

The First World War had ended with the defeat of Ottoman Empire. After the First World War, rumours were spread that a peace treaty was going to be imposed on Khalifa (spiritual head of the Islamic world) of Ottoman Empire. Gandhiji believed that by this Khilafat issue he could unite the Hindus and Muslims and launch a wide movement in India.

A **Khilafat Committee** was formed in Bombay under the leadership of Maulana Azad, Hakim Ajmal Khan and Hasrat Mohani. Muslim leaders, **Muhammad Ali** and **Shaukat Ali** began discussing with Gandhiji about a united mass action on the Khilafat issue. Gandhiji saw this as an opportunity of uniting Hindus and Muslims.

The Congress passed the resolution in its **Calcutta Session** in September 1920 to start a Non-Cooperation movement in support of Khilafat as well as for Swaraj.

## Need of Non-Cooperation Movement

Gandhiji in his famous book **Hind Swaraj** (1909) declared that British rule was established in India with the cooperation of Indians. If Indians refused to cooperate, British rule in India would collapse with in a year and Swaraj would come.

Mahatma Gandhi proposed the following strategy for the implementation of the Non-Cooperation as a Movement

- The movement would begin with a surrender of titles, honours and honorary posts by people.
- The movement would **boycott**[2] Civil Services, Army, Police, British Courts and Legislative Assemblies, School and Colleges and British goods.
- The British goods would be replaced by domestic goods or Swadeshi to promote the native cottage industries.
- In case of government suppression, Civil Disobedience Movement would be launched.

The Non-Cooperation Movement was adopted by the Congress during the **Nagpur Conference** in December 1920 and it began under the leadership of Mahatma Gandhi.

# Differing Strands within the Movement

In January 1921, the Non-Cooperation-Khilafat Movement started. Various social groups participated in the movement with their own specific aspirations.

## The Movements in the Towns

Non-Cooperation Khilafat Movement started in the cities with middle-class participation in which

- Students and teachers left government-controlled school and lawyers left courts.
- Foreign goods were boycotted. The merchants and traders refused to trade in foreign goods or finance foreign trade. As a result, the production of Indian textile mills and handlooms increased.
- Liquor shops were **picketed**[3].
- Council elections were boycotted in most provinces except Madras.

However, this movement gradually slowed down for many reasons like expensive *Khadi* clothes were not suitable for poor people and no alternative institutions were set-up. Finally the teachers and students had to resume their studies and jobs in government schools and lawyers joined back in government courts.

---

1 **Martial Law** Law of military government. When martial law is imposed, ordinary laws are suspended.

2 **Boycott** The refusal to deal and associate with people or participate in activities or buy and use things; usually a form of protest.

3 **Picketed** A form of demonstration or protest by which people block the entrance to a shop, factory or office.

## Rebellion in the Countryside

From cities, the Non-Cooperation Movement spread to the countryside.

### Peasant Movement in Awadh

In **Awadh, the Peasant Movement** developed under the leadership of **Baba Ramchandra** (a Sanyasi who had earlier been to in Fiji as an **indentured labourer**[4]**)**. This Peasant Movement demanded reduction of revenue, abolition of **begar**[5] and social boycott of oppressive landlords. In many places, **nai-dhobi bandhs** were organised by panchayats to deny services to all landlords.

In October, 1920 the **Oudh Kisan Sabha** was set-up. It was headed by Jawaharlal Nehru, Baba Ramchandra and a few others. Within a month, over 300 branches of this sabha had been set up in the villages around the region. As the peasant movement spread, the houses of *talukdars* (Indian land-holders) and merchants were attacked, bazaars were looted and grain hoards were taken over.

### Tribal Movement in Andhra Pradesh

Tribal peasants interpreted the message of Mahatma Gandhi and the idea of *Swaraj.* In the **Gudem Hills** of Andhra Pradesh, a **militant Guerrilla Movement** spread in the early 1920 under the leadership of **Alluri Sitaram Raju**. Raju convinced people to wear *'Khadi'* and give up drinking according to Gandhian ideas.

The **Gudem rebels**[6] attacked police stations, attempted to kill British officials and carried on **Guerrilla warfare**[7] for achieving Swaraj. Raju was captured and executed in 1924 and gradually he became a folk hero.

## Swaraj in the Plantations

According to **Indian Emigration Act** of **1859**, plantation workers were not permitted to leave the tea gardens without permission.

When the news of Non-Cooperation Movement spread to the plantantion, they left their job and headed towards their home. The plantation workers believed that in Gandhi Raj, everyone would be given land in their own village. However they were caught by the police and brutally beaten up.

# Towards Civil Disobedience

In February 1922, Mahatma Gandhi decided to withdraw the Non- Cooperation Movement as he felt that movement was turning violent in many places and Satyagrahis needed to be properly trained before they would be ready for mass struggles. **Chauri Chaura** incident was the main reason behind withdrawing the Non-cooperation Movement. The Chauri Chaura incident occurred at Chauri Chaura in Gorakhpur district of United Province on 4th February, 1922.

### Different Views within Congress

Some leaders within Congress were tired of mass struggle and wanted to participate in the election to the provincial councils set up by the **Government of India Act of 1919**. They felt that it was important to oppose British policies within the councils.

**CR Das** and **Motilal Nehru** formed the **Swaraj Party** within the Congress to argue for a return to council politics whereas some younger leaders like **Jawaharlal Nehru** and **Subhas Chandra Bose** argued for more strong mass agitation and for full independence. In this situation of internal debate and discussions, Two factors shaped Indian politics towards the late 1920 which were

(i) The first was the effect of the worldwide economic depression.

(ii) The second was agricultural prices which began to fall from 1926 and collapsed after 1930.

### Formation of Simon Commission

Simon Commission was constituted under **John Simon.** The main objective of **Simon Commission** was to review the functioning of the constitutional system in India and suggest changes in the system.

Indian leaders opposed the commission as there were no Indians in it. When the commission arrived in India in 1928, it was greeted with the slogan **Simon Go Back**. All parties including the Congress and the Muslim League participated in the demonstrations.

### Demand of Purna Swaraj

In October 1929, the Viceroy, Lord Irwin announced an uncertain offer of **dominion status**[8] for India and a **Round Table Conference** to discuss a future Constitution.

In December 1929, under the Presidency of Jawaharlal Nehru, the Lahore Congress formalised the demand of Purna Swaraj or full independence for India. It was declared that 26th January, 1930 would be celebrated as the Independence Day.

---

4 **Indentured Labour** Bonded labour where people agree to work to pay off for the debt.
5 **Begar** Labour that villagers were forced to contribute without any payment.
6 **Gudem Rebels** The people who participated in the militant Guerrilla Movement in the Gudem hills of Andhra Pradesh.
7 **Guerrilla Warfare** It is irregular military actions carried out by small usually independent forces.
8 **Dominion Status** It refers to semi-autonomous country within the British empire that is also called British commonwealth countries.

## The Salt March and the Civil Disobedience Movement

Mahatma Gandhi believed that salt was a powerful symbol that could unite the nation. On 31st January, 1930, Mahatma Gandhi sent a letter to Viceroy Irwin which claimed eleven demands. One of these eleven demands was to abolish salt tax.

The tax on salt and the government's monopoly over its production revealed the most cruel side of British rule. Irwin was not ready to talk upon the demands. Thus, Gandhiji took the decision to launch the movement.

### The Civil Disobedience Movement

On 12th March, 1930, alongwith 78 followers, Gandhiji started Salt March from **Sabarmati Ashram** for **Dandi**, the coastal town of Gujarat.

On 6th April, he reached Dandi and broke the Salt Law by boiling seawater and manufacturing salt. This marked the **beginning of the Civil Disobedience Movement.** As the movement spread,

- foreign clothes were boycotted.
- peasants refused to pay revenue and *chaukidari* taxes.
- village officials resigned.
- forest people violated forest laws in many places.

However, British government arrested all the leaders including Gandhiji.

### Calling Off the Civil Disobedience Movement

During Civil Disobedience Movement, peaceful Satyagrahis were attacked, women and children were beaten and about 1,00,000 people were arrested.

When **Abdul Gaffar Khan** was arrested on April 1930, several violent incidents took place in Peshawar. In this situation, Mahatma Gandhi call off the movement and signed a pact with Lord Irwin on 5th March, 1931. This was called **Gandhi-Irwin Pact**.

### Relaunching of Civil Disobedience Movement

In December 1931, Gandhiji went to London for the **Second Round Table Conference** but he returned disappointed as the British government refused to release the prisoners.

When Gandhiji came back in India, he found that Congress had been declared illegal and Abdul Ghaffar Khan and Jawaharlal Nehru were imprisoned.

As a result, Mahatma Gandhi relaunched the Civil Disobedience Movement. This movement was continued for a year and lost its momentum by the year 1934. Meaning of Swaraj was different for different social groups.

- In the countryside, rich peasant communities like the Patidars of Gujarat and the Jats of Uttar Pradesh were supporters of the Civil Disobedience Movement. They organised their communities to participate in boycott programmes. For them, the fight for Swaraj was a struggle against high revenues.
- The poor peasantry found it difficult to pay their rent to the landlords as the depression continued. They joined a variety of radical movements often led by Socialists and Communists in the hope that they would not have to pay the rent any further.
- Association like **Indian Industrial and Commercial Congress** and **Federation of the Indian Chamber of Commerce** and Industries under the leadership of GD Birla, Purushottam Thakur Das, etc supported the Civil Disobedience Movement in the hope that business restriction would be lifted.
  The Indian merchants and industrialists formed the Indian Industrial and Commerce Congress in 1920 and the Federation of the Indian Chamber of Commerce and Industries (FICCI) in 1927.
- The industrial working classes did not participate in the Civil Disobedience Movement in large numbers, except in the Nagpur region.
- A large number of women participated in this movement. In urban areas, women came from high-caste families. In rural areas, women came from rich peasant households. Women were inspired by Gandhiji's call and they began to see service to the nation as their sacred duty.

#### Formation of Hindustan Socialists Republican Army

Many nationalists did not believe in non-violent method for achieving freedom. In 1928, some nationalists like Bhagat Singh, Jatin Das and Ajoy Ghosh founded the Hindustan Socialists Republican Army (HSRA) in 1928 at a meeting in Ferozshah Kotla ground in Delhi.

## The Limits of Civil Disobedience

Dalits or untouchables and Muslims did not actively participated in this movement. For long time, the Congress had ignored the Dalits because of the fear of *Sanatanis*, the conservative high caste Hindus.

Gandhiji called Dalits **Harijan** or the **Children of God**. He believed that Swaraj would not come for hundred years if untouchability was not eliminated. He organised **Satyagraha** for them, to secure their entry into temples and access to public wells, tanks, roads and schools.

Gandhiji himself cleaned the toilets to dignify the work of *bhangi* (the sweepers). Gandhiji urged the upper class to change their mindset regarding the untouchables.

### Stand of Dalit Leaders

Dalit leaders wanted a different political solution to the problems of their community. **Dr BR Ambedkar** demanded reserved seats in educational institutions and a separate electorate that would choose Dalit members for Legislative Councils. Ambedkar organised the Dalits into the **Depressed Classes Association** in 1930. His views differed with Mahatma Gandhi at the Second Round Table Conference as Dr Ambedkar demanded separate electorate for Dalits.

When the British Government admitted Ambedkar's demand, Gandhiji strongly opposed it and began a fast unto death. Gandhiji believed that separate electorate for Dalits would slow down the process of their integration into the main society.

Ambedkar ultimately accepted Gandhiji's position and as a result, **Poona Pact** of September 1932 was signed. This pact gave the depressed classes reserved seats in Provincial and Central Legislative Council but the voting was to be done by the general electorate.

### Hindu-Muslim Clash

Some of the Muslim political organisations in India rarely participated in the Civil Disobedience Movement. After the decline of the Non-Cooperation and Khilafat Movement, a large section of Muslims felt separated from the Congress.

From the mid 1920, the Congress came to be more associated with openly Hindu religious nationalist groups like the **Hindu Mahasabha**. As a result, Hindu-Muslim communal clashes and riots occurred in various cities.

In 1930, Sir Muhammad Iqbal, the President of Muslim League demanded the importance of separate electorates for Mulims. He thought that it would safeguard their minority political interest. He justified the Muslim demand for the creation of a Muslim India within India.

### Difference between Hindu Mahasabha and Muslim League

The Congress and Muslim League made efforts to talk again for unity. In 1927, it appeared that such a unity could be possible. The only difference in the opinion of Congress and Muslim League was based on the representation in the future assemblies that were to be elected.

The leader of the Muslim League, **Muhammad Ali Jinnah** wanted reserved seats for Muslims in Central Assembly. He was willing to give up the demand for separate electorate for two conditions

(i) Muslims were assured reserved seats in the Central Assembly.

(ii) Representation would be in proportion to the population in Muslim dominated provinces (Bengal and Punjab).

In 1928, at the All Parties Conference, **MR Jayakar** of the Hindu Mahasabha strongly opposed the demands of Jinnah. Many Muslim leaders and intellectuals feared that the culture and identity of minorities could be submerged under the domination of Hindu majority.

## The Sense of Collective Belonging

Nationalist movements spread when people belonging to different regions and communities began to develop a sense of collective belongingness. It developed through the experience of united struggles. History, fiction, folklore, songs, popular prints and symbols, all played a part in the making of nationalism. It was seen in India during its freedom movement in the following ways

- The identity of a nation is most often symbolised in a figure or image. This image of **Bharat Mata** was first created by **Bankim Chandra Chattopadhyay** in 1870, when he wrote **Vande Mataram** for our motherland. Later, this song was included in his novel *Anandamath* and widely sung by the freedom fighters. The image of Bharat Mata was first painted by **Abanindranath Tagore**.
- Indian folk songs and folk tales sung by bard (wandering poets) played an important role for making the idea of nationalism.
- In Bengal, **Rabindranath Tagore** and in Madras, **Natesa Sastri** collected massive collection of folk tales and songs, which led the movement for folk revival.
- During the Swadeshi Movement, a **tricolour (red, green and yellow) flag** was designed in Bengal. It had eight lotuses representing eight provinces and a crescent moon representing Hindus and Muslims.
- By 1921, Gandhiji had designed the **Swaraj Flag**. It was a tricolour having a spinning wheel in the centre representing the Gandhian ideal of self help.

### Nationalism through Indian Ancient History

Another means of creating feeling of nationalism was explaining the meaning of history again. The nationalist writers urged the readers to take pride in India's great achievements in the past and struggle to change the miserable conditions of life under British rule.

But unification of people involved some problems. When the past that was being glorified was Hindu and the images celebrated were taken from Hindu **iconography,** the people of other communities felt left out.

## Conclusion

A growing anger against the Colonial Government brought together various groups and classes of Indians into a common struggle for freedom in the first half of the 20th century. However different expectations of diverse groups pose a constant threat to unity. The Congress under the leadership of Mahatma Gandhi tried to channel people's sufferings into organised and united movement for independence.

# Chapter Practice

## PART 1

## Objective Questions

### • Multiple Choice Questions

**1.** In India the growth of modern nationalism in intimately connected to the ............ .

(a) Western education
(b) Awarness of people
(c) Anti-colonial movement
(d) None of the above

***Ans.*** (c) In India the growth of modern nationalism is intimately connected to the Anti-colonial movement.

**2.** Identify the correct meaning of Satyagraha from the given options.

(a) Satyagraha means use of physical force to inflict pain.
(b) Satyagraha is a non-violent method of fighting against the oppression which does not inflict pain.
(c) Satyagraha means passive resistance and it is considered as a weapon of weak.
(d) Satyagraha means to search for truth and use physical force.

***Ans.*** (b) Satyagraha is a non-violent method of fighting against the oppression which does not inflict pain. It is a novel method of mass agitation, which stressed the principle of truth, tolerance, non-violence and peaceful protests.

**3.** Why did General Dyer order to open fire on a peaceful demonstration at Jallianwala Bagh? Choose the correct option.

(a) He ordered the open fire because he noticed a sudden unrest in the crowd.
(b) Because his objective was to produce a moral effect that can create fear in the minds of the Satyagrahis.
(c) Because he wanted to suppress the voice of the crowd.
(d) All of the above

***Ans.*** (b) General Dyer ordered to open fire because his objective was to produce a moral effect that can create fear in the minds of the Satyagrahis.

**4.** Who among the following were the prominent leaders during the Khilafat Movement? Identify the correct option.

(a) Maulana Mohammad Ali and Shaukat Ali
(b) Mohammad Ali Jinnah and Mahatma Gandhi
(c) Maulana Abdul Kalam Azad and Shaukat Ali
(d) Mohammad Ali Jinnah and Shaukat Ali

***Ans.*** (a) Maulana Mohammad Ali and Shaukat Ali were the prominent leaders during Khilafat Movement.

**5.** Who announced the vague offer of 'Dominion Status' for India in 1929? Identify the correct option.

(a) Lord Curzon (b) Lord William Bentick
(c) lord Irwin (d) Lord Mountbatten

***Ans.*** (c) In October 1929, the Viceroy, Lord Irwin announced the vague offer of 'Dominion Status' for India and a Round Table Conference to discuss a future Constitution.

**6.** Identify the personality with the help of clues given below

- He was a Sanyasi.
- Peasant Movement of Awadh developed under his leadership.
- He had earlier been a Fiji as an indentured labourer.

(a) Baba Ramachandra (b) Mahatma Gandhi
(c) Rabindranath Tagore (d) Abanindranath Tagore

***Ans.*** (a) The given information is about Baba Ramachandra.

**7.** Identify the movement with the given features and choose the correct option.

- It was started in 1930.
- The movement took place in Gujarat.
- This movement was started by Gandhiji.

(a) Non-Cooperation Movement
(b) Civil Disobedience Movement
(c) Peasant Movement
(d) Khilafat Movement

***Ans.*** (b) The given information is about Civil Disobedience Movement.

**8.** Choose the incorrectly matched pair from the given options.
(a) Salt March was initiated from- Nagpur
(b) Abdul Gaffar Khan was arrested- April 1930
(c) Mahatma Gandhi called off Civil Disobedience Movement- March 1931
(d) Civil Disobedience lost its momentum- 1934

***Ans.*** (a) Mahatma Gandhi started the Salt March from Sabarmati Ashram (not Nagpur) on 12th March, 1930 for Dandi, the coastal town of Gujarat.

**9.** Choose the correctly matched pair about the incidents with their year of occurrence from the given options.
(a) Indian Industrial and Commerce Congress was formed-1927
(b) Federation of the Indian Chamber of Commerce and Industries- 1920
(c) Poona Pact- 1932
(d) Mohammad Iqbal demanded Separate Electorates for Muslims- 1928

***Ans.*** (c) Poona Pact was signed in September 1932.

Indian Industrial and Commerce Congress was formed by the Indian merchants and industrialists in 1920.

Federation of the Indian Chamber of Commerce and Industries (FICCI) was formed in 1927.

In 1930, Mohammad Iqbal, the President of Muslim League demanded the importance of Separate Electorates for Muslims.

**10.** Match the following items given in Column A with those in Column B.

| Column A | Column B |
|---|---|
| A. Oudh Kisan Sabha was set up | 1. 1859 |
| B. Indian Emigration Act | 2. 1928 |
| C. Alluri Sitaram Raju was executed in | 3. 1924 |
| D. Arrival of Simon Commission | 4. 1920 |

**Codes**

| | A | B | C | D | | A | B | C | D |
|---|---|---|---|---|---|---|---|---|---|
| (a) | 3 | 4 | 2 | 1 | (b) | 4 | 1 | 3 | 2 |
| (c) | 2 | 3 | 1 | 4 | (d) | 1 | 2 | 4 | 3 |

***Ans.*** (b)

**11.** Match the following items given in Column A with those in Column B.

| Column A | Column B |
|---|---|
| A. 26th January, 1930 | 1. Gandhi-Irwin Pact |
| B. 31st January, 1930 | 2. Initiation of Salt March |
| C. 12th March 1930 | 3. Eleven demands sent to Viceroy Irwin by Gandhiji |
| D. 5th March, 1931 | 4. Would be celebrated as the Independence Day. |

Choose the correct answer from the options given below.

| | A | B | C | D | | A | B | C | D |
|---|---|---|---|---|---|---|---|---|---|
| (a) | 3 | 4 | 2 | 1 | (b) | 2 | 3 | 4 | 1 |
| (c) | 4 | 3 | 2 | 1 | (d) | 1 | 2 | 4 | 3 |

***Ans.*** (c)

**12.** Following image shows a place Chauri-Chaura in Gorakhpur where a peaceful demonstration in a bazaar turned into a violent clash with the police. After hearing this incident Mahatma Gandhi called off which of the following movement?

(a) Tribal Movement
(b) Non-Cooperation Movement
(c) Civil Disobedience Movement
(d) Poorna Swaraj Movement

***Ans.*** (b) Mahatma Gandhi called off the Non-Cooperation Movement after Chauri-Chaura incident.

## • Assertion-Reason MCQs

**Directions** (Q. 13-17) *Two statements are given in the question below as **Assertion** (A) and **Reason** (R). Read the statements and choose the appropriate option from the following options.*

**Codes**
(a) Both A and R are true and R is the correct explanation of A
(b) Both A and R are true, but R is not the correct explanation of A
(c) A is true, but R is false
(d) A is false, but R is true

**13.** **Assertion** (A) In February 1922, Mahatma Gandhi decided to withdraw the Non-Cooperation Movement.

**Reason** (R) Mahatma Gandhi felt that the movement was turning violent in many places and Satyagrahis need proper training for mass struggles.

***Ans.*** (a) In February 1922, Mahatma Gandhi decided to withdraw the Non-Cooperation Movement because he felt that the movement was turning violent in many places like at Chauri-Chaura and the Satyagrahis need proper training for such mass struggles. Hence, both assertion and reason statements justify each other.

**14.** **Assertion** (A) Some leaders within the Congress were tired of the Mass struggle and wanted to participate in the election to the Provincial Councils set up by the Government of India Act of 1919.

**Reason** (R) They felt that elections are necessary to establish democracy in India.

***Ans.*** (c) Some leaders with the Congress were tired of the mass struggle and wanted to participate in the election to the Provincial Councils set up by the Government of India Act of 1919 because they felt that it was important to oppose British policies within the Councils. Hence, the given statement A is true, but statement R is false.

**15.** **Assertion** (A) When Simon Commission arrived in India, it was greeted with the slogan 'Simon Go Back'.

**Reason** (R) Simon Commission was constituted under John Simon.

***Ans.*** (b) The Simon Commission was greeted with the slogan 'Simon Go Back' because it did not have a single Indian Member. It is true that Simon Commission was constituted under John Simon, but it is not a correct explanation for the given statement A.

**16.** **Assertion** (A) The Non-Cooperation Movement gradually slowed down for a variety of reasons in the cities.

**Reason** (R) As the boycott movement spread and people began discarding imported clothes and wearing only Indian ones, production of Indian Textile Mills and handlooms went up.

***Ans.*** (b) The Non-Cooperation Movement gradually slowed down for many reasons like expensive Khadi clothes were often more expensive than mass-produced mill cloth that the poor people could not afford to buy it.

In the Non-Cooperation Movement, foreign goods were boycotted and people started wearing only Indian clothes.

**17.** **Assertion** (A) Gandhiji entered into Gandhi-Irwin Pact on 5th March, 1931.

**Reason** (R) Abdul Ghaffar Khan and Jawaharlal Nehru were put in jail, the Congress was declared illegal, and a series of measures had been imposed to prevent meetings, demonstrations and boycotts.

***Ans.*** (b) With the signing of the Gandhi-Irwin Pact on 5th March 1931, Gandhiji consented to participate in the Round Table Conference in London. The New repressive measures by the British government declared the Congress illegal and put Abdul Ghaffar Khan and Jawaharlal Nehru into jail. Hence, both assertion and reason statements are true, but R is not the correct explanation of A.

## • Case based MCQs

**18.** Read the case/source given below and answer the questions that follow by choosing the appropriate option.

'To the altar of this revolution we have brought our youth as incense'

Many nationalists thought that the struggle against the British could not be won through non-violence. In 1928, the Hindustan Socialist Republican Army (HSRA) was founded at a meeting in Ferozeshah Kotla ground in Delhi.

Amongst its leaders were Bhagat Singh, Jatin Das and Ajoy Ghosh. In a series of dramatic actions in different parts of India, the HSRA targeted some of the symbols of British power. In April 1929, Bhagat Singh and Batukeswar Dutta threw a bomb in the Legislative Assembly. In the same year there was an attempt to blow up the train that Lord Irwin was travelling in. Bhagat Singh was 23 when he was tried and executed by the colonial government.

During his trial, Bhagat Singh stated that he did not wish to glorify 'the cult of the bomb and pistol' but wanted a revolution in society: 'Revolution is the inalienable right of mankind. Freedom is the imprescriptible birthright of all.

The labourer is the real sustainer of society ... To the altar of this revolution we have brought our youth as incense, for no sacrifice is too great for so magnificent a cause. We are content. We await the advent of revolution. Inquilab Zindabad!'

(i) Why Hindustan Socialist Republican Army was formed? With reference to the above context, infer the appropriate option.

(a) To fight against the British colonial rule with the principle of non-violence
(b) To fight against British colonial rule in India
(c) To achieve independence for the country through an armed rebellion if necessary
(d) Both (b) and (c)

***Ans.*** (d) Hindustani Socialist Republican Army was formed to fight against the British colonial rule in India and to achieve independence for the country through an armed rebellion if necessary.

(ii) Consider the following statements and find the incorrect from the given options.

I. Bhagat Singh and Batukeshwar Dutta threw a bomb in the Central Legislative Assembly.
II. Hindustan Socialist Republican Army was based on the principles given by Mahatma Gandhi.
III. Bhagat Singh wanted a revolution in the society.

**Codes**

(a) Only I (b) Only II
(c) Only III (d) Both II and III

**Ans.** (b) Statement II is incorrect. Hindustan Socialist Rebublican was not based on the Mahatma Gandhi's principle of Non-violence.

(iii) What lessons does Bhagat Singh's life have for modern-day India? Identify the correct option.
(a) He emphasised on socio-economic changes rather than changing political leaders.
(b) He inspired the masses to break social barriers of casteism.
(c) He taught people to shed away the fear of British rulers.
(d) All of the above

**Ans.** (d) All the given statements are correct.

(iv) The HSRA and Bhagat Singh focussed on which section of the society to bring a revolution? Identify the correct option.
(a) Labourers (b) Leaders
(c) Youth (d) Merchants

**Ans.** (c) The HSRA and Bhagat Singh focussed on youth to bring a revolution.

(v) During whose tenure as the Viceroy of India were the great martyrs Bhagat Singh, Sukhdev and Rajguru hanged? Choose the best suitable option.
(a) Lord Canning (b) Lord Irwin
(c) Lord Minto (d) Lord Curzon

**Ans.** (b) During the tenure of Lord Irwin, Bhagat Singh Sukhdev and Rajguru were hanged.

(vi) Which of the following were the Revolutionary activities of HSRA? Choose the correct option.
(a) Central Assembly Bombing Case.
(b) An attempt to blow up the train that Lord Irwin was travelling in.
(c) Both (a) and (b)
(d) Involved in Lahore Conspiracy Case

**Ans.** (c) The revolutionary activities of HSRA were Central Assembly bombing case and an attempt to blow up the train in which Lord Irwin was travelling.

# PART 2
# Subjective Questions

## • Short Answer (SA) Type Questions

**1.** Explain four points about Gandhiji's Satyagraha. **(CBSE 2011)**

*Or* Gandhiji's idea of Satyagraha emphasised the power of truth and the need to search for truth. In the Light of this statement assess the contribution of Gandhiji towards Satyagraha. **(CBSE 2017)**

**Ans.** Gandhiji's contribution towards Satyagraha and his idea of Satyagraha was

- It emphasised the power of truth and the need to search for truth.
- It suggested that if the cause was true and if the struggle was against injustice, then physical force was not necessary to fight the oppressor. Without being aggressive, the Satyagrahi could win the battle.
- By Satyagraha, one can win the oppressor even by appealing to the conscience. Oppressor should be made to see the truth.
- By Satyagraha, truth was bound to triumph (victory) ultimately. Gandhiji believed that this dharma of non-violence could unite all Indians.

**2.** Describe the implications of First World War on the economic and political situation of India. **(CBSE 2020)**

**Ans.** The implications of First World War on the economic and political situation of India were

**Economic Situation**

- It led to a huge increase in defence expenditure which was financed by war loans. It resulted in raising custom duties and the introduction of income tax.
- Increased prices of essential commodities led to extreme hardship for the common people.

**Political Situation**

- Forced recruitment of villagers into armies caused wide spread anger among them.
- There was acute food shortage due to failure of crops and influenza epidemic which resulted into death of millions of people.

**3.** What was the Rowlatt Act? How did it affect the National Movement?

*Or* What was Rowlatt Act? How did the Indians show their disapproval towards this Act? **(CBSE 2013, 10)**

**Ans.** Rowlatt Act was an oppressive act introduced by the British Government in 1919. It gave the Government enormous powers to repress political activities and allowed detention of political person without trial for two years.

The Rowlatt Act affected the National Movement and Indian show their disapproval towards this act in the following ways

- Rallies were organised in various cities, workers went on strike in railway workshops and shops were closed down.
- British administration suppressed the nationalists. As a result local leaders were picked up from Amritsar and Mahatma Gandhi was barred from entering Delhi.

**4.** What were the circumstances which led to Jallianwala Bagh incident? Describe in brief the reaction of the people immediately after the incident. **(CBSE 2009)**

***Ans.*** Circumstances that led to Jallianwala Bagh Incident were

- **Rowlatt Act** The Rowlatt Act (1919) was passed by the British Government despite the united opposition of the Indian members. This Act gave enormous powers to the government to repress political activities and allowed detention of any person without trial for two years.
- **Rowlatt Satyagraha** Gandhiji wanted non-violent civil disobedience against Rowlatt Act. Rallies were organised in different cities, workers went on strike and shop were closed down.
- **Martial Law** British administration imposed martial law in Amritsar due to popular upsurge. On 13th April, 1919, General Dyer fired at the innocent people who gathered in Jallianwala Bagh killing hundreds.

The reaction of people immediately after the incident was that crowds took to the streets and there were strikes, clashes with the police and attacks on government buildings.

**5.** Why was Non-Cooperation Movement started in 1920? Why did Gandhiji call off the movement in 1922? **(CBSE 2015)**

*Or* Why Gandhiji decided to withdraw the Non-Cooperation Movement? **(NCERT)**

***Ans.*** Non-Cooperation Movement was started by Gandhiji in 1920 because

- Gandhiji saw this movement as opportunity to unite Muslims and Hindus.
- He wanted a solution on Khilafat issue.
- The most important objective was the attainment of Swaraj.

Gandhiji called off Non-Cooperation Movement in 1922 because

- The movement became violent. At Chauri-Chaura (Gorakhpur) a peaceful demonstration in a bazar turned into a violent clash in which more than 20 policemen were killed.
- Gandhiji felt that the Satyagrahis needed to be properly trained before they would be ready for mass struggle.

**6.** How did plantation workers in Assam had their own understanding of Mahatma Gandhi and the notion of Swaraj? Explain. **(CBSE 2019)**

***Ans.*** The plantation workers in Assam had understood the notion of Swaraj in the following ways

- For plantation workers in Assam, freedom meant the right to move freely in and out of the confined space in which they were enclosed. Under the Inland Emigration Act of 1859 plantation workers were not permitted to leave the Tea Gardens without permission.
- Swaraj for plantation workers meant retaining a link the village from which they had come. When plantation workers heard of the Non-Cooperation Movement thousands of workers refused to obey their authorities, left the plantations and headed home.
- They believed that Gandhi Raj was coming and everyone would be given land in their own village. The plantation worker, however never reached their destination as they were caught by the police and brutally beaten up.

**7.** Who was Alluri Sitaram Raju? Explain his role in inspiring the rebels with Gandhiji's ideas. **(CBSE 2012)**

***Ans.*** Alluri Sitaram Raju was a tribal leader in the Gudem Hills of Andhra Pradesh. He started a Militant Guerrilla Movement in the early 1920s.

**Role of Aluri Sitaram Raju in Inspiring the Rebel**

Raju inspired the hill people. The hill people were enraged by the British policy. When the government began forcing them to contribute 'begar' for road building, the hill people revolted.

Raju talked of the greatness of Mahatma Gandhi. Inspired by Gandhiji's Non-Cooperation Movement, he persuaded people to wear Khadi and give up drinking. He did not believe in non-violence. He thought that India could be liberated only by the use of force.

**8.** What was the main objective of Simon Commission? Why was the commission rejected by the Indians? Discuss.

***Ans.*** The main objective of Simon Commission, constituted under John Simon, was to review the functioning of the constitutional system in India and suggest changes in the system.

The Commission was boycotted by the Indian leaders because

- There was no Indian member in this Commission.
- The terms of Commission's appointement did not give any indication of swaraj while the demand of Indians was only swaraj.

Thus, when the Simon Commission arrived in India in 1928, it was greeted with the slogan 'Go Back Simon'.

**9.** Explain the reason for the Lahore Session of the Congress in 1929 to be called the historical session.

*Or* Mention the main contents of Indian National Congress in December 1929 held under the leadership of Jawaharlal Nehru. **(CBSE 2014)**

**Ans.** Lahore Session of the Congress in 1929 is called the historical session as at this session, the Congress President Jawaharlal Nehru passed a resolution of declaring 'Purna Swaraj' in December 1929. In 1929, Viceroy Lord Irwin announced an uncertain offer of 'Dominian status' to India and a Round Table Conference to discuss a future Constitution. The expectations of the Congress were not met by this announcement. At that time liberals and moderates in Congress lost their influence and Radicals like Jawaharlal Nehru and Subhash Chandra Bose became more assertive in Congress.

After declaring 'Purna Swaraj' or complete independence, the Congress declared 26th January, 1930 as the Independence Day.

**10.** Why did Gandhiji launch the Civil Disobedience Movement? Give reasons.

**Ans.** Gandhiji launched the Civil Disobedience Movement because

- Mahatma Gandhi sent a letter (31st January, 1930) to Viceroy Irwin stating eleven demands. Some of these were of general interest, others were specific demands of different classes. However, Viceroy Irwin refused the demands. Thus, he decided to launch the movement.
- Another reason for launching the movement was the Salt Law. Gandhiji believed that the tax on salt and the Government monopoly over salt production was the most oppressive measure taken by the British Government. This law had to be removed. Thus, he broke the salt law by manufacturing salt by boiling water in Dandi and urged the people to refuse cooperation with the British. The Salt March marked the beginnning of the Civil Disobedience Movement.

**11.** Why did Mahatma Gandhi find in 'salt' a powerful symbol that could unite the nation? Explain. **(CBSE 2017, 16)**

**Ans.** Mahatma Gandhi found in salt a powerful symbol that could unite the nation because salt is consumed by everyone and is regarded as one of the most essential items of food. By levying tax on salt and establishing monopoly over its production, the communal power revealed the most oppressive face of them.

Gandhiji thought if any movement could be arranged against this oppression (monopoly over the production of salt) which affected people from all strata, it could unite the nation. He believed 'salt' had this power. So, he gave an ultimatum to the British Government, but Irwin was not ready to negotiate.

Gandhiji started his famous Salt March with his trusted 78 followers from the Sabarmati ashram towards Dandi, the coastal town of Gujarat. This marked the beginning of the Civil Disobedience Movement all over India.

In this way, 'salt' inspired the nation to rebel against the British.

**12.** Describe the role of poor peasantry in the 'Civil Disobedience Movement.' **(CBSE 2020)**

**Ans.** The role of poor peasantry in the Civil Disobedience Movement was

- As the economic depression continued the poor peasants found it difficult to pay the rent. They wanted the unpaid rent to the landlord to be remitted. Thus, they joined a variety of radical movements, often led by socialists and communists.
- They came in huge numbers to support Gandhiji and his followers. It was because of them that Civil Disobedience Movement could become a Mass movement.
- They launched 'no rent' campaign but it was not supported by the Congress. So, the relationship between the poor peasant and Congress remained uncertain.

**13.** Analyse the role of merchants and the industrialists in the Civil Disobedience Movement. **(CBSE 2010)**

**Ans.** The role of merchants and the industrialists in the Civil Disobedience Movement was

- They became powerful in the society and wanted to expand their business. So, they started opposing colonial policies that restricted their business. They wanted protection against imports of foreign goods and a rupee sterling foreign exchange ratio that would discourage imports.
- The industrialists criticised colonial control over the Indian economy and supported the Civil Disobedience Movement at its first stage. Most industrialists thought 'Swaraj' as a time when colonial restriction did not exist on business world. As a result trade and business would flourish without constraints.
- They gave financial assistance and refused to buy or sell imported goods.

**14.** Mention the efforts of Gandhiji to get Harijans their rights.

**Ans.** The efforts of Gandhiji for Harijans were

- Gandhiji organised Satyagraha to secure the entry of the untouchables into temples and access to public wells, tanks, roads and schools.
- Gandhi himself cleaned toilets to dignify the work of the bhangi (the sweepers) and persuaded the upper caste to change their heart and give up the sin of untouchability.

- Gandhiji signed Poona Pact (September 1932) with Dr Ambedkar. It gave the depressed classes reserved seats in Provincial and Central Legislative councils, but they were to be voted in by the general electorate.

**15.** Explain the role of Ambedkar in uplifting the dalits or the depressed classes. **(CBSE 2011)**

***Ans.*** The role of Ambedker in uplifting the dalit or the depressed classes was

- Dr BR Ambedkar joined active polities in 1930 and organised the Depressed Classes Association to uplift the dalits.
- He demanded separate electorates for dalits and reservation of seats in educational institutions for them.
- He signed the Poona Pact that gave reserved seats to the depressed classes or dalits in provincial and Central Legislative Councils.

**16.** Describe the cultural process through which nationalism captured people's imagination.

***Ans.*** There were variety of cultural processes through which nationalism captured people's imagination. These were history, fiction, folklore, songs, popular prints and symbols which played a part in the making of nationalism. The image of Bharat Mata helped to create an image in which people can identify the nation. Devotion to this mother figure came to be seen as evidence of one's nationalism. These cultural processes help in spread of nationalism as people began to believe that they all are part of the same nation and discover a sense of collective belongingness.

**17.** What type of flag was designed during the 'Swaraj Movement' in Bengal? Explain its main features. **(CBSE 2016)**

*Or* Who designed the Swaraj flag? What were the features of this flag? How was it used as a symbol of defiance? **(CBSE 2012)**

***Ans.*** At the time of Swadeshi or Swaraj Movement, a tricolour flag was designed in Bengal by Mahatma Gandhi. Its features were

- It had eight lotuses representing eight provinces of British India and a crescent moon representing Hindu-Muslim community.
- It had also tricolour, i.e. red, green and white. It had a spining wheel in the centre.

The flag represented Gandhian ideal of self-help and carrying the flag and holding it aloft during procession or marches, became a symbol of defiance.

## • Long Answer (LA) Type Questions

**1.** Who launched the Khilafat Movement? Why was the movement launched? **(CBSE 2012, 11)**

***Ans.*** The Khilafat Movement was a united struggle launched by Muhammad Ali and Shaukat Ali. Gandhiji saw this as an opportunity to bring Muslims under the umbrella of a unified national movement.

The Khilafat Movement (1919-1924) was a Pan-Islamic, political protest campaign launched by Muslims in British India to influence the British Government and to protect the Ottoman Empire during the aftermath of First World War.

The First World War had ended with the defeat of Ottoman Turkey. There was a fear that the power of the spiritual head of the Islamic world (Khalifa) would be curtailed. To defend his power, a Khilafat Committee was formed in Bombay in 1919. The Khilafat leaders put pressure upon the British Government to give better treatment to Turkey.

**2.** How did the 'Non-Cooperation Movement' spread in cities across the country? Explain its effects on the economic front. **(CBSE 2015)**

***Ans.*** The Non-Cooperation Movement was started by the Congress party in January 1921. Initially, this movement started with middle class participation in the cities.

Later, this movement spread when thousands of students, teachers and lawyers gave up their institutions and profession and joined the movement. This movement began in different cities across the country. The economic effects of Non-Cooperation Movement were

- As foreign goods and foreign clothes were boycotted, the import of foreign clothes halved between 1921 and 1922, and its value dropping from 102 crore to 57 crore rupees.
- many places, merchants and traders refused to trade in foreign goods or invest in foreign trade.
- As people discarded imported clothes and started to use Indian clothes, production of Indian textile mills and handlooms increased.

**3.** Why did Mahatma Gandhi launch the 'Non-Cooperation Movement? How did this movement unite the country? Explain. **(CBSE 2019)**

***Ans.*** Gandhiji launched the Non-Cooperation Movement in 1920 because

He saw this movement as an opportunity to bring Muslims under a unified national movement. When young Muslim leaders like Muhammad Ali and Shaukat Ali approached him about the possibility of a united movement against the British rule.

- Gandhiji thought through the Non-Cooperation Movement, British rule in India would collapse within a year and Swaraj would come.

Thus, at the Congress Session in Nagpur in December 1920, the Non-Cooperation programme was finalised and Gandhiji launched the Non-Cooperation Movement.

This movement united the country as

- The Non-Cooperation Movement spread from the cities to the countryside. Different sections of our society interpreted this movement differently. The name of Gandhiji invoked to sanction all actions and aspirations.
- In Awadh, peasants under the leadership of Baba Ram Chandra revolted against the talukdars and the landlords who demanded very high rent and different taxes from them. The peasant demanded reduction of revenue, abolition of begar and social boycott of oppressive landlords.
- In Gudem hills of Andhra Pradesh, Alluri Sitaram Raju inspired by Gandhiji's ideals and started militant Guerrilla movement for achieving Swaraj.

**4.** Why did Mahatma Gandhi start the Civil Disobedience Movement'? How did this movement unite the country ? Explain. **(CBSE 2019)**

***Ans.*** Gandhiji launched the Civil Disobedience Movement because Lord Irwin ignored Gandhi's eleven demands including the abolition of the Salt Tax. Gandhiji's 'Salt March' marked the beginning of the Civil Disobedience Movement all over India.

The Civil Disobedience Movement came into force in various parts of the country and united different groups in the country as it was widely spread in the following ways

- With the spread of the movement, foreign cloth was boycotted and liquor shops were picketed. Peasants refused to pay revenue and chaukidari taxes. Village officials resigned from their post. Forest people violated forest law.
- In the countryside, rich peasant communities viz, Patidars of Gujarat and the Jats of Uttar Pradesh became the supporters of the Civil Disobedience Movement.
- The poorer peasantry, often led by the socialist and the communist, joined a variety of radical movements for the remission of their unpaid rent to the landlords.
- Industrialists led by Purshottamdas Thakurdas and GD Birla supported the Civil Disobedience Movement. Moreover railway workers, dock workers, mine workers from Chotta Nagpur and large number of women from all over the India participated in the Civil Disobedience Movement.

**5.** 'The Civil Disobedience Movement was different from the Non-Cooperation Movement.' Support the statement with examples. **(CBSE 2016)**

***Ans.*** The Civil Disobedience Movement was different from the Non-Cooperation Movement as

| Non-Cooperation Movement | Civil Disobedience Movement |
|---|---|
| Non-Cooperation Movement was launched in 1921 by Gandhiji. | Civil Disobedience Movement was launched in 1930. |
| It was started with middle class participation. | It was first supported by the industrialists like GD Birla and Purshottamdas Thakur das. |
| Due to Khalifa issues, Muslim Community participated in Non-Cooperation Movement on large scale. | The growing proximity of the Congress Party and Hindu Mahasabha prevented the Muslims to participate in Civil Disobedience Movement. |
| The Non-Cooperation Movement was withdrawn by Gandhiji due to violent incident at Chauri-Chaura. | The Civil Disobedience Movement was withdrawn in 1931, when Gandhiji signed 'Gandhi-Irwin Act. |
| In this movement women did not participate in large scale. | Large scale participation of women is one of the most significant features of the Civil Disobedience Movement. |

**6.** Explain the role of women in the Civil Disobedience Movement.

***Ans.*** The role of women in the Civil Disobedience Movement was

- During Gandhiji's Salt March, thousands of women participated in marches, manufactured salt and picketed foreign cloth and liquor shops. Many went to jail. In urban areas, these women were from high caste educated family e.g. Sarojini Naidu, Satyavati Devi, Kamala Nehru, Vijaylakshmi Pandit, Kasturba Gandhi, etc. In rural areas, women came from rich peasant households. In Bengal the women's participation increased in nationalism.
- In 1930, women rallied before Bethune College, Calcutta in support of Gandhiji's Civil Disobedience Movement.
- In Bombay, large section of women of Gujarati community was influenced by Gandhiji's idealism and participated in National Movement.

However, all these participations were symbolic as women did not hold any position of authority for a long time.

## • Case Based Questions

**1.** Read the case/source given below and answer the questions that follows.

The movement started with middle-class participation in the cities. Thousands of students left government-controlled schools and colleges, headmasters and teachers resigned, and lawyers gave up their legal practices. The council elections were boycotted in most provinces except Madras, where the Justice Party, the party of the non-Brahmans, felt-that entering the council was one way of gaining some power- something that usually only Brahmans had access to.

The effects of non-cooperation on the economic front were more dramatic. Foreign goods were boycotted, liquor shops picketed, and foreign cloth burnt in huge bonfires. The import of foreign cloth halved between 1921 and 1922, its value dropping from ₹ 102 crore to ₹ 57 crore. In many places merchants and traders refused to trade in foreign goods or finance foreign trade. As the boycott movement spread, and people began discarding imported clothes and wearing only Indian ones, production of Indian textile mills and handlooms went up. **(CBSE 2020)**

(i) Explain the role of 'Justice Party' in boycotting of Council elections.

(ii) How was the effects of 'Non-Cooperation on the economic front' dramatic? What was the main cause for boycotting foreign goods during Non-Cooperation Movement?

(iii) Explain the effect of Boycott movement on foreign textile trade.

***Ans.*** (i) The role of 'Justice Party' is that it did not boycotted the council elections. It was the party of non-Brahmans. The party thought that council elections was a opportunity for them to enter the councils and gaining some power.

(ii) The effects of Non-Cooperation Movement were dramatic on economic front as foreign goods were boycotted, foreign clothes were burnt and foreign trade and financing foreign trade was refused.

The main cause for boycotting foreign goods during Non-Cooperation Movement was to challenge the well-established economic and power structure of Britishers.

(iii) The effects of Boycott movement on foreign textile trade were

- People began discarding imported clothes.
- People started to wear only Indian clothes.
- The import of foreign clothes halved between 1921 and 1922.

**2.** Read the sources given below and answer the questions that follow. **(CBSE 2020)**

**Source-A The Salt March and The Civil Disobedience Movement**

Mahatma Gandhi found in salt a powerful symbol that could unite the nation. On 31st January, 1930, he sent a letter to Viceroy Irwin stating eleven demands. Some of these were of general interest; while others were specific demands of different classes, from industrialists to peasants.

(i) How did Gandhiji react to the Salt Law ?

***Ans.*** Gandhiji reacted by demanding to abolish the Salt Law as salt was something consumed by the rich and the poor alike. It was one of the most essential items of food and British government had monopoly over it production and it levied tax on salt monopoly over its production. Mahatma Gandhi declared the most oppressive face of the British rule.

**Source-B How Participants saw the Movement**

In the countryside, rich peasant communities - like the Patidars of Gujarat and Jats of Uttar Pradesh - were active in the movement. Being producers of commercial crops, they were very hard hit by trade depression and falling prices.

(ii) Why did the rich peasants become supporters of the Civil Disobedience Movement ?

***Ans.*** Rich peasants became supporters of the Civil Disobedience Movement as for them fight for Swaraj was a struggle against high revenues. Being producers of commercial crops, rich peasants were very hard hit by the trade depression and falling prices. They found it impossible to pay government's revenue demand which the British government did not want to reduce.

**Source-C The Limits of Civil Disobedience Movement**

When the Civil Disobedience Movement started there was an atmosphere of suspicion and distrust between communities.

(iii) Examine the limits of the Civil Disobedience Movement.

***Ans.*** The limits of the Civil Disobedience Movement were

- Dalits or untouchables were not moved by the abstract concept of swaraj, so they did not join in this movement.
- As relations between Hindus and Muslims worsened, some of the political organisations of Muslims did not join the movement.

## • Map Based Questions

**1.** Mark and locate the following on the given map of India. **(CBSE 2014)**

(i) A place where the Congress Session was held in 1920. **(CBSE 2017)**

(ii) A place where the Congress Session was held in 1927. **(CBSE 2017)**

***Ans.*** (i) 1920-Calcutta, Nagpur (ii) 1927-Madras

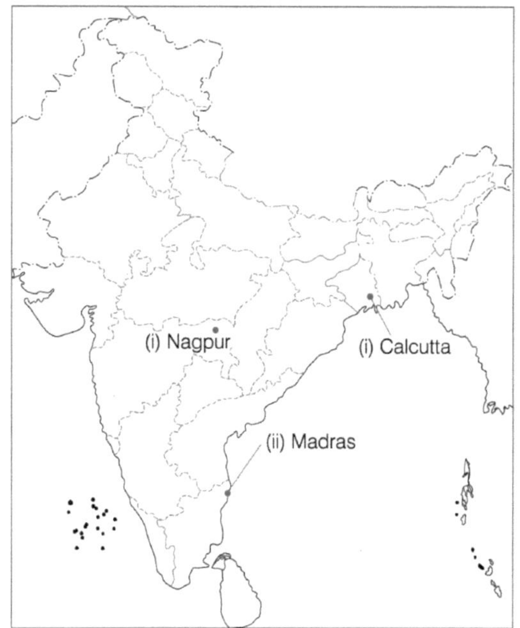


**2.** Idendify the place marked on the map with the help of information given below.

(i) Jallianwala Bagh incident

(ii) Calling of the Non-Cooperation Movement

(iii) Civil Disobedience Movement

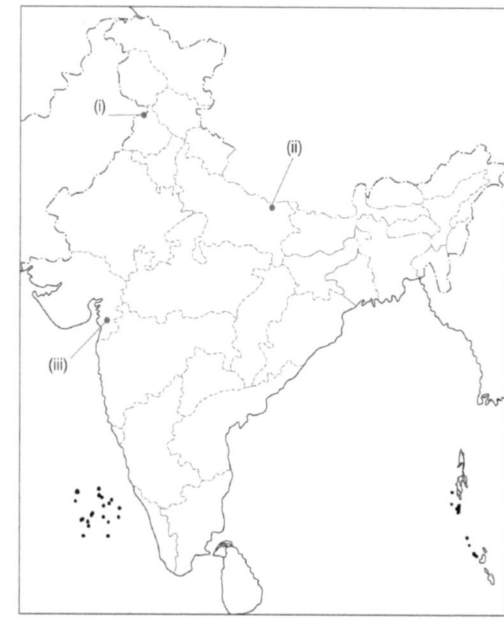


***Ans.*** (i) Amritsar 1919-(Punjab) (ii) Chauri-Chaura (UP) 1922 (iii) Dandi (Gujarat)

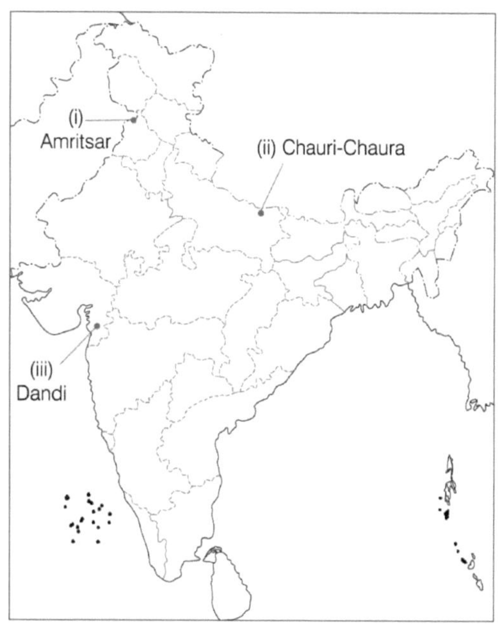

**3** Mark and locate the following in given map of India.

(i) Movement of Indigo planters

(ii) Peasant Satyagarha

(iii) Cotton mill workers Satyagraha

***Ans.*** (i) Champaran 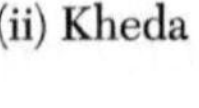 (ii) Kheda

(iii) Ahmedabad

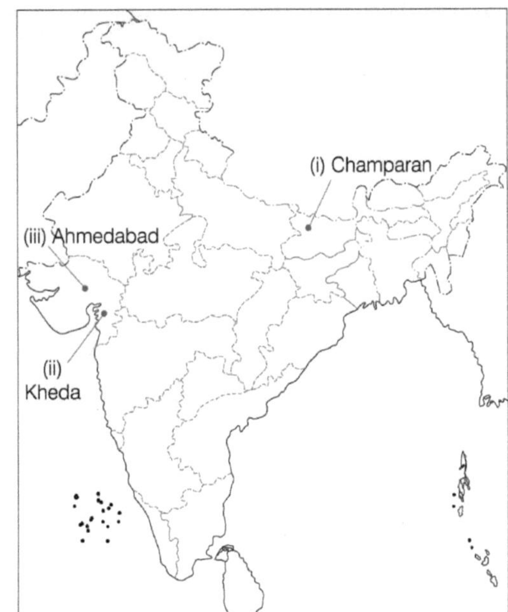

# Chapter Test

## Objective Questions

**1.** Who was responsible for the infamous Jallianwalla Bagh incidence on 13th April, 1919 at Amritsar?

(a) Warren Hastings (b) General Dyer
(c) Lord Cornwallis (d) William Bentick

**2.** To launch broad based movement in India, who felt the need to bring Hindus and Muslims close together?

(a) Jawaharlal Nehru (b) Bal Gangadhar Tilak
(c) Mahatma Gandhi (d) Lala Lajpat Rai

**3.** The nation is most often symbolised in which of the forms?

(a) History and fiction (b) Figures or images
(c) Popular prints (d) Folklore or songs

**4.** Find the incorrect statement.

(a) In Awadh, the Peasant Movement was developed under Pt Jawaharlal Nehru.
(b) Khilafat Movement was started in 1921.
(c) Ambedkar organised the Dalit into the Depressed Classes Association in 1930.
(d) In 1921, Gandhiji had designed a tricolour Swaraj Flag.

**5.** Consider the following statements and choose the correct option.

I. A khilafat committee was formed in Bombay in March 1919.

II. Jallianwala Bagh massacre took place on 13th April, 1920.

III. Simon commission was constituted by Mahatma Gandhi.

**Codes**

(a) Only I (b) Both I and II
(c) Only III (d) All of these

## Short Answer Type Questions

**6.** When and where did Mahatma Gandhi successfully organise Satyagraha Movements just after arriving in India?

**7.** Suggest at least three differences between the Civil Disobedience and the Non-Cooperation Movement.

**8.** Explain some economic effects of the Non-Cooperation Movement.

**9.** Explain the effects of 'World Wide Economic Depression' on India towards late 1920s.

**10.** Describe various problems in unifying people in India by the end of the 19th century.

## Long Answer Type Questions

**11.** Explain the reaction of the business class towards the Civil Disobedience Movement.

**12.** How did the Civil Disobedience Movement came into force in various parts of the country? Explain with examples.

**13.** "Dalit participation was limited in the Civil Disobedience Movement." Examine the statement.

## Answers

**1.** (b) General Dyer **2.** (c) Mahatma Gandhi **3.** (b) Figures or images

**4.** (a) In Awadh, the Peasant Movement was developed under Pt Jawaharlal Nehru.

**5.** (a) Only I

CHAPTER 02

# The Making of a Global World*

### In this Chapter...


- The Pre-Modern World
- The 19th Century (1815-1914)
- The Inter-War Economy
- Rebuilding a World Economy : The Post-War Era


Globalisation is an economic system, which is hardly 50 years old but the making of the global world has a long history. To understand phenomena of Globalisation, it is required to understand the history of trade, migration, people's search for work, the movement of capital, etc.

## The Pre-Modern World

Human societies have steadily become more interlinked. From ancient times, travellers, traders, priests and pilgrims travelled vast distances for various reasons, like

- to gain knowledge
- for more opportunities
- for religious or spiritual fulfilment
- to escape from ill-treatment

They carry with themselves goods, money, ideas, skills, values, inventions and even germs and diseases. By the 13th century, a strong link was established between the countries.

An active coastal trade linked the Indus Valley Civilizations with West Asia in the early 3000 BC. For more than a millennia, *Cowries* (sea shells) used as a form of currency from the Maldives to China and East Africa.

### Silk Routes Link the World

**Silk routes**[1] were existed since before the Christian era and flourished till the 15th century. The silk routes are good examples of pre-modern trade and cultural links between the distant parts of the world, *i.e.* linking Asia with Europe and North Africa. Along the silk routes, the silk cargoes from China, Indian spices and textiles, gold and silver from Europe were carried to different parts of the world.

The Buddhist preachers, Christian missionaries and later on, Muslim preachers travelled along these routes. These routes proved to be a great source of trade and cultural links between distant parts of the world.

### Food Travels : New Crops Introduced

Traders and travellers introduced new crops to the land they visited. Foods like potatoes, soya, groundnuts, maize, tomatoes, chillies, sweet potatoes were introduced in Europe and Asia after America was discovered by Christopher Columbus.

Noodles travelled West from China and became spaghetti. Europe's poor began to eat better and live longer after the introduction of potatoes. Arab traders took pasta to Sicily, an island in Italy.

1 **Silk Route** The route taken by traders to carry silk cargoes from China to the West.

* This chapter should be assessed in the **Periodic Test** only and will not be evaluated in the Board Examination.

Ireland's poor peasants depended upon the potatoes and when the Irish potato famine occurred around 1 million people died of starvation in Ireland and many had migrated in search of work.

## Conquest, Disease and Trade

The pre-modern world shrank after European sailors found a sea route to Asia and America in the 16th century. The Indian subcontinent was central to the trade, but the entry of Europeans helped to expand this trade towards Europe.

Precious metal, silver, found in the mines of Peru and Mexico enhanced Europe's wealth and financed its trade with Asia. Many expeditions were taken in search of **El Dorado**, the fabled city of gold in South America.

The Spanish and Portuguese were the first Europeans to conquer America in mid-16th century. The conquest of America was possible through the deadly disease smallpox that the Spanish conquerors carried on their person.

America's original inhabitants had no immunity against this disease. As a result, thousands of European moved to America and slaves captured in Africa worked in **plantation**[2] of cotton and sugar for European market.

India and China until 18th century were among the world's richest countries and the main centres of world trade. However, with Indian's colonisation and China's restriction of overseas contacts, Europe emerged as the centre of world trade.

# The 19th Century (1815-1914)

In the 19th century, economic, political, social, cultural and technological factors interacted in complex ways. It changed the society and reshaped its external relations immensely.

Economists identify three types of movement or flows within international economic exchanges

(i) The flow of trade in goods (especially cloth and wheat).
(ii) The flow of labour due to migration of people in search of employment.
(iii) The movement of capital for short-term or long-term investments over long distances.

All these flows affected people's lives significantly.

## A World Economy Takes Shape

In the late 18th century industrialisation and population growth had increased the demand for foodgrains in Britain. This situation resulted in the increase in foodgrain prices.

### Corn Laws and its Effects

Due to the pressure from the landowners, the government restricted the import of corn. These laws were commonly known as Corn Laws.

After the introduction of the Corn Laws, food prices became **exorbitant**[3] (unreasonably high). Industrialists and people living in towns were unhappy with high food prices. They forced the British Government to abolish the Corn Laws. After the abolition of the Corn Laws, food could be imported into Britain at much cheaper rate than before.

British agriculture was unable to compete with imports. Vast areas of land were uncultivated and thousands of people lost their livelihood. They came to the cities in search of works or migrated overseas. The effects of abolition of Corn Laws were

- Food could be imported into Britain more cheaply than it could be produced in Britain.
- As food prices fell, consumption in Britain increased.
- From the mid-19th century, faster industrial growth in Britain led to higher incomes and more demand for food.
- Around the world in Eastern Europe, Russia, America and Australia, land was cleared to cultivate more foodgrains to meet the increasing demand of Britain.
- New railways and harbours were needed to export agricultural products.
- Increasing number of workers needed more homes and settlements.
- Due to the demand for labour, millions of people migrated from Europe to America and Australia in the 19th century in search of a better life.
- Capital flowed from financial centres such as London.
- By the 1890, a **global agricultural economy** had developed.
- Sometimes, food came from thousands of miles away by railways or ships.
- The effects of abolition of corn laws also affected India as some change occured in West Punjab. In India, the British rulers transformed Punjab into a fertile agricultural land by developing irrigation system for growing wheat and cotton for export.

Regional commodities developed so fast that between 1820 and 1914, world trade had multiplied 25 to 40 times. About, 60% of this trade comprised primary products i.e. agricultural products like wheat and cotton and minerals like coal.

2 **Plantation** Estate for cultivation of cash crops like tea, coffee, cotton, tobacco, sugarcane, etc.
3 **Exorbitant** Going far beyond what is fair, reasonable; to high, expensive, etc.

### Role of Technology in 19th Century World

Technology or new inventions like **railways, steamships** and the **telegraph** had a great impact on the transformation of 19th century world.

Faster railways, lighter wagons and larger ships helped to move food more cheaply and quickly from far away farms in America, Australia or New Zealand to final markets of Europe.

### Role of Technology in Meat Transportation

Till the 1870s animals were shipped live from America to Europe and then slaughtered when they arrived there. Live animals took up a lot of space in ship and many animals also died in voyage, fell ill and became unfit to eat.

The development of **refrigerated ships** greatly helped to transport the perishable food items over long distances. Frozen meat was exported from America, Australia, New Zealand to different European countries.

The role of technology in meat transportation decreased the price of meat in European market and the cost of shipping. Meat (sometimes butter and egg) became a daily diet for the poor. This better living conditions created social peace within the country and support for imperialism in the colonies.

## Colonialism in the Late 19th Century

Trade flourished and markets expanded in the late 19th century. The European conquest in 19th century led many painful economic, social and ecological changes in the colonised countries.

In many parts of the world, expansion of trade led to loss of freedoms and livelihood. Britain, France, Germany, Belgium and later USA became colonial powers.

## Rinderpest or the Cattle Plague

In Africa, a fast-spreading disease of cattle plague or rinderpest destroyed a large number of cattle in the 1890s. The disease spread like 'forest fire' in the whole of Africa and killed 90 per cent of the cattle.

## Indentured Labour Migration from India

Indentured labour means a bonded labourer under contract to work for an employer for a specific amount of time, to pay off his passage to a new country or home. In the 19th century, lakhs of Indian and Chinese indentured labourers went to work on plantations, in mines and in different construction projects around the world. Most Indian indentured workers came from the present-day regions of Eastern Uttar Pradesh, Bihar, Central India and Tamil Nadu. In mid-19th century, these regions of India experienced many social changes like cottage industries declined, land rents rose and lands were cleared for mines and plantations. All these forced the poors to migrate in search of work.

### Destinations of Indian Indentured Migrants

The main destinations of Indian indentured migrants were the Caribbean Islands mainly Trinidad, Guyana, Surinam, Mauritius and Fiji besides other places near home. Tamil migrants went to Ceylon and Malaya. Some indentured workers were recruited in Assam's tea plantations.

### Condition of Indentured Labourer

Recruitment of indentured labourers was done by agents engaged by employers and paid a small commission.

Agents recruited indentured labourers by promising them better living conditions, more money and other benefits. However, when they arrived at the plantations, labourers found harsh conditions.

### Changes in Cultural Scene in 19th Century

19th century indenture has been described as a 'new system of slavery'. Although, living and working conditions were harsh, workers discovered their own ways of surviving. They developed new forms of festivals and other forms of entertainment by combining their different cultural forms.

**Riotous Carnival (Hosay[4]) in Trinidad,** the protest religion of **Rastafarianism**, which was made famous by Jamaican singer Bob Marley, Chutney music of Trinidad and Guyana are all examples of cultural fusion.

### Descendants of Indentured Labourers

Many indentured labourers permanently settled in the countries where they had gone after their contracts ended. So, there are large communities of people of Indian descent in these countries.

For example, Nobel Prize winner writer like VS Naipaul, etc. are descended from indentured labourers from India. The system of indentured labour was abolished in 1921.

## Indian Entrepreneurs Abroad

Indian bankers were amongst the many groups of bankers and traders, who financed export agriculture in Central and South-East Asia. **Shikaripuri Shroffs**, **Nattukottai Chettiars** were some famous Indian bankers.

Indian traders and moneylenders also followed European colonisers into Africa. Hyderabadi Sindhi traders developed flourishing trades at busy ports worldwide. They usually sold local and imported curios (rare objects) to tourists.

4 **Hosay** A riotous carnival in Trinidad when workers of all races and religions join to celebrate.

## Indian Trade, Colonialism and the Global System

Fine cottons from India were exported all over the Europe. With industrialisation, British cotton manufacturers began to expand. The industrialists pressurised the government to restrict cotton imports from India and protect local industries. Due to this, the flow of fine Indian cotton in Britain began to decline.

### Indian Trade and Colonialism

The British Government introduced high **tariffs**[5] on import of cotton cloth. From the early 19th century, British manufacturers also began to seek overseas markets for their cloth. As a result, the Indian textile industry was adversely affected. Indian textile faced stiff competition in other international markets. Consequently, India's share in International cotton textiles exports declined from 30% in 1800 to 3% in 1870.

As the exports of manufactures declined rapidly, export of raw materials increased equally fast. Between 1812 to 1871, the share of raw cotton exports increased from 5% to 35%.

British forced the farmers of India to produce indigo and opium. Indigo used for dyeing cloth was exported to Britain. Opium grown (from the 1820) in India was exported to China. The money earned through opium sale was used by Britain to finance its tea and other imports from China.

### Trade Relationship Between India and Britain

Over the 19th century, the British manufactures were available in large numbers in the Indian market. Foodgrains and raw material which were exported from India to Britain increased.

The value of British exports to India was much higher than the value of British imports from India. Thus, Britain had a **trade surplus** with India and used this surplus to balance its trade deficits with other countries. This trade surplus of Britain helped to pay the home charges i.e. private **remittances**[6] of British officials, traders, interest payments on external debt and pensions of British officials in India.

# The Inter-War Economy

The First World War (1914-18) was mainly fought in Europe but it had impact on whole world. It was fought between two power blocs. On one side were the **Allies**[7] – Britain, France, Russia (later joined by the US) and on the opposite side were the Central Powers – Germany, Austria-Hungary and Ottoman Turkey. World's leading industrial nations joined the war and tried to do the greatest possible destruction on their enemies.

The First World War was the first modern industrial war. For the first time, modern weapons like machine guns, tanks, aircraft, chemical weapons etc were used on a massive scale.

### Impacts of the First World War

- During the war, 9 million were dead and 20 million were injured.
- Household incomes also declined due to the death or injury of the earning members of the family and women had to take the jobs.
- Britain borrowed large sums of money from US banks as well as the US public. This made the USA an international creditor from an international debtor.

## Post-War Recovery

The post-war recovery was difficult. After the war, Britain found it difficult to recapture its earlier position of dominance in the Indian market and to compete with Japan Internationally. Britain faced an economic crisis and was burdened with huge external debts. This led to many British workers being out of work in 1921.

The wheat exports from Eastern Europe were disrupted during the war, as a result wheat production in Canada, America and Australia expanded.

After the war, production in Eastern Europe revived and created a **glut**[8] in wheat output. Grain prices fell, rural incomes declined and farmers fell deeper into debt.

## Rise of Mass Production and Consumption

After a short period of economic trouble, the US economy resumed its strength in the early 1920s. During that period, mass production became a characteristic feature of industrial production in USA.

### First Mass Production of Cars

Car manufacturer **Henry Ford** adapted the 'assembly line' method of a Chicago slaughter house to his new car plant in Detroit. He realised that this method would allow a faster and cheaper way of producing vehicles. This assembly line method forced the worker to repeat a single task mechanically and continuously which is dictated by the conveyor belt.

5 **Tariff** Tax imposed on a country's imports from the rest of the world. Tariffs are levied at the point of entry i.e. at the border or the airport.
6 **Remittance** An amount of money that is sent as a payment for something.
7 **Allies** The First World War fought between two power blocs. Allies were Britain, France and Russia later joined by the US formed an alliance.
8 **Glut** Supply of something in excess.

As a result, Henry Ford's cars came off the assembly line at three-minute intervals. The T-Model Ford was the world's first mass-produced car. Ford paid high wages to the workers to do **monotonous**[9] tasks, but recovered this cost through faster production. Car production in the US hike from 2 million in 1919 to more than 5 million in 1929.

Mass production lowered cost and prices of engineered goods like refrigerators, washing machines, radios, gramophone players etc. The housing and consumer increase created scope of large number of employment and incomes in the US and as a result, it became the largest overseas lender.

## The Great Depression

The Great Depression began around 1929 and lasted till the mid-1930s. During this period, most of the countries of the world experienced **catastrophic**[10] declines in production, employment, income and trade. The agricultural sector, in general was the worst affected.

### Factors Responsible for Depression

A combination of several factors were responsible for the depression

- Agricultural overproduction remained a problem. This decreased the prices of agricultural products. Farmers tried to expand production by bringing a larger volume of produce to the market to maintain their overall income. But, this further decreased the prices of agricultural products in the market.
- In the mid-1920s, many countries financed their investment through the loans they got from the USA. American capitalists stopped all loans to European countries.

### Effects of Great Depression

- In Europe, the depression led to the failure of some major banks and collapse of currencies like Sterling.
- The US was severely affected by the depression, as the banks had cut domestic lending and called back loans.
- Farms could not sell their harvests, households were ruined and businesses collapsed.
- The US banking system collapsed because the banks were unable to recover investments, collect loans and repay depositors.
- The US attempted to protect its economy in the depression by doubling the import duties, which hit the world trade badly.

## India and the Great Depression

Due to the Great Depression, India's export and imports declined to half (50 per cent) and prices of primary products like wheat and jute fell sharply between 1928 and 1934. The colonial government refused to reduce revenue demands, so the peasants became the worst suffers.

During this period India became an exporter of precious metals, especially gold. It promoted global economic recovery and helped to speed up Britain's recovery but did not help the Indian peasants to improve their conditions.

Across India, peasants condition became worst. People having fixed income faced less problem due to the price fall. In 1931, Mahatma Gandhi launched the Civil Disobedience Movement as a result of depression.

## Rebuilding a World Economy : The Post-War Era

The Second World War resulted in immense devastation in human and economic terms. It broke out after two decades of the First World War (1939-45). It was fought between the Axis Powers (Nazi Germany, Japan and Italy) and the Allies (Britain, France, Soviet Union and USA).

At least 60 million (about 3 per cent of the world's 1939 population) people were killed and millions were injured in this war.

### Post-War Reconstruction

Vast parts of Europe and Asia were devastated and several cities were destroyed by the war, therefore reconstruction became long and difficult task.

Two crucial influences shaped post-war reconstruction

(*i*) The US emerged as the world's dominant political economic and military power in the Western world.

(*ii*) Soviet Union became super power. It defeated Nazi Germany. It transformed itself from an agricultural country into a world power. As a leader of the Communist bloc, Soviet Union posed a great threat to the Capitalist economy.

## Post-War Settlement and the Bretton Woods Institutions

From inter-war economic experiences, two key lessons were drawn by the economists and politicians. These were

(*i*) The first lesson was that an industrial society based on mass production needed mass consumption. Mass consumption needed high and stable income. Stable income required steady and full employment, for which government should take necessary steps.

(*ii*) The second lesson was related to a country's economic links with other countries. The target of full employment could be achieved only if government had the power to control flows of goods, capital and labour.

---

**9 Monotonous** Something which is boring because it is always the same.

**10 Catastrophic** A terrible disaster.

It was supported by the United Nations Monetary and Financial Conference held in July, 1944 at Bretton Woods in New Hampshire, USA.

### Establishment of IMF and World Bank

The Bretton Woods Conference established the **International Monetary Fund** (IMF) to deal with external surpluses and deficits of its member nations. The International Bank for Reconstruction and Development (known as **World Bank**) was set up to finance post-war reconstruction.

The IMF and World Bank are referred as the Bretton Woods Institutions or Bretton Woods twins. They commanded financial operations in 1947 and the decision making in these Constitutions were mostly controlled by the Western Industrial powers.

The International Monetary System is the system linking national currencies and monetary system. Under this system, the national currencies followed the fixed **exchange rates**[11] and were fixed to the US dollar.

## The Early Post-War Years

The Bretton Woods System inaugurated an era of stable growth of trade and income for the Western industrial nations and Japan.

World trade grew annually at over 8% between 1950-1970 and incomes at nearly 5%. The unemployment rate of this period was averaged less than 5% in most industrial countries. Developing countries were in hurry to catch up with the advanced industrial countries.

## Decolonisation and Independence

When the Second World War ended, many countries were still under European colonial rule. Over the next two decades, most colonies in Asia and Africa became free and emerged as independent nations. But independence did not bring freedom from poverty or a lack of resources to these countries. Their economies and societies suffered a lot by long periods of colonial rule.

The IMF and the World Bank were designed to meet the financial needs of the industrial countries. But as Europe and Japan rapidly rebuilt their economies, they grew less dependent on the IMF and the World Bank. Therefore, from the late 1950s, the Bretton Woods Institutions began to shift their attention more towards developing countries.

### Condition of Developing Nations

Newly independent countries were trying to lift their population out of poverty. But after many years of decolonisation, they are still controlled by the international agencies which are dominated by the former colonial powers like US and France.

Most developing countries did not benefit from fast growth like the Western economies in the 1950s and 1960s. Thus, they organised themselves as a group, the Group of 77 (or G-77) countries to demand a New International Economic Order (NIEO).

By the NIEO, they meant a system that would give them

- real control over their natural resources
- More development assistance
- fairer prices for raw materials
- better access for their manufactured goods in developed countries' markets

## End of Bretton Woods and the Beginning of 'Globalisation'

From the 1960s, the rising cost of US's overseas involvements weakened its finances and competitive strength. The US dollar could not maintain its value in relation to gold.

This eventually led to the collapse of the system of **fixed exchange rates**[12] and the introduction of a system of **floating exchange rates**.

### Change in International Financial System

From the mid-1970s, the international financial system changed. The developing countries were then forced to borrow from Western commercial banks and private lending institutions. This change led to periodic debt crises, unemployment i.e., lower incomes and increased poverty in Africa, Latin America and also in the industrial world.

From the late 1970s, MNCs also began to shift production operations to low-wage Asian countries.

### New Economic Policy in China

China had been cut off from the post-war world economy since its revolution in 1949. But new economic policies in China and the collapse of the Soviet Union and Soviet-style communism in Eastern Europe brought many countries back in the world economy.

Wages were comparatively low in countries like China. Thus, they became attractive destinations for investment by Foreign MNCs. In the last two decades, countries like China, India and Brazil have achieved rapid economic development.

11 **Exchange Rates** They link national currencies of international trade. There are broadly two kinds of exchange rates : fixed exchange rate and floating exchange rate.

12 **Fixed Exchange Rates** When exchange rates are fixed and governments intervene to prevent movements in them.

# Chapter Practice

## PART 1 Objective Questions

### • Multiple Choice Questions

**1.** Which among the following countries were among the world's richest countries and the main centres of trade? Choose the correct option:

(a) India and China (b) China and Japan
(c) China and Britain (d) India and Japan

***Ans.*** (a) India and China until the 18th century were among the world's richest countries and the main centres of world trade.

**2.** Who wrote in May 1634 that small pox signalled God's blessing for the colonists: '... the natives ... were near all dead of small pox, so as the Lord had cleared our title to what we possess'. Identify the correct option.

(a) Alfred Crosby (b) John Winthorp
(c) MW Ridley (d) Michael Fitzgerald

***Ans.*** (b) John Winthorp , the first governor of the Massachusetts Bay colony in New England, wrote these words.

**3.** Identify the reason which made the transport of perishable products over long distances possible, from the given options.

(a) Steam Ships (b) Refrigerated ships
(c) Airline Services (d) Refrigerated Trains

***Ans.*** (b) The development of refrigerated ships greatly helped to transport the perishable food items over long distances.

**4.** Which of the following statements is appropriately associated with World War I ?

(a) Britain borrowed large sums of money from US banks as well as the US public.
(b) The First World War was mainly fought in Europe but it had impacted on the whole world.
(c) First World War was the first modern industrial war.
(d) All of the above

***Ans.*** (d) All the given statements are correct about First World War.

**5.** Which of the following would be provided to the developing countries by the New International Economic Order (NIEO)? Identify the correct option.

(a) More development assistance.
(b) Real control over their natural resources
(c) Fixed exchange rates
(d) Both (a) and (b)

***Ans.*** (d) NIEO would provide more development assistance and real control over natural resources.

**6.** Identify the method from the following information.

- This method was used in Chicago slaughterhouse.
- This method forced the workers to repect a single task.
- This method was faster and cheaper way of producing goods.

(a) Assembly line (b) Mass production
(c) Line production (d) None of these

***Ans.*** (a) The given information is about Assembly line method.

**7.** Choose the correctly matched pair from the given options.

(a) 1845 – European powers meet in Berlin to divide-up Africa between themselves.
(b) 1921 – Indentured Labour abolished
(c) 1939 – First World War
(d) 1890 – Potato Famine in Ireland

***Ans.*** (b) Indentured labour was abolished in 1921.

**8.** Choose the correctly matched pair from the given options.

(a) Remittance – Supply of something in excess.
(b) Glut – An amount of money that is sent as a payment for something.
(c) Catastrophic – A terrible disaster
(d) Tariff – A riotous carnival

***Ans.*** (c) Catastrophic means a terrible disaster.

Remittance here means an amount of money that is sent as a payment for something.

Glut here means supply of something in excess.

Tariff means a tax imposed on a country's imports from the rest of the world. Tariffs are levied at the point of entry i.e. at the border or the airport.

**9.** Match the following.

| | Column I | | Column II |
|---|---|---|---|
| A. | Global agricultural economy | 1. | 1929 |
| B. | First World War | 2. | 1914-18 |
| C. | Great Depression | 3. | 1890 |
| D. | Civil Disobedience Movement | 4. | 1931 |

**Codes**

| | A | B | C | D | | A | B | C | D |
|---|---|---|---|---|---|---|---|---|---|
| (a) | 2 | 3 | 4 | 1 | (b) | 3 | 2 | 1 | 4 |
| (c) | 4 | 3 | 2 | 1 | (d) | 1 | 4 | 3 | 2 |

*Ans.* (b)

**10.** Match the following:

| | List-I | | List-II |
|---|---|---|---|
| A. | First World War | 1. | US banking system collapsed |
| B. | Great Depression | 2. | First Modern industrial war |
| C. | Second World Post War Reconstruction | 3. | Bretton Woods Institutions |
| D. | IMF and World Bank | 4. | US emerged as the world's dominant power |

**Codes**

| | A | B | C | D | | A | B | C | D |
|---|---|---|---|---|---|---|---|---|---|
| (a) | 2 | 4 | 3 | 1 | (b) | 2 | 1 | 4 | 3 |
| (c) | 4 | 3 | 2 | 1 | (d) | 3 | 1 | 4 | 2 |

*Ans.* (b)

**11.** Following image depicts hungry children digging for potatoes in a field that has already been harvested, hoping to discover some leftovers. Identify the time period in which around 1,000,000 people died of starvation in Ireland due to Great Irish Potato Famine, and double the number emigrated in search of work.

(a) 1842-1844 (b) 1845-1849
(c) 1850- 1853 (d) 1854- 1858

*Ans.* (b) The time period of Great Irish Potato Famine was 1845 to 1849.

**12.** Following image depicts a prospective buyer carefully inspecting slaves lined up before the auction. To attract buyers, slaves were often dressed in their best clothes. Identify the year in which this image was illustrated in London News.

(a) 1849 (b) 1850 (c) 1851 (d) 1852

*Ans.* This image was illustrated in London News in 1849.

## • Assertion-Reason MCQs

**Directions** (Q. Nos. 13-17) *Each of these questions contains two statements,* **Assertion** *(A) and* **Reason** *(R). Each of these questions also has four alternative choices, any one of which is the correct answer. You have to select one of the codes (a), (b), (c) and (d) given below.*

**Codes**

(a) Both A and R are true and R is the correct explanation of A
(b) Both A and R are true, but R is not the correct explanation of A
(c) A is true, but R is false
(d) A is false, but R is true

**13. Assertion** (A) Most of the TVs, mobile phones and toys we see in the shops seem to be made in China.

**Reason** (R) Industries are relocated to China due to the low-cost structure of the Chinese economy most importantly its low wages.

*Ans.* (a) Most of the TVs, Mobile Phones and toys we see in the shops are made in China because of the low-cost structure of the Chinese Economy most importantly its low wages. Hence, both assertion and reason statements are true and justify each other.

**14. Assertion** (A) Developing countries are now forced to borrow from Western commercial banks and private lending institutions.

**Reason** (R) Periodic debt crises in the developing world and lower incomes and increased poverty are evident, especially in Africa and Latin Africa.

**Ans.** (a) Due to change in International Financial System after the mid 1970s, developing countries are now forced to borrow from western commercial banks and leading institutions. This has resulted into periodic debt crises in the developing world and lower incomes and increased poverty, especially evident in Africa and Latin Africa. Hence, both the assertion and reason statements are true and justify each other.

**15.** **Assertion** (A) Worldwide spread of MNCs was a notable feature of the 1950s and 1960s.

**Reason** (R) US businesses expanded worldwide and Western Europe and Japan also recovered to become industrial economies.

**Ans.** (b) Worldwide spread of MNCs was a notable feature of the 1950s and 1960s because high import tariffs imposed by different government forced MNCs to locate their manufacturing operations and became domestic producers in as many as countries as possible.

On the other hand, many MNCs came up during the 1950s and 1960s as US businesses expanded worldwide and Western Europe and Japan also recovered to become industrial economies. Hence, both assertion and reason are true, but reason is not the correct explanation of assertion.

**16.** **Assertion** (A) During the Great Depression of 1929, in general, agricultural regions and communities were the worst affected.

**Reason** (R) The fall in agricultural prices was greater and more prolonged than that in the prices of industrial goods.

**Ans.** (a) During the Great Depression, agricultural regions and communities were the worst affected because the fall in agricultural prices was greater and more prolonged than that in the prices of industrial goods. Hence, both assertion and reason statements are true and justify each other.

**17.** **Assertion** (A) In Africa, in the 1890s, a fast-spreading disease of Cattle Plague or rinderpest had a terrifying impact on people's livelihoods and the local economy.

**Reason** (R) There was widespread European imperial impact on colonized societies.

**Ans.** (b) In Africa, in the 1890s, a fast spreading disease of Cattle Plague or rinderpest had a terrifying impact on people's livelihoods and the local economy. This is a good example of the widespread European imperial impact on colonized societies. Hence, both assertion and reason statements are true, but reason is not the correct explanation of assertion.

## • Case Based MCQs

**18.** Read the case/source given and answer the questions that follow by choosing the correct option.

When the Second World War ended, large parts of the world were still under European colonial rule. Over the next two decades most colonies in Asia and Africa emerged as free independent nations. They were, however, overburdened by poverty and a lack of resources, and their economies and societies were handicapped by long periods of colonial rule. The IMF and the World Bank were designed to meet the financial needs of the industrial countries. They were not equipped to cope with the challenge of poverty and lack of development in the former colonies. But as Europe and Japan rapidly rebuilt their economies, they grew less dependent on the IMF and the World Bank. Thus, from the late 1950s the Bretton Woods institutions began to shift their attention more towards developing countries. As colonies, many of the less developed regions of the world had been part of Western empires. Now, ironically, as newly independent countries facing urgent pressures to lift their populations out of poverty, they came under the guidance of international agencies dominated by the former colonial powers.

Even after many years of decolonisation, the former colonial powers still controlled vital resources such as minerals and land in many of their former colonies. Large corporations of other powerful countries, for example the US, also often managed to secure rights to exploit developing countries' natural resources very cheaply.

(i) Why the Bretton Woods Institutions were established? Choose the correct option from the following:

(a) To promote the International Trade
(b) To reconstruct the economies damaged during the Second World War
(c) To improve the adverse Balance of Payment situation of the non member countries
(d) All of the above

**Ans.** (b) The motive behind the establishment of the Bretton Woods Institutions was to provide funds to member countries for economic reconstruction and development of the economies ruined by World War II.

(ii) What factors led to decolonisation after the Second World War? With reference to the above context, infer the appropriate option.

(a) After World War-II, European countries lacked the wealth and political support necessary to suppress the revolts.
(b) There were strong independence movements in colonies.
(c) Both (a) and (b)
(d) Financial needs of European countries were not favoured as they were colonial powers.

**Ans.** (c)

(iii) Which of the following countries has an effective right of veto over key IMF and World Bank decisions? Select the best suitable option from the following reference to the context:

(a) France (b) Australia (c) Russia (d) USA

*Ans.* (d) USA has an effective sign of veto over key IMF and World Bank decision.

(iv) Why did the Bretton Woods Institutions shift their focus from industrial countries to colonies? Identify from the given options.

(a) As upliftment of poor countries was a central notion.
(b) Because industrial countries had rebuilt their economies.
(c) Because financial support was a need for establishment of administration in colonies.
(d) As industrial countries tried to establish their control on Bretton Woods Institutions.

*Ans.* (b) The Bretton Woods Institutions shift their focus from industrial countries to colonies because industrial countries had rebuilt their economies.

(v) How did Bretton Woods Institutions failed in maintaining the idea of decolonisation? Choose the correct option.

(a) The European rulers played a dominant role in Bretton Woods Institutions.
(b) As its focus was to improve the European industrial centres.
(c) Through Bretton Woods Institutions, European rulers continued their control over colonies resources.
(d) All of the above

*Ans.* (c)

(vi) **Assertion** (A) World Bank and IMF were established after the Second World War.
**Reason** (R) Second World War caused an immense amount of economic destruction and many parts of Europe and Asia were destroyed.

**Codes**

(a) Both A and R are true and R is the correct explanation of A
(b) Both A and R are true, but R is not the correct explanation of A
(c) A is true, but R is false
(d) A is false, but R is true

*Ans.* (b) World Bank and IMF were established after the Second World War. On the other hand, Second World War has caused 'an immense amount of economic destruction and many parts of Europe and Asia were destroyed. Hence, both assertion and reason statements are true, but reason is not the correct explanation of assertion.

# PART 2
# Subjective Questions

## • Short Answer (SA) Type Questions

**1.** Describe the significance of silk routes in the pre-modern period in the field of trade cultural exchange and religion. **(CBSE 2014)**

*Ans.* The significance of silk routes were

- The silk routes are good examples of pre-modern trade and cultural links between the distant parts of the world, *i.e.* linking Asia with Europe and North Africa.
- Along the silk routes, the silk cargoes from China, Indian spices and textiles, gold and silver from Europe were carried to different parts of the world.
- The Buddhist preachers, Christian missionaries and later on, Muslim preachers travelled along these routes.
- These routes proved to be a great source of trade and cultural links between distant parts of the world.

**2.** 'Food offers many examples of long distance cultural exchange'. Justify this statement. **(CBSE 2011)**

*Ans.* Food offers many examples of long distance cultural exchange in the following ways

- Traders and travellers introduced new crops to the lands they travelled.
- Ready food stuffs in distant parts of the world might share common origins. It is believed that noodles travelled West from China to become spaghetti.
- Arab traders took 'pasta' to Sicily in Italy.
- Many of our common foods like potatoes, soya, groundnuts, maize, tomatoes, chillies were not known to us. These foods came from American Indians and we became gradually dependent on these.

**3.** Explain any three effects of scraping Corn Laws in Britain. **(CBSE 2020)**

*Ans.* Three effects of scraping Corn Laws in Britain were

- After the Corn Laws were abolished, food could be imported into Britain more cheaply than it could be produced within the country.
- British agriculture was unstable to compete with imports. Vast areas of land were now left uncultivated and thousands of men and women were thrown out of work. They migrated to the cities or other countries in search of work.
- As the food prices fell, consumption in Britain rose. From the mid 19th century, faster industrial growth in Britain also led to higher incomes and therefore, more food imports.

**4.** Explain three reasons for the attraction of Europeans to Africa. **(CBSE 2012)**

***Ans.*** The three reasons for the attraction of European to Africa were

(i) Africa had abundant land and was rich in mineral resources. Its population was relatively small.

(ii) The Europeans were hoping to establish plantations and mines in Africa to produce crops and minerals for export to Europe.

(iii) In Africa, industrial revolution did not take place. Africans were militarily weak and backward. Europeans thought that they could easily capture the country and use its resource and people for their own profit.

**5.** Describe the impact of 'Rinderpest' on people's livelihood and local economy in Africa in the 1890s.

***Ans.*** Rinderpest was a cattle plague spread by Asian cattle taken to Africa to feed the Italian soldiers by the European colonisers. The impact of 'rinderpest' on people's livelihood and local economy in Africa in the 1890s was

- **Economic Impact** Rinderpest killed 90 per cent of the cattle. This virtually destroyed the African economic system based on cattle and land. Africans, who worked rearing cattle, were unemployed and forced to earn their livelihood by working in mines and on plantations set-up by the Europeans.
- **Impact on Livelihood** Using this plague advantage, colonising nations successfully monopolised cattle resources. By this, they strengthen their power and forced Africans into the labour market.

**6.** Who were indentured labourers? How were they recruited? Explain condition of the indentured labourers who went to work in different parts of the world. **(CBSE 2013, 12)**

*Or* Write a short note on indentured labourers.

***Ans.*** Indentured labourers were bonded labourers under contract to work for an employer for a specific amount of time, to pay off their passage to a new country or home.

They were recruited by agents engaged by employers and were paid a small commission.

The condition of the indentured labourers in different parts of the world was very pathetic in the following ways

- They were subjected to harsh, inhuman and unsympathetic conditions.
- If they were unwilling to migrate, they were captured by agents.
- If they were caught while escaping, they faced severe punishment.
- They have very few legal rights.
- Deductions were made from their wages, if the work was found unsatisfactory.

**7.** Mention any three circumstances that compelled Indians and Chinese to work as indenture labour in plantation and mines. **(CBSE 2016)**

***Ans.*** In the 19th century, hundreds of thousands of Indians and Chinese labourers went to work on plantations in mines and in different construction projects as indentured labour around the world. The circumstances that compelled them to work as indentured labour were

(i) Decline of cottage industry

(ii) Increase in land rents

(iii) Unemployment, poverty and indebtedness

Due to these reasons, poor were forced to migrate in search of work. The prospective migrants were tempted by the false promises of the agents and became indentured labourers.

**8.** Describe the economic condition of Britain after the 'First World War'. **(CBSE 2018)**

***Ans.*** The economic condition of Britain after the First World War was

- Britain which was a leading economy of the world before the First World War faced a prolonged crisis. While Britain was pre-occupied with war, industries had developed in Japan and India. After the war, Britain found it difficult to recapture its earlier position.
- Britain has borrowed liberally from the USA for its war time expenditure, thus at the end of the war, Britain was burdened with huge external debt.
- After the war, production in Britain contracted which led to huge job losses. In 1921, one in every five British workers was out of work. Anxiety and uncertainty about work became an enduring part of the post-war time.

**9.** Examine how the First World War transformed the US from being an international debtor to an international creditor.

***Ans.*** The First World War has transformed the US from being an international debtor to an international creditor in the following ways

- During the war, industries were restructured to produce war related goods. The US became the big supplier of war needs. So, the war helped to boost the US economy.
- The war led to the snapping of economic links between some of the world's largest economic powers which were now fighting with each other to pay for them.
- Due to war, Britain borrowed large amount of money from US banks.

**10.** Describe the great economic hardship that prevailed in Europe during the 1830s. **(CBSE 2019)**

***Ans.*** Economic hardships that prevailed in Europe during the 1830s were

- The first half of the nineteenth century saw an enormous increase in population all over Europe. Migration of rural people to the cities further made the situation worse.
- Small producers in towns faced stiff competition from import of cheap machine-made goods from England. This competition was mainly faced by the textile production as it was carried out mainly in homes or small workshops which were partly mechanised.
- Some regions of Europe which were under the feudal rule, the condition of the peasants was not good. The rise of food prices and bad harvest led to widespread pauperism in town and country.

**11.** How did Bretton Woods inaugurate an era of unprecedented growth in trade?

*Or* Explain the role of Bretton Woods institutions in post-Second World War settlement. **(CBSE 2020)**

***Ans.*** Bretton Woods inaugurated an era of unprecedented growth in trade by establishing International Monetary Fund and Bank for Reconstruction and Development known as world Bank

The Bretton Woods Conference established the International Monetary Fund (IMF) to deal with external surplus and deficits of its member nations. The conference established the World Bank to finance post-war reconstruction.

The IMF and World Bank were referred as the Bretton Woods Institutions or the twins of the Bretton Woods. Both these institutions commenced financial operations in 1947. Decision making in these institutions was controlled by the Western industrial powers.

**12.** How did housing and consumer boom lead to prosperity in the US?

***Ans.*** The housing and consumer boom in the 1920s created the basis of prosperity in the US in the following ways

- Large investments in housing and household goods seemed to create a cycle of higher employment and incomes. This led to rising consumption demand, more investment and again more employment and incomes.
- In 1923, the US resumed exporting capital to the rest of the world and became the largest overseas lender.
- US imports and capital exports boosted European recovery and world trade and also it enhanced the income growth over the next six years.

**13.** What are MNCs? Why MNCs choose China as an alternative location for investment?

***Ans.*** Multinational Corporations (MNCs) are large companies that operate in several countries at the same time.

The first MNCs were established in 1920s. The MNCs choose China as an alternative location of investment because

- Availability of skilled and unskilled labours/ workers at low wages
- Less cost of production
- China has the largest population besides labour. They also formed a large consumer base.

**14.** Analyse any three factors that make globalisation more fair. **(CBSE 2019)**

***Ans.*** Fair globalisation means that the benefits of the globalisation must be shared by all equally. The ways to make globalisation fair in India are

(i) Government needs to care about the labour laws so that workers get their trade union rights.

(ii) Government can negotiate with WTO for fairer rules and can align with developing countries to stand against the domination of developed countries.

(iii) Supporting the small producers to improve their performance so that they remain viable in the face of competition from MNC.

**15.** Why did Group 77 countries demand a New International Economic Order? Explain. **(CBSE 2010)**

***Ans.*** Group 77 countries demanded a New International Economic Order (NIEO) because

- They wanted to revise the International Economic System in favour of the developing countries.
- They wanted a system that would give them a real control over their natural resources.
- They wanted to set up a system under which they could get a fairer price for raw materials and better access for their manufactured goods in the developed countries' market.

## • Long Answer (LA) Type Questions

**1.** Describe the role of technology in transformation of the world in the 19th century. **(CBSE 2019)**

***Ans.*** Technology has played an important role in transformation the world economy in the 19th century in the following ways

- Technology can be regarded as the primary source in economic development. The railways, steamships, the telegraph were important inventions in the nineteenth century.

- The technological advances were the result of larger social, political and economic factors. For example, colonisation stimulated new investment and improvements in transport system.
- Faster railways, lighter wagon and large refrigerated ships helped move food more cheaply and quickly from America, Australia or New Zealand to final markets in different European countries.
- The reduced shipping costs lowered meat prices in Europe. The poor in Europe could consume a more varied diet which included meat, butter and eggs.
- Better living condition in Europe as a result of technology promoted social peace within the country and people started to support the policies of imperialism.

**2.** Describe the condition of indentured labour that migrated from India during the nineteenth century.

**Ans.** The condition of indentured labour that migrated from India during the 19th century was

- The conditions of these workers were very bad and their wages were extremely low.
- Agents tempted the prospective migrants by providing false information about final destinations. They did not tell them about the harsh modes of travel, the nature of the work and living and working conditions.
- There was long working hours for the labourers and children who were more than the age of five years were also expected to work with their parents.
- The indenture labour was nothing but a 'new system of slavery'. On arrival of the working place the labourers found completely different environment which they imagined.
- Sometimes the labourers could not finish the work which they were allotted. If they could not complete it, they were prosecuted and sent to jail.
- Their wages were deducted if their works were considered to be unsatisfactory. Many tried to escape, but if they caught, they faced severe punishment.

**3.** How did Henry Ford revolutionise mass production in the US? Explain.

**Ans.** Henry Ford revolutionise mass production by adopting the assembly line of a Chicago slaughterhouse to his new car plant in Detroit. The assembly line allowed a faster and cheaper way of producing vehicles. It forced workers to repeat a single task mechanically and continuously which is dictated by the conveyor belt. This increased their efficiency in the single task and the speed of production too.

As a result, Henry Ford's cars came off the assembly line at three-minute intervals. However, standing in front of the conveyor belt, no worker could delay the motion or take a break. In the beginning, many workers quit since they could not cope up with the stress of work. Thus, Henry Ford paid high wages to the workers who do that monotonous tasks, but recovered this cost through faster production. Due to this mass production, car production in the US hiked from 2 million in 1919 to more than 5 million in 1929.

**4.** Why the year 1929 known as the Great Depression? Explain the main factors responsible for the Great Depression.

*Or* Explain the causes of Great Depression. **(NCERT)**

**Ans.** The year of 1929 came to be known as the Great Depression because during this period most parts of the world experienced catastrophic declines in production, employment, income and trade.

The Great Depression was caused by several factors which were

- Many countries financed their investments through loans from the US. In the early 1920s, the economy of the US was strong. But the over production in industrial and agricultural sectors led to the depression.
- There was a sudden growth in the purchase of refrigerators, washing machines, radios, gramophone players, etc through hire-purchase. With the fall in prices and the prospect of depression, US banks slashed domestic lending and called back loans.
- Farms could not sell their harvests, households were ruined and business collapsed. The consumerist prosperity of 1920s disappeared.
- As a result of falling incomes, many households could not repay what they had borrowed. They even were forced to give up their homes, cars and other consumer durables.

**5.** Explain the impact of the Great Depression on India during the early twentieth century. **(CBSE 2020)**

**Ans.** The impact of the Great Depression on India during the early twentieth century was

- The depression immediately affected Indian trade. India's exports and imports nearly halved between 1928 and 1934. As international prices crashed, prices in India also plunged. Between 1928 and 1934 wheat prices in India fell by 50 per cent.
- Peasants and farmers suffered more than urban dwellers. Agricultural prices fall sharply, but the colonial government refused to reduce revenue demands.
- Peasants producing for the world market were the worst hit. As gunny exports collapsed, the price of raw jute crashed more than 60 per cent.

- Peasants who borrowed in the hope at better times or to increase output in the hope of higher income suffered a lot.
- Across India, peasants' indebtedness increased. Jute producers fell deeper and deeper into debt. They used up their savings, mortgaged lands and sold their valuables like jewellery to meet their expenses.

**6.** Explain what is referred to as the G-77, countries. In what ways can G-77 be seen as a reaction to the activities of the Bretton Woods twins? **(NCERT)**

***Ans.*** The G-77 is a coalition of developing nations.

They have demanded a New International Economic Order (NIEO) in which they have a real control over their natural resources.

By NIEO, they got more development assistance and fairer prices for raw materials, and better access to the markets in developed countries for their manufactured goods.

G-77 was seen as a reaction to the activities of the Bretton Woods twins because the Bretton Woods twins, IMF and World Bank were mainly setup to favour the developed nations. As a result most developing countries did not benefit from the fast growth that the Western economics experienced in the 1950s and 1960s. So, they organised themselves as a group-the group of 77 of G-77 to demand a new economic order.

The developing nations organised themselves into G-77 so as to gain real control over their natural resources. They also wanted a better opportunity for their manufactured goods in the markets of developed nations.

## • Case Based Questions

**1.** Read the given case/source and answer the following questions.

**Source A Decolonisation and Independence**

At the same time, most developing countries did not benefit from the fast growth the Western economies experienced in the 1950s and 1960s. Therefore, they organised themselves as a group i.e. the Group of 77 (or G-77) to demand a New International Economic Order (NIEO). By the NIEO they meant a system that would give them real control over their natural resources, more development assistance, fairer prices for raw materials and better access for their manufactured goods in developed countries' markets.

(i) What is NIEO? Explain the objectives of developing countries.

***Ans.*** NIEO is the New International Economic Order. It was a set of proposal put forward during the 1970's by the developing countries with the following objectives

- To revise the international economic system in favour of the developing countries.
- These countries wanted to set up a system under which they could get fairer prices for raw materials and better access for their manufactured goods in the developed countries markets, etc.

**Source B Indentured labour Migration from India**

Recruitment was done by agents engaged by employers and paid a small commission. Many migrants agreed to take up work hoping to escape poverty or oppression in their home villages. Agents also tempted the prospective migrants by providing false information about final destinations, modes of travel, the nature of the work and living and working conditions. Often migrants were not even told that they were to embark on a long sea voyage. Sometimes agents even forcibly abducted less willing migrants.

(ii) How were the indentured workers exploited by the recruiting agents?

***Ans.*** Recruiting agents exploited indentured workers by providing them false information about final destination, modes of travel, the nature of work and living and working conditions. Sometimes agent even forcibly captured less willing migrants.

**Source C The Great Depression**

The Great Depression began around 1929 and lasted till the mid-1930s. During this period, most parts of the world experienced catastrophic declines in production, employment, incomes and trade. The exact timing and impact of the depression varied across countries.

But in general, agricultural regions and communities were the worst affected. This was because the fall in agricultural prices was greater and more prolonged than that in the prices of industrial goods.

(iii) Which factors was responsible for the Great Depression in 1929?

***Ans.*** The main factor responsible for the depression in 1929 was agricultural overproduction. This decreased the prices of agricultural products. To handle this situation, farmers tried to expand production by bringing a larger volume of produce to the market. But this further decreased the price of agricultural products.

**2.** Read the given case/source and answer the following questions.

The Bretton Woods conference established the International Monetary Fund (IMF) to deal with external surpluses and deficits of its member nations. The International Bank for Reconstruction and Development (popularly known as the World Bank) was set up to finance post-war reconstruction: The IMF and the World Bank are referred to as the Bretton Woods institutions or sometimes the Bretton Woods twins. The post-war international economic system is also often described as the Bretton Woods system. The IMF and the World Bank commenced financial operations in 1947.

Decision- making in these institutions is controlled by the Western industrial powers. The US has an effective right of veto over key IMF and World Bank decisions.

The international monetary system is the system linking national currencies and monetary system. The Bretton Woods system was based on fixed exchange rates. In this system, national currencies, e.g., the Indian rupee, were pegged to the dollar at a fixed exchange rate. The dollar itself was anchored to gold at a fixed price of $35 per ounce of gold.

(i) Which institutions were established by the Bretton Woods conference ? Why the International Monetary Fund (IMF) was set up?

(ii) What was the Bretton Woods system?

(iii) What decision was taken at Bretton Woods in New Hampshire, USA?

***Ans.*** (i) International Monetary Fund and the International Bank for Reconstruction and Development, popularly known as World Bank were established by the Bretton Woods Conference.

The IMF was set up to promote International Monetary Cooperation.

(ii) The Bretton Woods System was a system based on fixed exchange rates. In this system, national currencies i.e. the Indian rupees were pegged to the dollar at a fixed exchange rate.

(iii) In Bretton Woods Conference New Hampshire USA, decision was taken for establishing World Bank and International Monetary Fund (IMF) to preserve Global economical stability and full employment in the industrial world.

# Chapter Test

## Objective Questions

**1.** Which of our common foods were not known to our ancestors until about 5 centuries ago?
(a) Sweet potatoes
(b) Groundnut and maize
(c) Soya, chillies and tomatoes
(d) All of these

**2.** Where animals are not slaughtered for food at the starting point?
(a) America (b) Australia (c) New Zealand (d) Europe

**3.** Which of the following statements is associated with IMF ?
(a) The Bretton Woods Conference established the IMF.
(b) The conference was held in May 1945.
(c) The IMF and the World Bank commenced financial operation in 1948.
(d) The conference was held at Bretton Woods in New Hampshire, UK.

**4.** Find the incorrect statement.
(a) The Great Depression began around 1939 and lasted till the mid 1980s.
(b) The system of indentured labour was abolished in 1921.
(c) Rinderpest arrived in Africa in late 1880s.
(d) The First World War fought in 1914-18.

**5.** Choose the correctly matched pair from the given options.
(a) 1870's – Rinderpest arrived in Africa
(b) 1924 – Indentured Labour Abolished
(c) 1918 – Second World War
(d) 1947 – Chinese Communist Revolution

## Short Answer Type Questions

**6.** What was the impact of technology on food availability?

**7.** The G-77 group of nations demand a New International Economic Order. Why?

**8.** What is rinderpest? Who brought it to Africa? How did rinderpest help the Europeans to conquer Africa?

**9.** 'The global transfer of diseases became instrumental in colonisation of Africa and South America'. Explain the statement.

**10.** 'The First World War was a modern industrial War'. Explain.

## Long Answer Type Questions

**11.** Analyse the effects of the First World War on the world economy.

**12.** Give three examples to show that the world changed with the discovery of new sea routes of America.

## Answers

**1.** (d) All of these
**2.** (d) Europe
**3.** (a) The Bretton Woods Conference established the IMF.
**4.** (c) Rinderpest arrived in Africa in late 1880s.
**5.** (c) 1918 – Second World War

CHAPTER 03

# The Age of Industrialisation*

### In this Chapter...

- Before the Industrial Revolution
- Hand Labour and Steam Power
- Industrialisation in the Colonies
- Factories Come Up
- The Peculiarities of Industrial Growth
- Market for Goods

The industrialisation is considered to be the backbone of economic development. Modernisation began with the age of industrialisation in Europe. The industrialisation is often associated with the growth of factory industry.

## Before the Industrial Revolution

History of industrialisation started with the establishment of first factories. But there is a problem with such idea. There was large-scale industrial production even before factories began in England and this production was not dependent on factories. This phase of industrialisation is known as **proto-industrialisation**[1].

### Expansion of World Trade

In the towns, urban crafts and trade **guilds**[2] were very powerful. Different guilds were granted the rights of production and trade for a specific products by the rulers.

These guilds controlled the production and restricted the entry of new merchants in the trade. The new merchants thus moved to countryside for expanding production and persuaded them to produce for international market. With the expansion of world trade and the aquisition of colonies in different parts of the world, the demand for goods began growing. World trade expanded at a very fast rate during the 17th and 18th century.

In the countryside, the income of poor peasants and artisans was not sufficient, so they began working for the merchants.

### Proto-Industrialisation System as a System of Commercial Exchange

The proto-industrial system was a network of commercial exchange. It was controlled by the merchants. Income from proto-industrial production supplemented peasants income from cultivation. A merchant clothier in England first purchased wool from a wool **stapler**[3] and supplied it to the spinners. The thread that was spun was taken in different stages of production to weavers, **fullers**[4] and then to dryers.

The finished products passed through several stage and reached the market of London. Gradually, London came to be known as a **finishing centre**. At each stage of production 20-25 members were employed by each merchants.

The goods were produced by a vast number of producers working within their family farms, instead of factories.

---

1 **Proto-industrialisation** Period before or beginning of industrialisation.

2 **Guilds** An association of skilled workers that maintained control over production, regulated competition and prices in the trade of specific products.

3 **Stapler** A person who 'staples' or sorts wool according to its fibre.

4 **Fuller** A person who 'fulls' i.e. gathers cloth by pleating.

* This chapter should be assessed in the **Periodic Test** only and will not be evaluated in the Board Examination.

## The Coming Up of the Factory

The earliest factories in England came up by the 1730s. However, the number of factories multiplied in the late 18th century. **Cotton textile** was the main industry at that time.

A series of inventions in the eighteenth century increased the **efficacy**[5] of each step of the production process which included **carding**[6], **twisting**, **spinning** and **rolling**. Richard Arkwright is credited to create the cotton mill. Within the mill, all the processes were carried out at one place. In the 19th century, factory system increased largely in England.

## The Pace of Industrial change

Cotton and metal became the most dynamic industries in Britain. Cotton was the leading sector in the first phase of industrialisation upto the 1840s followed by iron and steel industry.

The new machinery and industries could not easily displace traditional industries. At the end of 19th century, less than 20 per cent of the total workforce was employed in technologically advanced industrial sectors.

Textile was a dynamic sector, but a large portion of the output was not produced within factories. Most of the textiles were primarily produced within domestic units. Ordinary and small innovations were seen in non-mechanised sectors like food processing, building, furniture making, production of implements, pottery, glasswork and tanning.

The technological changes occurred slowly. They did not spread largely across the country. Merchants and industrialists were cautions about using new expensive technology. **James Watt** improved the steam engine produced by Newcomen and patented the new engine in 1781.

**Mathew Boulton** manufactured the new model of steam engine. But it was not easily accepted by the industrialists. At the beginning of the 19th century, there were only 321 steam engines all over the England.

# Hand Labour and Steam Power

In Britain, there was no shortage of human labour. Poor peasants and **vagrants**[7] moved to the cities in search of jobs so workers were available at low wages. In many industries, the demand for labour was seasonal. For example, gas works and breweries, book binding and printing, ship repairing, etc needed seasonal labour.

## Preference for Handmade Products

A range of products could be produced only with hand labour. These required human skill, instead of mechanical technology. In Victorian Britain, handmade products which were refined symbolised a class. Handmade products were preferred by the aristocrats and the **bourgeoisie**[8]. These handmade products were better finished and carefully designed. Machine made goods were exported for the people of colonies.

## Life of the Workers

The life of workers at that time was pathetic as

- The possibility of getting a job depended on existing networks of friendship and relations.
- Many job seekers had to wait for weeks, spending nights under bridges and in night shelters set up by private individuals.
- After the busy season was over, labourers looked for even odd jobs which were difficult to find till the mid-19th century.
- The wages increased in the early 19th century, but this increase was balanced by an increase in prices of commodities.
- The income of workers depended on the number of days of their work.
- About 10 per cent of the urban population was extremely poor till the mid-19th century.

### Technology and Employment

The fear of unemployment made workers unfriendly to the introduction of new technology. When the **Spinning Jenny**[9] was introduced in the woollen industry, women who survived on hand spinning began opposing new machines.

After the 1840, building activities like construction of railways, roads, railway lines, etc increased in the cities which needed large-scale employment.

The number of labourers employed in the transport industry doubled in the 1840s which again doubled in the next 30 years.

# Industrialisation in the Colonies

British colonies like India industrialised with the development of factory industries and non-mechanised sector.

5 **Efficacy** The power to produce a desired result or effect.
6 **Carding** The process in which fibres, such as cotton or wool, are prepared prior to spinning.
7 **Vagrants** A person who has no home or job, especially one who begs.
8 **Bourgeoisie** Middle class with its perceived materialistic values or conventional attitudes.
9 **Spinning Jenny** This machine was devised by James Hargreaves in 1764, which speeded up the spinning process and reduced labour demand. By turning one single wheel, a worker could set in motion a number of spindles and spin several threads at the same time.

## The Age of Indian Textiles

Silk and cotton products of India dominated the international market before the age of machine industries. Armenian and Persian merchants took the goods from Punjab to Afghanistan, Eastern Persia and Central Asia.

**Surat, Masulipatnam and Hooghly** were the most important ports, which were used for trade. Many Indian merchants and bankers were involved in financing production, carrying goods and supplying to exporters.

By the 1750s, with the arrival of the European companies, the Indians started losing their control over the trade. The European companies were gaining power by securing a variety of concessions from local courts. Some of the companies got monopoly rights to trade. All this resulted in a decline of the old ports like Surat and Hooghly, and emergence of new ports like Bombay and Calcutta. This change was an indication of the growth of new colonial power.

## Situation of Weavers

In 1760s, the Indian fine textiles were in great demand in Europe. So, the East India Company was keen on expanding textile exports from India.

In 1760s and 1770s, the East India Company faced problems in getting a regular supply of goods for export. This is because it faced competition from the French, Dutch, Portuguese and local traders. After the Company established its political power it developed a system of management and control. By this system, it started to eliminate its competitors and tried to assert a monopoly over right to trade.

The company adopted a system of loans to the weavers to prevent them dealing with other buyers. In many places of Bengal and Carnatic, weavers left villages and migrated to different villages. Sometimes, they even revolted against the Company and refused to take loans.

### Gomasthas

The East India Company started appointing gomasthas i.e. paid servant to supervise weavers, collect supplies and examine the quality of the cloth. The new *gomasthas*, having no social links with the villages, acted arrogantly and punished the weavers for delay in supplies. They marched into villages with **sepoys**[10] and peons and often punished the weavers by beating with stick.

## Manchester Comes to India

In 1811-12, the share of cotton textile industry was 33 per cent of India's export and by 1850-51, it was just 3 per cent. In the 19th century, textile industries in England developed. The industrialists pressurised the government to impose import duties on cotton textiles, so that Manchester goods could sell in Britain without facing any competition. At the same time industrialists persuaded the East India Company to sell British manufactures in Indian markets. By 1870s, cotton import from England was over 50 per cent of the value of Indian imports.

### Problems Faced by Indian Weavers

The problems faced by Indian weavers were

- Indian export market collapsed. The local market was filled with Manchester goods (goods imported from Britain). These imported cotton goods were so cheap that Indian weavers could not easily compete with them.
- As cotton exports from India increased due to the Civil War in USA, weavers in India did not get sufficient and good quality cotton and they were forced to buy raw cotton from Britain at higher prices.

# Factories Come Up

**Cotton** and **jute** mills were the first to be established in India. The **first cotton mill** was set up in 1854 in **Bombay** and the **first jute mill** was set up in 1855 in **Bengal**.

In North India, Elgin Mill was started in Kanpur in 1860s and a year later, first cotton mill was setup in Ahmedabad. By 1874, the **first spinning and weaving mill** of Madras began production. Most of these industries were set-up by Indian entrepreneurs.

## The Early Entrepreneurs

From the late 18th century, the British in India began exporting opium to China and took tea from China to England.

Many Indian businessmen were involved in this trade. Some famous industrialists of 19th century were Dwarkanath Tagore, Dinshaw Petit, Jamsetjee Nusserwanjee Tata, Shiv Narayan Birla (Grandfather of GD Birla), Seth Hukumchand, etc.

Dwarkanath Tagore set up six joint stock companies in the 1830s and 1840s. JN Tata set up first iron and steel works in India at Jamshedpur in 1912. Seth Hukumchand set up the **first Indian jute mill** in Calcutta in 1917.

### Colonial Limitations Over Indian Merchants

As colonial power gained control over Indian trade, the scope of business for Indian merchants became limited. Indian merchants were not allowed to trade with Europe in manufactured goods.

**10 Sepoy** This is how the British pronounced the word *sipahi*, meaning an Indian soldier in the service of the British.

Indian merchants were allowed to export only raw materials and foodgrains like cotton, opium, wheat and indigo which were required by the British. European Managing Agencies controlled a large sector of Indian industries till the First World War. Some of them were Bird Heiglers & Co. Andrew Yule and Jardine Skinner & Co. In most cases, Indian financiers provided the capital while the European Agencies made all investment and business decision.

## Migration of Workers in Search of Jobs

With the expansion of factories, the demand for workers increased. Peasants and artisans who found no work in the village went to the industrial centres in search of work. Many workers travelled distant places in the hope of work in the mills. For example, from the United Provinces, they even went to work in Bombay or Calcutta.

The problems faced by workers were

- Getting job was not easy.
- Number of workers were more as compared to jobs.
- Entry to the mills was restricted.

Industrialists employed a jobber to get new recruits. Jobber was an old and trusted worker. Jobber got people from his village, ensured them jobs, helped them settle in the city and provided them money in times of crisis.

The Jobber became a person with some authority and power. He controlled the lives of workers and demanded money and gift for his favour.

# The Peculiarities of Industrial Growth

The European industrialists were mainly interested in industrial products which they could export. These products were not for sale in India.

Indian businessmen began setting up industries in the late 19th century and by the first decade of the 20th century, a series of changes affected the pattern of industrialisation.

These were

- As swadeshi movement became stronger, the nationalist leaders urged the people to boycott foreign goods.
- Industrialists in India started cotton cloth production and the British mills became busy to produce goods for the army as the First World War started.
- India began shifting from yarn to cloth production, as India's yarn export to China has declined due to production of Chinese and Japanese mills which flooded chinese market.
- New factories were set up during the war to supply war needs and Indian industrial production increased.
- After the war, Manchester could never capture its old position and the economy of Britain was collapsed.

## Small-Scale Industries Predominate

Large industries were mainly located in Bengal and Bombay and formed only a small segment of the economy.

Over the rest of the country, small-scale production continued to predominate. **Handicrafts** production actually expanded in the 20th century by adopting new technology like looms with a **fly shuttle**[11].

Amongst weavers some produced coarse cloth while others wove finer qualities. The coarse cloth was purchased by the poor. Its demand fluctuated due to bad harvests or famines.

The finer varieties were bought by the rich. Famines did not affect the sale of fine varieties such as Baluchari and Banarasi saris. Mills could not imitate the **intricate**[12] designs of the weavers.

# Market for Goods

Advertisement, labelling and calendars were used to popularise products by both British and Indian manufactures. Advertisement through newspapers, magazines and hoardings were used by the producers to expand their market. Advertisement makes products appear desirable and necessary. It played a very significant role from the very beginning of the industrial age, for developing a new consumer culture.

### Initial Stages of Advertising in India

When Manchester industrialists began selling cloth in India, they put labels on the cloth bundles 'MADE IN MANCHESTER'. Sometimes, the images of Indian Gods, Goddesses (e.g. Krishna, Saraswati) were used on these labels.

By the late 19th century, manufacturers were printing calendars to popularise their products as calendars were used even by people who could not read. Besides, the images of Gods, figures of important persons, emperors and nawabs were used in advertisements and calendars. Advertisements sometimes became a medium of the nationalist message of Swadeshi which guaranteed the quality of the product.

## Conclusion

The age of industries has meant major technological changes, growth of factories and the making of a new industrial labour force. Small-scale production and hand technology also played key role in the industrial landscape.

---

**11 Fly Shuttle** It is a mechanical device used for weaving, moved by means of ropes and pullies. It is used by weavers to operate large looms.
**12 Intricate** It is the thing which is very complicated and detailed.

# Chapter Practice

## PART 1

## Objective Questions

### • Multiple Choice Questions

**1.** Which of the following industries became the most dynamic industries in Britain?

(a) Cotton and Jute
(b) Cotton and Metal
(c) Metal and Pottery
(d) Metal and Glasswork

***Ans.*** (b) Cotton and Metal became the most dynamic industries in Britain. Cotton was the leading sector in the first phase of industrialisation up to the 1840's followed by Iron and steel (Metal) Industry.

**2.** Which of the following is not a reason why industrialists in the 19th century Europe preferred hand labour over machines?

(a) There was abundance of labour so there were low wages.
(b) Hand labour produced uniform and standardised goods for a mass market.
(c) Machines required huge capital investment.
(d) Industries where demand was seasonal, industrialists preferred hand labour.

***Ans.*** (b) Some industrialists in nineteenth century Europe prefer hand labour over machines because

- Machines were costly, ineffective, difficult to repair and needed huge capital investments.
- Labour was available at low wages at that period of time.
- In seasonal Industries only seasonal labour was required.

Thus, option (b) is not an appropriate reason.

**3.** In Victorian Britain, the upper classes- aristocratic class and bourgeoisie preferred hand made goods. Identify the reason from the given options.

(a) They were made from imported material.
(b) As they were better finished.
(c) Only upper class could afford the expensive handmade items.
(d) The Handmade goods came to symbolise refinement and class.

***Ans.*** (d) Handmade goods were preferred by the aristocratic and bourgeoisie class as it symbolises refinement and class. These handmade products were better finished and carefully designed as compared to machine made products.

**4.** What made workers become hostile to the Spinning Jenny? Identify the correct reason from the given options.

(a) Common people had not yet accepted the machine-made products.
(b) Handmade goods were still popular.
(c) It had reduced the demand for labour.
(d) As low wages were offered to the labour.

***Ans.*** (c) The fear of unemployment and reduced demand of labour made the workers hostile or unfriendly to the introduction of new technology in the form of Spinning Jenny.

**5.** Why did the weavers suffer from a problem of raw cotton? Identify the correct option.

(a) Raw Cotton exports increased
(b) Cotton crop Perished
(c) Local Markets shrank
(d) Export Market collapsed

***Ans.*** (a) The weavers suffer from a problem of raw cotton because the cotton exports from India increased due to the Civil War in USA. Thus, the weavers were forced to buy raw cotton from Britain at higher prices.

**6.** Why it was difficult to get a job in a factory despite expansion of factories? Choose the correct option.

(a) Employers were looking for only skilled workers and they rejected inexperienced workers.
(b) The number of jobs were less than the number of job seekers.
(c) Employers wanted educated workers.
(d) Employers didn't prefer migrants.

***Ans.*** (b) It was difficult to get a job in a factory because the number of jobs were less than the number of job seekers.

**7.** Identify the person with the help of clues.

- He got people from the village
- He ensured people with jobs.

- He helped people to settle in cities.

(a) Stapler (b) Fuller
(c) Jobber (d) Gomasthas

*Ans.* (c) Jobber got people from his village, ensured them jobs, helped them settle in the city and provided them money in times of crises.

**8.** Choose the correctly matched pair about the events and their year:

(a) James Hargreaves invents the Spinning Jenny – 1764
(b) James Watt patents the Steam Engine – 1771
(c) Richard Arkwright creates the first cotton mill – 1781
(d) Earliest factories started in England – 1790's

*Ans.* (a) James Hargreaves invented the Spinning Jenny in 1764.

**9.** Match the following items given in List I with those in List II.

| List I (Year) | List II (Events) |
|---|---|
| A. 1854 | 1. J.N. Tata set up the Iron and Steel works of India. |
| B. 1855 | 2. First Spinning and Weaving Mill of Madras starts production. |
| C. 1874 | 3. First Jute Mill comes up in Bengal. |
| D. 1912 | 4. First Cotton Mill is set up in Bombay. |

**Codes**

| | A | B | C | D | | A | B | C | D |
|---|---|---|---|---|---|---|---|---|---|
| (a) | 1 | 2 | 3 | 4 | (b) | 3 | 1 | 4 | 2 |
| (c) | 2 | 3 | 4 | 1 | (d) | 4 | 3 | 2 | 1 |

*Ans.* (d)

**10.** Match the following items given in List I with those in List II.

| List I (Terms) | List II (Description) |
|---|---|
| A. Efficacy | 1. The process in which fibres are prior to spinning. |
| B. Carding | 2. A person who has no home or job. |
| C. Vagrants | 3. Middle class with its perceived materialistic values. |
| D. Bourgeoisie | 4. The power to produce a desired result or effect. |

**Codes**

| | A | B | C | D | | A | B | C | D |
|---|---|---|---|---|---|---|---|---|---|
| (a) | 2 | 3 | 4 | 1 | (b) | 4 | 1 | 2 | 3 |
| (c) | 3 | 4 | 1 | 2 | (d) | 2 | 1 | 3 | 4 |

*Ans.* (b)

**11.** Following image shows the homeless in London applying for tickets to stay overnight in a workhouse. These shelters were maintained under the supervision of the Poor Law Commissioners for the 'destitute, wayfarers, wanderers and foundling'. Identify the year in which this image was painted by Samuel Luke Fildes.

(a) 1871 (b) 1872 (c) 1874 (d) 1877

*Ans.* (c) The given image was painted in 1874.

**12.** Following image marked the decline of the old trading order and growth of the colonial economy. Identify the trading ports that grew during the 1780s.

(a) Bombay and Calcutta
(b) Madras and Calcutta
(c) Gujarat and Madras
(d) Gujarat and Bombay

*Ans.* (a) The trading ports that grew during the 1780s were Bombay and Calcutta.

## • Assertion-Reason MCQs

**Direction** (Q. Nos. 13-17) *Each of these questions contains two statements,* ***Assertion*** *(A) and* ***Reason*** *(R). Each of these questions also has four alternative choices, any one of which is the correct answer. You have to select one of the codes (a), (b), (c) and (d) given below.*

**Codes**

(a) Both A and R are true and R is the correct explanation of A
(b) Both A and R are true but, R is not the correct explanation of A
(c) A is true, but R is false
(d) A is false, but R is true

**13.** **Assertion** (A) In 1760s and 1770s, the East India Company faced problems in getting a regular supply of goods for export.

**Reason** (R) Emergence of new ports was an indication of the growth of new colonial powers.

***Ans.*** (b) In the 1760s and 1770s, the East India Company faced problems in getting a regular supply of goods for export. This is because it faced competition from the French, Dutch, Portuguese and local traders. On the other hand, emergence of new ports like Bombay and Calcutta was an indication of the growth of new colonial powers. Hence, both Assertion and Reason statements are true but Reason is not the correct explanation of Assertion.

**14.** **Assertion** (A) With the expansion of factories, the demand for workers increased.

**Reason** (R) Many worker travelled distant places in the hope of work in the mills.

***Ans.*** (a) With the expansion of factories, the demand for workers increased and due to this many workers travelled distant places in the hope of work in the mills. Hence, both Assertion and Reason are true and Reason is the correct explanation of Assertion.

**15.** **Assertion** (A) The period of industrialisation before the first factories came up in Europe is termed as proto-industrialisation.

**Reason** (R) This period was marked by merchants from towns getting products made in villages.

***Ans.*** (a) The period of industrialisation before the first factories came up in Europe is termed as proto-industrialisation as this period was marked by merchants from towns getting products made in villages. Hence, both Assertion and Reason statements are true and Reason is the correct explanation of Assertion.

**16.** **Assertion** (A) When the Spinning Jenny was introduced in the woolen industry, women who survived on hand spinning began opposing new machines.

**Reason** (R) The fear of unemployment made workers unfriendly to the introduction of new technology.

***Ans.*** (a) When Spinning Jenny was introduced in the woolen industry, the women who survived on hand spinning opposed new machines because of the fear of unemployment due to the introduction of new technology. Hence, both Assertion and Reason are true and Reason is the correct explanation of Assertion.

**17.** **Assertion** (A) By the 1750s, with the arrival of the European companies the Indians started losing their control over the trade.

**Reason** (R) There was a decline of the old ports like Surat and Hooghly and the emergence of new ports like Bombay and Calcutta.

***Ans.*** (b) By the 1750s, with the arrival of the European companies, the Indians started losing their control over the trade. On the other hand, there was decline of the old ports like Surat and Hooghly and emergence of the new ports like Bombay and Calcutta. Hence, both Assertion and Reason are true but Reason is not the correct explanation of Assertion.

## • Case Based MCQs

**18.** Read the case/source given and answer the questions that follow by choosing the correct option.

Will Thorne is one of those who went in search of seasonal work, loading bricks and doing odd jobs. He describes how job-seekers walked to London in search of work: 'I had always wanted to go to London, and my desire ... as stimulated by letters from an old workmate ... who was now working at the Old Kent Road Gas Works ... I finally decided to go ... in November, 1881. With two friends I started out to walk the journey, filled with the hope that we would be able to obtain employment, when we get there, with the kind assistance of my friend ... we had little money when we started, not enough to pay for our food and lodgings each night until we arrived in London. Some days we walked as much as twenty miles and other days less. Our money was gone at the end of the third day ... For two nights we slept out - once under a haystack and once in an old farm shed ... On arrival in London we tried to find ... my friend ... but ... were unsuccessful. Our money was gone, so there was nothing for us to do but to walk around until late at night, and the try to find some place to sleep. We found an old building and slept in it that night. The next day, Sunday, late in the afternoon, we got to the Old Kent Gas Works and applied for work. To my great surprise, the man we had been looking for was working at the time. He spoke to the foreman and I was given a job.'

(i) What was the status of human labour in Britain? Select the best suitable option from the following with reference to the context.

(a) There was limited number of workers.
(b) There was no shortage of labour.
(c) Labour had to be imported .
(d) There was uneven distribution of labour.

***Ans.*** (b) There was no shortage of labour in Britain.

(ii) What kinds of production demanded seasonal labour? Identify the best suitable option from the following.

(a) Steel and iron (b) Cotton and textiles
(c) Handmade goods (d) Bookbinders and printers

***Ans.*** (d) Bookbinders and printers demanded seasonal labour.

(iii) What was the possibility of getting a job with abundance of labour in cities such as London? With reference to the above context, infer the appropriate option.

(a) Jobs were given on the basis of merit system.
(b) Jobs were given who were registered with a particular factory.
(c) A job depended on existing networks of friendship and kin relations in a factory.
(d) All of the above

*Ans.* (c) The possibility of getting a job in London was depended on existing networks of friendship and kin relations in a factory.

(iv) What were the problems workers faced during the Industrialisation? Identify the best suitable option from the following.

(a) Migration from one place to another in search of suitable job.
(b) Spending nights under bridges or in night shelters.
(c) Preferences given to the unskilled labour in the industries.
(d) Both (a) and (b)

*Ans.* (d)

(v) Two statements are given in the question below as **Assertion** (A) and **Reason** (R). Read the statements and choose the appropriate option.

**Assertion** (A) Seasonality of work in any industries meant prolonged periods without work.

**Reason** (R) The lives of the workers was adversely affected and they returned towards rural areas.

**Codes**

(a) Both A and R are true and R is the correct explanation of A
(b) Both A and R are true, but R is not the correct explanation of A
(c) A is true, but R is false
(d) A is false, but R is true

*Ans.* (a) Seasonality of work in any industry meant prolonged periods without work. After the busy season was over, the poor were on the streets again. This had an adverse impact on their lives as most of them returned towards their rural areas when the demand for labour opened up there. Hence, both Assertion and Reason are true and Reason is the correct explanation of Assertion.

(vi) Which of the following aspect is correct regarding the given source? Identify the correct option

(a) It is extracted from 'Comers and Goers'.
(b) It is quoted by Raphael Samuel.
(c) It shows the realities of the Victorian City.
(d) All of the above

*Ans.* (d) All the given statements are correct.

PART 2

# Subjective Questions

## • Short Answer (SA) Type Questions

**1.** Explain the meaning of the term 'Industrial Revolution'.

*Ans.* The term 'Industrial Revolution' stands for those developments and inventions which revolutionised the technique and organisation of production in the later half of the 18th century. This Industrial Revolution replaced the previous domestic system of production by the new factory system. In place of manual and animal power, new machines and steam power were used for producing things. This revolution replaced cottage industries by factories, hand labour by machine work and craftsmen and artists by capitalists and factory owners.

**2.** How did factory production began in England?

*Ans.* The factory production began in England with the establishment of early factories by the 1730s. The number of factories increased dramatically in the late 18th century. During this period, cotton was the first good whose production was flourished. It was followed by the rapid establishment and expansion of the iron and steel industry.

The driving force of industrialisation was the inventions and technological changes of the 18th century. This innovation increased the efficiency at each stage of production and enhanced the output produced per worker, especially in the case of cotton and other textile industry.

Richard Arkwright laid the foundation of the factory system by creating the cotton mill. The spinning Jenny and other devices were invented to speed up textile production. This allowed more careful supervision over the production process, proper check over quality and regulation of labour force employed. Thus, in the late 19th century, factories increasingly became an intimate part of the Britain.

**3.** Highlight any three benefits of industrialisation on the society.

*Ans.* The benefits of industrialisation on the society can be are

- Industrialisation leads to improved standards of the entire society as a whole and improves of the economic conditions.
- It leads to prosperity in the form of the availability of better and more foods, clothing and gave longer life

expectancy, freedom from hard physical work, more and better facilities for development of intellectual capabilities of individual.

- It produce employment, wealth and technical skill. It provided modern conveniences, medical advances, changes in lifestyle, education, transportation development, etc.

**4.** Describe the conditions of workers in Europe after the industrial revolution. **(CBSE 2019)**

***Ans.*** The conditions of workers in Europe after the industrial revolution were

- In most of the industries, the demand for labour was seasonal. The actual possibility of getting a job depended on existing networks of friendship and relations.
- The workers were getting very low wages.
- Factories employed large number of women. With technological development women gradually lost their industrial jobs.
- Most of the workers were living in slums. Factory or workshop owners did not provide housing facilities to the migrant workers.

**5.** Explain how were Indian merchants and bankers involved in the export trade in the early 18th century. **(CBSE 2012)**

***Ans.*** Indian merchants and bankers were involved in the export trade in early 18th century in the following ways

- They were financing production, carrying goods and supplying exporters.
- The supply merchants linked the port towns to the inland regions.
- They gave advances to the weavers, procured the woven cloth from weaving villages and carried the supply to the ports.
- At the port, the big shippers and export merchants had brokers who negotiated the price and bought goods from the supply merchants operating inland.

**6.** Mention any three restrictions imposed by the British Government upon the Indian merchants in the 19th century.

***Ans.*** The restrictions imposed by the British Government upon the Indian merchants in the 19th century were

(i) The British Government developed a system of management and control that would eliminate competition and restrict the space within which Indian merchants could function.

(ii) Indian merchants were not allowed to trade with Europe in manufactured goods.

(iii) Indian merchants had to export mostly raw materials like raw cotton, opium, wheat and indigo required by the British. They were also gradually thrown out of the shipping business.

**7.** Critically examine how the British companies gradually asserted monopoly rights in India.

***Ans.*** British companies gradually asserted monopoly rights in India in the following ways

- The company appointed paid gomasthas to supervise weavers, collect supplies and examine the quality of cloth.
- The company introduced the system of advances to the weavers to prevent company weavers from dealing with other buyers.
- The company introduced a system of management and control that would eliminate competition, control costs and ensure regular supplies of cotton and silk goods.

**8.** Examine the causes of clashes between weavers and *gomasthas* in many weaving villages.

***Ans.*** The causes of clashes between the weavers and the gomasthas were

- The gomasthas gave loans to the weavers to purchase the raw material for their production. Those who took loans had to hand over the product timely to the gomasthas. They had no option to sell their products to other traders.
- Often the price given by the gomasthas (dictated by the company) was miserably low and the loans the weavers had accepted tied them to company. Weavers along with village traders revolted and opposed the company official and sometimes migrated to other villages.
- The gomasthas had no feelings to the weavers. They marched into villages with sepoys and peons and punished the weavers.

Thus, clashes between the weavers and gomasthas became very common.

**9.** Describe any three major problems faced by Indian cotton weavers in the nineteenth century. **(CBSE 2018)**

***Ans.*** The major problems that the Indian weavers faced in the nineteenth century were

(i) Their export market collapsed and the local market shrank.

(ii) The local market was flooded with Manchester goods (goods imported from Britain). These imported cotton goods were so cheap that Indian weavers could not easily compete with them.

(iii) Due to the Civil War in USA, weavers in India did not get sufficient supply of raw cotton and they were forced to buy raw cotton at high prices. In this situation, weaving was not profitable.

**10.** How did many Indian entrepreneurs survive despite of tight economic controls imposed by the British Government? **(CBSE 2012)**

**Ans.** Many Indian entrepreneurs survived despite of tight economic controls imposed by the British Government by adopting the following ways

- Some merchants traded with Burma, Middle East and East Africa accumulated capital through other trade networks.
- Some merchants operated within India, carrying goods from one place to another, banking money, transferring funds between cities and financing traders.
- When opportunities of investment in industries opened up, many Indian entrepreneurs set up their own factories.

**11.** Explain the role of European Managing Agencies in India.

**Ans.** Role of European Managing Agencies in India was

- European Managing Agencies (e.g. Bird Heiglers and Co., Andrew Yule, Jardine Skinner and Co.) dominated industrial production in India. They were interested in certain kinds of products which could be exported.
- By acquiring land at cheap rates from the colonial government, they established tea and coffee plantations.
- They invested money in mining, indigo and jute. These products were not for sale in India. Most of these products were used for export trade.
- Till the First World War, these agencies controlled a large sector of Indian industries.
- These agencies mobilised capital, set up joint stock companies and managed them.

**12.** Describe the role of 'Jobbers' in the beginning of twentieth century in India.

**Ans.** Jobbers were people employed by industrialists to recruit the right people from among the job seekers. Very often the jobber was an old and trusted worker. They played an important role in the mills of India in the beginning of the twentieth century in the following ways

- He got people from his village and ensured them jobs.
- He helped people to settle them in the city. He provided money in times of crisis.
- Jobbers became persons with some authority and power. He began demanding money and gifts for his favour and started to control the lives of workers.

**13.** Why did industrial production in India increase during the First World War?

*Or* Explain the impact of the First World War on industrial production in India. **(CBSE 2015)**

**Ans.** Industrial production in India was impacted or increased during the First World War due to the following reasons

- British industries were busy with war production to meet the needs of the army and they stopped British goods in other countries like-India. It was a good opportunity for Indian industries to fill in empty markets with their own products. Suddenly, Indian industries had a vast home market to supply.
- As the war continued, Indian factories were called upon to supply war needs like-jute bags, cloth or army uniform, tents and leather boots, etc.
- The increased demand for a variety of products led to the setting up of new factories. Production was also increased by the old industries. Many new workers were employed and forced to work more hours.

**14.** Give reasons why British industries failed to recapture their old hold on the Indian market after the First World War.

**Ans.** British industries failed to recapture their old hold on the Indian market after the First World War because

- During the war years, Indian industries gradually consolidated their position by substituting foreign manufacturers and capturing the home market.
- The nationalist movement had gained ground under Mahatma Gandhi and his call for use of Swadeshi products was largely supported.
- Countries like Japan, US and Germany had modernised and Britain could not compete with them.

Thus, British economy fell down after the world war and cotton production and exports of cotton cloth fell dramatically.

**15.** 'Despite stiff competition from machine- made thread, the Indian handloom production not only survived, but also saw a steady growth in the 20th century'. Explain reasons in favour of your answer. **(CBSE 2012)**

*Or* How did handloom cloth production expand steadily in the 20th century? Explain. **(CBSE 2014)**

**Ans.** Despite stiff competition from machine-made thread, the Indian weavers survived and expanded steadily in the 20th century due to following reasons

- Indian weavers began to use fly shuttle which increased productivity per worker, speeded up production and reduced labour demand.
- Among the weavers, some produced coarser cloth while others wove finer varieties. The finer varieties were bought by the rich and the sale of Banarasi and Baluchari saris was not affected by famines or droughts.
- Mills could not imitate specialised weaves like saris with woven borders, famous lungis and handkerchiefs of Madras, etc.

## • Long Answer (LA) Type Questions

**1.** What was proto industrialisation? In what ways the proto-industrial production helped the poor farmers in countryside?

**Ans.** The proto industrial system was a part of a network of commerical exchanges. In the seventeenth and eighteenth centuries with the expansion of world trade and acquisition of colonies, the demand for goods expanded. But the merchants could not set up business in towns due to the strict restriction imposed by guilds. So the merchants turned to the countryside.

Proto-industrialisation helped the poor farmers in the countryside in the following ways

- The peasants and cottagers looked for alternative ways for their survival.
- Many had small land holdings, which couldn't provide work for all the members.
- When merchants came around and offered money to produce goods for them, peasants eagerly accepted.
- By working for the merchants, they could remain in the countryside and also could cultivate their own small plots of land.

In this way, proto-industrial production supplemented the shrinking income of the poor peasants and raised their standard of living.

**2.** Describe the role of 'technology' in transformation of the world in the nineteenth century.

**Ans.** The role of technology in transformation of the world in the nineteenth century was

- Technological advancement through the invention of railways, steamships, telegraph etc transformed the nineteenth century world. Faster railways, lighter wagons and larger ships helped move food more cheaply and quickly from far away farms to final markets.
- Development of new technology like refrigerated ships enabled the transport of perishable foods like meat, egg more quickly than before. As a result poor of European countries got better food. This brought social peace and also support for imperialism.
- Industrialisation forced people to migrate from rural areas to urban areas in search of jobs in the factories. It encouraged the spirit of individualism among both men and women. Collective values of rural life began to fade out in urban areas.
- It further widened the gap between rich and poor. The factory workers were forced to live in unhealthy slum areas of cities instead of pollution free rural landscape.
- Industrialisation forced the entire household i.e. woman and children to work, child labour became a major problem of the society.

**3.** Describe the life of workers during the nineteenth century in England.

**Ans.** The life of workers during the nineteenth century in England was

- **Low Wages** The workers were getting very low wages. Till the mid-nineteenth century, about 10% of the population was extremely poor. The abundance of labour in the market affected the lives of the workers.
- **Women Workers** Factories employed large number of women. With technological development women gradually lost their industrial jobs.
- **Overcrowded Cities** Most of the workers were living in slums. As the new possible job opportunities were in the cities, number of people from countryside travelled towards the cities in search of work.
- **Seasonal Work** In most of the industries, the demand for labour was seasonal. The actual possibility of getting a job depended on existing networks of friendship and kin relations. Many of the workers had to wait for weeks spending nights under bridges or night shelters.

**4.** Why did the export of Indian textile decline at the beginning of the nineteenth century? Explain any three reasons. **(CBSE 2020)**

**Ans.** By the end of the 19th century, export of Indian textile industry started to decline due to the following reasons

- **East India Company Gained Power** Once the East India Company established political power, it asserted a monopoly right to trade. It proceeded to develop a system of management and control that would eliminate competition, control costs and ensure regular supplies of cotton and silk goods.
- **Growth of Cotton Industries in England** As cotton industries developed in England, industrial group became worried about the imports from other countries. They pressurised the government to impose import duties on cotton textile, so that Manchester goods could easily sell in Britain without facing any competition from outside.
  Further the industrialists persuaded the East India Company to sell British products forcefully in Indian market.
- **The Result of Two Edge Policy** To sell British products in India the East India Company followed a two edged policy, i.e. no taxes on imports but high taxes on exports. Due to this policy, local Indian market shrank and flooded with cheap Manchester machine made products.
- **Shortage of Raw Material** Due to the American Civil War, cotton supplies from the US cut off and Britain turned to India for cotton supplies. As raw cotton exports from India increased, Indian weavers faced the problem due to the shortage of raw materials for textile industry.

**5.** Describe the role of early entrepreneurs of India in the development of industries. **(CBSE 2019)**

**Ans.** The role of early entrepreneurs of India in the development of Industries was

- From the late 18th century, the British in India began exporting opium to China and took tea from China to England. Many Indian businessmen were involved in this trade.
- In the nineteenth century many cotton mills, jute mills, spinning and weaving mills were set up and most of these were set up by Indian entrepreneurs.
- In Bengal Dwarkanath Tagore, in Bombay Dihshaw Petit and Jamsetjee Nusservanjee Tata built huge industrial empire by accumulating their initial wealth partly from exports of China and partly from raw cotton exports to England. Other businessmen like Seth Hukumchand, J.N. Tata set up Jute mill, Iron and Steel factories in India.
- Some merchants from Madras traded with Burma and some others traded with the Middle East and East Africa.
- Some entrepreneurs operated within India, carry goods from one place to another, banking money, transferring funds between cities and financing other traders. When opportunities of investment were opened up, many factories were set up.

**6.** By the first decade of the 20th century, a series of changes affected the pattern of industrialisation in India. Explain. **(CBSE 2013, 2008)**

**Ans.** By the first decade of the 20th century, a series of changes affected the pattern of industrialisation in India in the following ways

- **Effect of Swadeshi and Boycott Movement** After the partition of Bengal, Swadeshi Movement was developed. It has two sides i.e. positive and negative. In the positive side, nationalists urged people to use only swadeshi goods and in the negative side they mobilised people to boycott foreign goods.

  This movement had an immense effect on economy. There was an increase in the demand of Indian goods, specially clothes.
- **Aim of Industrial Groups** Industrial groups organised themselves to protect their collective interests. They pressurised the government to increase tariff protection and grant other concessions.
- **Decline of Exports to China** From 1906, the export of Indian yarn to China declined as produce from Chinese and Japanese mills flooded the Chinese markets. Thus, industrialist in India began shifting from yarn to cloth production. Cotton goods production in India doubled between 1900 and 1912.
- **Result of First World War** Till the First World War, industrial growth was slow. British mills became busy with war production, thus Manchester imports to India declined. Suddenly, Indian mills got a vast home market to supply. As the war prolonged, Indian factories had to supply different war needs. This led to set up new factories and multiple shifts for the old factories.

  Indian industry developed immensely at that period. After the war, Manchester could not recapture its old position in Indian market.

**7.** 'We find that from the very beginning of the industrial age, advertisements played a vital role in expanding the markets for products.' Explain the statement in the context of pre-independence period of our country.

**Ans.** From the very beginning of the industrial age, advertisements played a vital role in expanding the markets for products in the following ways

- The Manchester industrialists began selling their cloth in India by putting labels on the cloth bundles. When buyers saw such labels on the cloth like 'Made In Manchester', they felt confident about buying the cloth.
- The manufacturers also used images of Indian Gods, Goddesses and important personalities on these labels. These images helped to make the foreign products somehow familiar to Indian people.
- In the late 19th century, the British manufacturers used calendars to popularise their products.

  Unlike newspapers and magazines, calendars were being used even by illiterate people.
- Indian manufacturers even advertised the nationalist message which was clear and specific. For example, 'if you care for the nation then buy products that Indians produce'. Advertisement became a medium of the message of Swadeshi.

## • Case Based Questions

**1.** Read the given cases/sources and answer the following questions.

**Source A Hand Labour and Steam Power**

In Victorian Britain, the upper classes-the Aristocrats and the Bourgeoisie preferred things produced by hand. Handmade products came to symbolise refinement and class. They were better finished, individually produced and carefully designed. Machine-made goods were for export to the colonies.

(i) Evaluate the preference of handmade products by the Aristocrats and Bourgeoisie in England.

**Ans.** The upper class-the aristocrats and the bourgeoisie preferred things produced by hand because it symbolised refinement and class. They were better finished, designed and individually produced.

**Source B Life of the Workers**

The abundance of labour in the market affected the lives of workers. As news of possible jobs travelled to the countryside, hundreds tramped to the cities. The actual possibility of getting a job depended on existing networks of friendship and kin relations. If you had a relative or a friend in a factory, you were more likely to get a job quickly. But not everyone had social connections. Many job-seekers had to wait weeks, spending nights under bridges or in night shelters.

(ii) 'The abundance of labour in the market affect the lives of the workers'. Explain in the context of 19th century Britain?

**Ans.** The abundance of labour in the market affected the lives of the workers during the 19th century as news of possible jobs travelled to the countryside, poor peasants and vagrants moved to the cities in large numbers. But the actual possibility of getting a job depended on existing networks of friendship and kin relations. But not everyone had social connections. Many job seekers had to wait for weeks, spending sleepless nights under bridges or in night shelters.

**Source C Manchester comes to India**

Cotton weavers in India thus faced two problems at the same time: their export market collapsed and the local market shrank, being glutted with Manchester imports. Produced by machines at lower costs, the imported cotton goods were so cheap that weavers could not easily compets with them. By the 1850s, reports from most weaving regions of India narrated stories of decline and desolation.

(iii) What kind of problems were faced by Indian cotton weavers? Describe.

**Ans.** The problems faced by the Indian weavers were

- Their export market collapsed.
- The local market shrank due to the low cost machine made British products.

**2.** Read the given case/source and answer the following questions.

In the countryside poor peasants and artisans began working for merchants. This was a time when open fields were disappearing and commons were being enclosed. Cottagers and poor peasants who had earlier depended on common lands for their survival, gathering their firewood, berries, vegetables, hay and straw, had to now look for alternative sources of income. Many had tiny plots of land which could not provide work for all members of the household.

So, when merchants came around and offered advances to produce goods for them, peasant households eagerly agreed, by working for the merchants, they could remain in the countryside and continue to cultivate their small plots. Income from proto-industrial production supplemented their shrinking income from cultivation. It also allowed them a fuller use of their family labour resources. This proto-industrial system was thus part of a network of commercial exchanges. It was controlled by merchants and the goods were produced by a vast number of producers working within their family farms, not in factories. At each stage of production 20 to 25 workers were employed by each merchant. This meant that each clothier was controlling hundreds of workers.

(i) What is proto-industrial system? Discuss its importance.

(ii) Which phase of industrialisation is called Proto-industrialisation and why?

(iii) Explain the main features of proto-industrialisation.

**Ans.** (i) The proto-industrial system was a network of early form of commercial exchange before industrialisation. It was controlled by the merchants.

It was important as the peasant could cultivate their own small patches of land and yet could earn some supplementary income by producing for the merchants. This allowed them to make better use of the available family resources.

(ii) The early phase of industrialisation in which large-scale production was carried out for international market not at factories but in decentralised units is called proto-industrialisation. It is called proto-industrialisation because products are made by hand only.

(iii) The main features of proto-industrialisation were

- It was controlled by merchants or guilds who had monopoly rights to produce and trade goods.
- Generally family members were involved in the production process and the production was carried out in countryside.

# Chapter Test

## Objective Questions

**1.** Who set up six joint-stock companies in Bengal in the 1830s and 1840s?
(a) Dwarkanath Tagore
(b) JN Tata
(c) Jamsetjee Jeejeebhoy
(d) R D Tata

**2.** In the year 1931, which of the following locations has highest concentration of large scale industries in India?
(a) Madras
(b) Punjab
(c) Bombay
(d) Bengal

**3.** Which image of God was most commonly used to popularise baby products?
(a) Ram
(b) Shiva
(c) Krishna
(d) Hanuman

**4.** Find the incorrect option.
(a) During the World War I, local industries captured the home market.
(b) The first cotton mill was set up in 1854 in Bombay.
(c) First Jute mill was set up in 1856 in, Surat.
(d) Iron and Steel works were set up in Jamshedpur in 1912.

**5.** Choose the correctly matched pair from the given options.
(a) Hoogly — Most important old port for trade
(b) Spinning Jenny — Introduced in Jute mills
(c) Gomasthas — Appointed by Indian merchants
(d) Sepoy — Indian soldier in the service of Industrialists

## Short Answer Type Questions

**6.** What was trade guild? Explain.

**7.** The First World War created dramatically a new situation for Indian industries. Analyse how this happened by giving three situations.

**8.** Why did the poor peasants and artisans in the countryside begin to work for the merchants from the towns?

**9.** "Series of changes affected the pattern of industrialisation in India by the early twentieth century." Analyse the statement.

**10.** Explain any three effects of population growth in England in late eighteenth century.

## Long Answer Type Questions

**11.** Explain giving four reasons why the industrialists of Europe preferred hand labour over machines during the 19th century.

**12.** The Indian cotton export market collapsed and the local market shrank in the beginning of the 19th century. Why?

# Answers

**1.** (a) Dwarkanath Tagore
**2.** (d) Bengal
**3.** (c) Krishna
**4.** (c) First Jute mill was set up in 1856 in, Surat.
**5.** (a) Hoogly — Most important old port for trade

CHAPTER 01

# Minerals and Energy Resources*

### In this Chapter...


- What is a Mineral?
- Classification of Minerals
- Conservation of Minerals
- Energy Resources


## What is a Mineral?

A homogeneous, naturally occurring substance with a definable internal structure is called mineral. Rocks are the combinations of minerals. Some rocks consist of single mineral, but most of them consist of several minerals in different quantity.

The formation of minerals depend upon physical and chemical conditions that in turn, results in a wide range of colours, hardness, crystal forms, lustre and density of a particular mineral. Minerals are found in varied forms in nature, ranging from the hardest diamond to the softest talc.

For better understanding of Earth's landforms, Geographers study minerals as part of the earth's crust. Geologists study the formation, age and composition (Physical and Chemical) of minerals.

Materials of daily use are made of minerals like toothpaste contain silica, limestone, phosphate, etc. Minerals are needed by our body too and are also the basis of all economic activities. They are also studied to know the formation, age and composition of the earth.

## Mode of Occurrence of Minerals

Minerals are usually found in **ores**. An ore is a naturally occurring material having one or more minerals in sufficient concentration so that their extraction is done successfully.

Mineral generally occur in the following forms

- **Veins and Lodes** In igneous and metamorphic rocks, minerals occur in cracks, crevices, faults or joints. Smaller occurences are called veins and larger are called lodes. These veins and lodes are formed when minerals in liquid/molten and gaseous forms are forced upward through cavities towards the earth's surface. They cool and solidify when they reach the earth's surface and fill in the cracks, crevices, faults or joints. Metallic minerals like tin, copper, zinc and lead are obtained from it.
- **Beds or Layers** In sedimentary rocks, minerals occur in the form of beds or layers due to deposition, accumulation and concentration in horizontal layers of the rock. Coal, some forms of iron ore, gypsum, potash salt and sodium salt are also found in these beds or layers. These minerals (except coal and iron ore) are formed due to evaporation, especially, in arid regions.
- **Decomposition of Surface Rocks** When decomposition of surface rocks and the removal of soluble constituents takes place, it leaves a residual mass of weathered material containing mineral ores. Bauxite is formed by the decomposition of surface rocks.

* The theoretical aspect of this chapter should be assessed in the **Periodic Test** only and will not be evaluated in Board Examination. However, the map items of this chapter as given in the map list will be evaluated in Board Examination.

- **Alluvial Deposits** Some minerals are found in sands of valley floors and at the base of hills. These are known as **placer deposits[1]**. They are not corroded by water, e.g. gold, silver, platinum and tin.
- **Ocean Waters** These contain many minerals. Common salt, magnesium and bromine are derived from ocean waters, whereas manganese nodules occur in ocean beds.

> **Rat Hole Mining**
>
> It is a type of mining that is done by diging long narrow tunnels to reach the coal deposits under the ground. It is practiced in Jowai and Cherapunjee.
>
> The practice of Rat hole mining is declared illegal by National Green Tribunal.
>
> But in most of the tribal areas of the North-East India, minerals are owned by individuals or communities.
>
> In Meghalaya, there are large deposits of coal, iron ore, limestone and dolomite, etc. Rat hole mining is done here.

### Distribution of Minerals in India

In India, there are found large variations in occurrence of minerals. It is because of the differences in the geological structure, processes and time involved in the formation of minerals.

The distribution of minerals in India is

- **Peninsular Plateau** Peninsular rocks contain most of the reserves of coal, metallic minerals, mica, non-ferrous mineral and non-metallic minerals.
- **Gujarat and Assam** Sedimentary rocks on the Western and Eastern flanks of the Peninsula which are found in Gujarat and Assam have most of the petroleum deposits.
- **Rajasthan** Rajasthan with the rock systems of the peninsula has many reserves of **non-ferrous minerals[2]**.
  - **Northern Plains** There is very little or no minerals of economic value in vast alluvial plains of the North India.

## Classification of Minerals

Minerals are mainly classified as metallic, non-metallic and energy minerals.

### Metallic Minerals

Minerals containing metals are called metallic minerals, like gold, silver, tungsten, etc. *They are of two types*

#### (i) Ferrous Minerals

Metallic minerals having iron content are called ferrous minerals. These minerals account for about three-fourth of the total value of the production of metallic minerals. India exports a fairly large amount of ferrous minerals. These minerals provide a strong base for the development of **metallurgical industries**.

The distribution of major ferrous mineral, iron ore and manganese is

#### Iron Ore

It is the basic mineral and the backbone of industrial development. India has abundant resources of good quality iron ore. The finest iron ore is **magnetite**. It has a very high iron content upto 70%. Magnetite has excellent magnetic qualities, especially valuable in the electrical industry.

**Haematite** ore has an iron content upto 50-60%. It is the most important industrial iron ore in terms of the quantity used.

### Iron Ore Belts in India

The major iron ore belts in India are

- **Odisha-Jharkhand Belt** In Odisha, high grade haematite ore is found in Badampahar mines in the Mayurbhanj and Kendujhar districts.
- In the adjoining Singbhum district of Jharkhand haematite iron ore is mined in Gua and Noamundi.
- **Odisha has the largest share in iron ore production** in India i.e. 52% in 2016-17.
- **Durg-Bastar-Chandrapur Belt** It lies in Chhattisgarh and Maharashtra. Very high grade haematites are found in the famous **Bailadila range** of hills in the Bastar district of Chhattisgarh.
- The range of hills comprises of 14 deposits of super high grade haematite iron ore. It has the best physical properties needed for making steel. Iron ore from these mines is exported to Japan and South Korea *via* Vishakhapatnam port.
- **Ballari-Chitradurga-Chikkamagaluru-Tumakuru Belt** This belt in Karnataka has large reserves of iron ore. The Kudremukh mines are located in the Western Ghats of Karnataka. They are a 100% export unit and are known to be one of the largest in the world.
- The ore from this belt is transported as slurry through a pipeline to a port near Mangaluru.
- **Maharashtra-Goa Belt** It includes the state of Goa and Ratnagiri district of Maharashtra. Though, the ores are not of very high quality, yet they can be efficiently used. From this belt, iron ore is exported through Marmagao port.

1 **Placer Deposits** Minerals which occur as alluvial deposits brought down by the river such as gold, silver, tin etc.

2 **Non-Ferrous minerals** Minerals that do not contain iron content are called non-ferrous minerals.

### Manganese

It is a metallic element used in manufacturing of steel and ferro-manganese alloys. Nearly 10 kg of manganese is used to manufacture one tonne of steel. It is also used in manufacturing insecticide, bleaching powder and paints. **Madhya Pradesh has the largest share in manganese production** in India, i.e. 27% in 2016-17.

### (ii) Non-Ferrous Minerals

Minerals that do not contain iron content are called non-ferrous minerals. The reserves and production of non-ferrous minerals in India is not sufficient.

These minerals include copper, lead, zinc, bauxite, gold etc which are vital for various industries like metallurgical, engineering and electrical industries. The distribution of non-ferrous minerals i.e. copper and bauxite is discussed below

### Copper

It is an important mineral due to its excellent electrical conductivity. It is used in manufacturing of electrical cables and in electronics and chemical industries. The leading producers of copper in India are **Khetri mines** in **Rajasthan**, **Balaghat** mines in **Madhya Pradesh** and **Singhbhum** district of **Jharkhand**.

### Bauxite

Bauxite ore is used for obtaining aluminium. It is formed by decomposition of a wide variety of rocks rich in aluminium silicates.

Bauxite is a clay-like substance from which alumina is extracted and later alumina developed into aluminium.

Aluminium is known for its strength and lightness. It is widely used in manufacturing of utensils, electrical goods, etc.

**Amarkantak plateau**, **Maikal hills** and the **plateau region of Bilaspur-Katni** are the main regions of bauxite deposits in Madhya Pradesh. **Odisha is the largest bauxite producing state in India** with 49% of the country's total production in 2016-17.

Panchpatmali deposits in Koraput district are the most-important centres of bauxite deposits in Odisha.

## Non-Metallic Minerals

The basic characteristic of non-metallic minerals is that they do not yield new products on melting. Mica is an important non-metallic mineral.

### Mica

It is used in electrical and electronics industries due to its di-electric strength, low power loss factor, insulating properties and resistance to high voltage. Mica occurs in the form of plates or leaves, which can be split into thin sheets. Mica can be clear, black, green, red, yellow or brown.

Its deposits are mainly found in the Northern edge of the Chota Nagpur plateau. Koderma-Gaya-Hazaribagh belt of Jharkhand is the leading producer of mica. Other mica producing regions are Ajmer (Rajasthan) and Nellore (Andhra Pradesh).

### Rock Minerals

**Limestone** is a rock mineral found in sedimentary rocks. It is composed of calcium carbonates or calcium and magnesium carbonates.

Limestone is used for smelting iron ore in blast furnaces of steel plants and is the basic raw material for manufacturing of cement. Rajasthan has the largest share in limestone production in India i.e. 21%, in 2016-17.

#### Hazards of Mining

Mining is a hazardous industry. It is known as a killer industry due to the following reasons

- Risk to life due to collapse of roofs, overflow of water, fire is always there inside the mines.
- Dumping of waste and slurry leads to land degradation, soil erosion and increases the stream and river pollution.
- Mining causes respiratory diseases and pulmonary disorder to miners.

## Conservation of Minerals

Mineral resources are finite (exhaustible) and non-renewable. So, there is need to conserve our mineral resources and use it judiciously in the following ways

- Mineral resources should be used in planned and sustainable manner.
- Technologies should be developed to use lower grade ores at lower costs.
- Metals should be recycled and alternative materials like scrap metal should be used so that minerals can be conserved.

## Energy Resources

Resources which are used as power to run industries are called energy resources. Fuel minerals like coal, petroleum, natural gas, uranium and electricity can generate energy. **Energy resources**[3] can be classified as conventional or non-conventional sources.

**Conventional Sources** like firewood, cattle dung cake, coal and petroleum, natural gas and electricity (both hydel and thermal) have been used for a long time.

3 **Energy Resources** Resources which are used as power to run industries are called energy resources.

Non-conventional sources of energy have come into use recently. These include wind power, solar energy, tidal energy, geothermal energy, atomic energy and biogas energy. They are freely available, usually inexhaustible and renewable.

## Conventional Sources of Energy

Some prominent conventional sources of energy are

### Coal

It is the most abundantly available fossil fuel in India. It fulfills a greater amount of energy needs of the country. It is because India is highly dependent on coal for meeting its commercial energy needs.

Coal is a bulky material (of large size for its weight), which loses weight on use as it is reduced to ash. Thus, heavy industries and thermal power stations are located on or near the coalfields.

Coal is used for power generation, to supply energy to industry and for domestic needs. Coal is formed by the compression of plant materials over millions of years.

The degree of compression formed due to pressure of upper layers of the Earth and the depth at which compression takes place results in the formation of different types of coal.

Depending on the degrees of compression, the depth and time of burial during its formation, there are following varieties of coal

- **Peat** It is formed by decaying of plants in swamps. It has a low carbon content and low heating capacity and high moisture content.
- **Lignite** It is a low grade brown coal. It is soft and has high moisture content. It is used for electricity generation. The important lignite reserves are in Neyveli in Tamil Nadu.
- **Bituminous** It is the most popular coal in commercial use. High grade bituminous coal is ideal for use in metallurgy. It has special value for smelting iron in blast furnaces. It is found in greater depths.
- **Anthracite** This is the highest quality hard coal.

### Occurrence of Coal in India

In India, coal occurs in rock series of the following two main geological ages

- **Gondwana Coal** This coal was formed over 200 million years ago. This type of coal is used in metallurgy. The major sources of Gondwana coal are located in the Damodar valley (West Bengal-Jharkhand). In this belt, Jharia, Raniganj and Bokaro are important coal fields.
  Coal deposits are also present in the Godavari, Mahanadi, Son and Wardha valleys.
- **Tertiary Coal** This coal was formed 55 million years ago. This type of coal is found in the North-Eastern states of Meghalaya, Assam, Arunachal Pradesh and Nagaland.

### Petroleum

It is also known as mineral oil and 'liquid gold'. It is the second highest energy source (after refining into various products like furnace oil, diesel, petrol, kerosene, etc) used in India after coal. It is used as a fuel.

Petroleum refineries provide raw materials for synthetic textile, fertiliser, chemical industries, lubricants and fuel due to which it is called 'Nodal Industry'.

### Occurrence of Petroleum in India

Natural occurrence of petroleum in India is associated with **anticlines**[4] and **fault traps** of tertiary rocks. In anticline, folding or dome region, oil is trapped in the crest (top portion) of the upfold (stratified rocks).

The oil bearing layer is a porous limestone or sandstone through which oil may flow. But it is prevented from rising or sinking by intervening non-porous layers surrounding the oil occurrences.

**Mumbai high**, **Gujarat** and **Assam** are major oil producers of India. Ankeleshwar is the most important oil field in Gujarat. Assam is the oldest oil producing state of India. Important oil fields of Assam are **Digboi**, **Naharkatiya** and **Moran-Hugrijan**.

### Natural Gas

It is a clean energy resource as it gives out very little carbon and pollutants on burning. It is found with or without petroleum. As compared to coal and petroleum products, it burns with a very low emission of harmful gases and other pollutants.

It is used as a source of energy as well as an industrialist material in the petrochemical industry. Natural gas is mainly used by the fertiliser and power industies. Use of Compressed Natural Gas (CNG) for vehicles to replace liquid fuel is also increasing.

### Occurrence of Natural Gas

The offshore region of the **Krishna–Godavari** basin has the largest amount of natural gas currently available in India.

It is also available along the **West coast in Mumbai high**, in **Gulf of Cambay** and in **Andaman and Nicobar islands**.

### Electricity

It has a wide range of application in today's world. The per capita consumption of electricity in a place is considered as an index of development. There are two ways through which electricity is generated.

4 **Anticline** A formation of rocks raised up by folding into a broad arch so that the strata slopes downwards on both sides from a common centre.

These are

(*i*) Thermal electricity is generated by burning **fossil fuels**[5], (coal, petroleum, natural gas etc) that supplies energy to drive turbines. The thermal power stations use non-renewable resources i.e. fossil fuels for generating electricity.

(*ii*) **Hydro electricity**[6] is generated by flowing water. This energy is pollution free and commonly used all over India by constructing multi-purpose projects, like Bhakra Nangal, Damodar valley, the Kopili Hydel Project, etc.

## Non-Conventional Sources of Energy

The excessive use of non-renewable resources causes several environmental problems. Hence, a shift towards renewable resources is necessary.

Some prominent non-conventional sources of energy are

### Nuclear or Atomic Energy

It is generated by altering the structure of atoms that releases heat and energy which is used to generate electric power. Uranium and thorium are found in Aravalli ranges of Rajasthan and Jharkhand and monazite sands of Kerala which are used for generating nuclear or atomic energy.

### Solar Energy

India is a tropical country. It has enormous possibilities of tapping solar energy. It is used for a variety of purposes like electric power generation (using photovoltaic panels) and for heating purposes.

It is fast emerging as a fuel source in rural and remote places, thereby reducing their dependence on fire wood and dung cakes. The cow dung cake then be used as manure in agriculture.

### Wind Power

India has great potential of wind power. The largest wind form cluster is located in Tamil Nadu from Nagar coil to Madurai. Apart from these, Andhra Pradesh, Karnataka, Gujarat, Kerala, Maharashtra and Lakshadweep have important wind farms. Nagarcoil and Jaisalmer (Rajasthan) are very famous for effective use of wind energy in India.

### Biogas

It is generated by the decomposition of organic matter like shrubs, farm waste, animal and human wastes in biogas plants. It has higher thermal efficiency than Kerosene, dung cake and charcoal. It is cheap, environment friendly and prevents loss of trees used for firewood.

It is used as a fuel for cooking and lighting in rural areas. It also provides improved quality of manure. Biogas plants are set up by municipal, cooperatives and also by individuals. Biogas plants are also known as 'Gobar gas plants' in rural India.

### Tidal Energy

It is the energy generated by movement of oceanic tides, which can be harnessed to generate electricity. To produce electricity, flood gate dams are built across inlets from where water enters during high tide. The gates are closed, once enough water flows in after the tide falls outside the flood gate.

The water retained inside the gate is made to flow out through a pipe that carries it through a power generating turbine. In India, the Gulf of Khambhat, the Gulf of Kutch in Gujarat on the Western coast and Gangetic delta in Sunderban regions of West Bengal provide ideal conditions for utilising tidal energy.

### Geo-thermal Energy

It refers to the heat and electricity produced by using the heat from the interior of the Earth. Geothermal energy exists because the Earth grows hotter with increase in depth. At some places, this geothermal gradient is so high that high temperatures are found at a shallow depth.

Groundwater present in these areas absorb heat from the rocks and becomes hot and rises as steam. This steam is used to drive turbines for the generation of electricity. Parvati valley near Manikarn in Himachal Pradesh and Puga valley in Ladakh are two experimental projects to produce geothermal energy.

## Conservation of Energy Resources

Since, energy is a basic requirement for economic development, we need to conserve it. To have sustainable development, we need to promote energy conservation by avoiding wastage and to increase the use of renewable energy sources. So, we should conserve energy resources by

- using public transport systems instead of individual vehicles.
- switching off electrical appliances when not in use.
- using power-saving devices.
- using non-conventional sources of energy.

5 **Fossil Fuels** Fuels formed by the decomposition of organic matter in the earth's crust or seabed.

6 **Hydroelectricity** Electricity generated by running water such as fast moving rivers.

# Chapter Practice

PART 1
## Objective Questions

### • Multiple Choice Questions

**1.** Which of the following is the basic mineral and the backbone of industrial development?
(a) Zinc ore
(b) Iron ore
(c) Manganese ore
(d) Silver ore

*Ans.* (b) Iron ore is the basic mineral and the backbone of industrial development.

**2.** Which is the finest iron ore with a very high content of iron?
(a) Magnetite (b) Haematite
(c) Lignite (d) None of these

*Ans.* (a) Magnetite is the finest iron ore with a very high content of iron.

**3.** The Badampahar mine in Mayurbhanj and Kendujhar district is situated in which of the following Indian state?
(a) Karnataka
(b) Odisha
(c) Chhattisgarh
(d) Jharkhand

*Ans.* (b) The Badampahar mine in Mayurbhanj and Kendujhar district is situated in Odisha.

**4.** Iron ore is exported to Japan and South Korea via which port?
(a) Chennai
(b) Vishakhapatnam
(c) Haldia
(d) Mangaluru

*Ans.* (b) Iron ore is exported to Japan and South Korea via Vishakhapatnam port.

**5.** Which of the following minerals is obtained from ocean waters?
(a) Common Salt (b) Bromine
(c) Magnesium (d) All of these

*Ans.* (d) All the given minerals i.e. common salt, bromine and magnesium are obtained from ocean waters.

**6.** Large reserves of natural gas have been discovered in which place in India?
(a) Arabian Sea
(b) Andaman and Nicobar Islands
(c) Krishna Godavari Basin
(d) Gulf of Mannar

*Ans.* (c) Large reserves of natural gas have been discovered in Krishna Godavari Basin in India.

**7.** Which type of sand in Kerala is rich in thorium?
(a) Monazite sands
(b) Gypsum sands
(c) Silica sands
(d) Black sands

*Ans.* (a) Monazite sand in Kerala is rich in thorium.

**8.** Where is the largest wind farm cluster located in India?
(a) Andhra Pradesh (b) Kerala
(c) Karnataka (d) Tamil Nadu

*Ans.* (d) The largest wind farm cluster is located in Tamil Nadu.

**9.** In India, the Gulf of Khambhat, the Gulf of Kachchh and the Gangetic delta provide ideal condition for utilising which energy?
(a) Tidal energy
(b) Wind energy
(c) Solar energy
(d) Non-conventional energy

*Ans.* (a) In India, the Gulf of Khambhat, the Gulf of Kachchh and the Gangetic delta provide ideal condition for utilising tidal energy.

**10.** Which of the following is true for geothermal energy?

(a) Experimental projects are set up in Puga valley, Ladakh.
(b) Aravalli ranges of Rajasthan have small reserves of it.
(c) It develops in regions where there is low temperature.
(d) They are good sources for exhaustible conventional fuels.

*Ans.* (a) It is true for geothermal energy that experimental projects are set up in Puga valley, Ladakh.

**11.** Choose the correct option. **(CBSE 2020)**

(a) Chandrapur thermal power plant – Odisha
(b) Mayurbhanj iron ore mines – Amarkantak
(c) Kalol oil fields – Gujarat
(d) Bauxite – Jharkhand

*Ans.* (c) Kalol oil fields are located in Gujarat.

**12.**

| | List I | | List II |
|---|---|---|---|
| A. | Ferrous minerals | 1. | Potash |
| B. | Non-ferrous minerals | 2. | Uranium |
| C. | Non-metallic menerals | 3. | Nickel |
| D. | Energy minerals | 4. | Bauxite |

| | A | B | C | D | | A | B | C | D |
|---|---|---|---|---|---|---|---|---|---|
| (a) | 3 | 4 | 1 | 2 | (b) | 1 | 3 | 2 | 4 |
| (c) | 1 | 2 | 3 | 4 | (d) | 1 | 4 | 3 | 2 |

*Ans.* (a)

**13.** What work do the following picture show?

(a) Construction work in progress
(b) Mining
(c) Trapping of nuclear energy
(d) Conservation of minerals

*Ans.* (b) Mining is shown in the given picture.

**14.** Consider the following statement about Bauxite.

I. From bauxite, a clay like substance alumina is extracted.
II. Jharkhand is largest bauxite producer of India.
III. Ballari-Chitradurga belt is famous for bauxite reserves in India.

Which of the above statement is/are correct?

(a) Only I
(b) II and III
(c) I and III
(d) All of these

*Ans.* (a) Statement I is correct. Statement II and III are incorrect as Odisha is the largest bauxite producer in India (2016-17). Ballari-Chirtadurga-Chikkamagaluru-Tumakuru belt in Karnataka has large reserves of iron ore.

**15.** Arrange the following manganese producing states from highest to lowest production.

I. Odisha
II. Madhya Pradesh
III. Karnataka
IV. Andhra Pradesh

**Codes**

(a) II, I, III, IV
(b) I, II, III, IV
(c) III, II, I, IV
(d) II, III, IV, I

*Ans.* (a) The correct sequence of manganese producing states from highest to lowest production is Madhya Pradesh, Odisha, Karnataka and Andhra Pradesh.

## • Assertion-Reason MCQs

**Direction** (Q. Nos. 16-17) *Each of these questions contains two statements,* **Assertion** *(A) and* **Reason** *(R). Each of these questions also has four alternative choices, any one of which is the correct answer. You have to select one of the codes (a), (b), (c) and (d) given below.*

**Codes**

(a) Both A and R are true and R is the correct explanation of A
(b) Both A and R are true, but R is not the correct explanation of A
(c) A is true, but R is false
(d) A is false, but R is true

**16.** **Assertion** (A) Flood gate dams are built across rivers so that water flows into inlet and gets trapped during high tides.

**Reason** (R) Trapped water flows back via a pipe that carries it through a power generating turbine.

*Ans.* (d) A is false as floodgate dams are built across inlets so that during high tide water flows into the inlet and gets trapped when the gate is closed. R is true as trapped water flows back via a pipe that carries it through a power generating turbine.

**17.** **Assertion** (A) Mica is a mineral made up of plates or leaves.

**Reason** (R) Mica deposits are found in the Northern edge of the Chota Nagpur Plateau.

*Ans.* (b) Mica is a mineral made up of plates or leaves. On the other hand, mica deposits are found in the Northern edge of the Chota Nagpur Plateau. Thus, R is not the correct explanation of A.

## • Case Based Question

**18.** Read the case/source given and answer the questions that follow by choosing the correct options.

Energy is required for all activities. It is needed to cook, to provide light and heat, to propel vehicles and to drive machinery in industries. Energy can be generated from fuel minerals like coal, petroleum, natural gas, uranium and from electricity. Energy resources can be classified as conventional and non-conventional sources. Conventional sources include: firewood, cattle dung cake, coal, petroleum, natural gas and electricity (both hydel and thermal). Non-conventional

sources include solar, wind, tidal, geothermal, biogas and atomic energy. Firewood and cattle dung cake are most common in rural India. According to one estimate more than 70 per cent energy requirement in rural households is met by these two; continuation of these is increasingly becoming difficult due to decreasing forest area. Moreover, using dung cake too is being discouraged because it consumes most valuable manure which could be used in agriculture.

(i) Which of the following statement is true about conventional energy resources?
(a) They cause minimum pollution.
(b) They are available in limited quantity.
(c) Cattle dung is the most used energy in the world.
(d) There are sufficient reserves of conventional energy sources.

*Ans.* (b) Conventional energy resources are available in limited quantity.

(ii) Which of the following resources does not generate energy?
(a) Coal (b) Fuel
(c) Natural gas
(d) None of the above

*Ans.* (d) All the given resources are used to generate energy.

(iii) Which of the following energy is non-conventional source of energy?
(a) Firewood
(b) Tidal energy
(c) Natural gas
(d) Petroleum

*Ans.* (b) Tidal energy is non-conventional source of energy.

(iv) Firewood and cattle dung cake are most common energy in rural India because
(a) they are easily available
(b) they are non-conventional
(c) they produces high energy
(d) None of the above

*Ans.* (a) Firewood and cattle dung cake are most common energy in rural India because they are easily available.

(v) How India can reduce its dependence over countries for energy?
(a) Promoting non-conventional source of energy
(b) Promoting efficient use of resources
(c) Both (a) and (b)
(d) None of the above

*Ans.* (c) India can reduce its dependence over countries for energy by promoting non-conventional sources of energy and efficient use of resources.

(vi) **Assertion** (A) About 70 per cent energy required in countryside households are met by firewood and cattle dung cake.

**Reason** (R) Cattle dung cake is valuable for use as manure in agriculture.

**Codes**
(a) Both A and R are true and R is the correct explanation of A
(b) Both A and R are true, but R is not the correct explanation of A
(c) A is true, but R is false
(d) A is false, but R is true

*Ans.* (b) About 70 per cent energy required in countryside households are met by firewood and cattle dung cake. On the other hand, cattle dung cake is valuable for use as manure in agriculture. Thus, R is not the correct explanation of A.

PART 2

# Subjective Questions

## • Short Answer (SA) Type Questions

**1.** Explain any three types of formations in which minerals occur.

**Ans.** Three main types of formations in which mineral occurs are

(i) **Veins and Lodes** Smaller occurrences are called veins and larger ones are called lodes. In igneous and metamorphic rocks minerals may occur in the cracks, crevices, faults or joints.

(ii) **Beds or Layers** In sedimentary rocks, minerals occur in bed or layers. They are formed as a result of deposition, accumulation and concentration in horizontal strata. (layers)

(iii) **Placer Deposits** Certain minerals occur as alluvial deposits in sands of valley floors and the base of hills as placer deposits.

**2.** Which state is the largest producer of manganese in India? Mention any four uses of manganese. **(CBSE 2013)**

*Or* Which is the largest producer of manganese in India? Mention two uses of manganese. **(CBSE 2017)**

**Ans.** Odisha is the largest producer of manganese in India.

Uses of manganese are as follows

(i) It is used in the manufacturing of ferro-manganese alloy.

(ii) It is used in the manufacturing of bleaching powder.

(iii) It is used in insecticides, paint industries and manufacturing of batteries.

(iv) It is used in manufacturing of steel. Nearly 10 kg of manganese is required to manufacture one tonne of steel.

**3** Name the non-metallic mineral which can split easily into thin sheets. Mention its uses. **(CBSE 2014)**

**Ans.** Mica is the non-metallic mineral which can be split easily into thin sheets as it occurs in the form of plates or leaves of different colors.

Uses of Mica are as follows

(i) It is used in paints as a pigment extender. It also helps to brighten the tone of coloured pigments.

(ii) It is used in electrical and electronic industry due to its di-electric strength, insulating properties and resistance to high voltage.

(iii) It is used in making toothpaste and cosmetics due to its shiny and glittery appearance.

**4.** What are the uses of limestone? Mention names of two states of India which are major producers of limestone.

**Ans.** The uses of limestone are as follows

- It is used in cement industry. It is because it is the raw materical of cement.
- It is essential for smelting iron ore in the blast furnace in a steel plant.

Rajasthan (largest producer) Madhya Pradesh, Andhra Pradesh and Karnataka are important states which are major producers of limestone.

**5.** India is fairly rich in mineral resources, however its distribution is uneven. Comment.

**Ans.** India is fairly rich in mineral resources, however its distribution is uneven. This can be said with the help of following examples

(i) Gujarat and Assam have petroleum deposits as oil is found in sedimentary rocks on the Western and Eastern flanks of the peninsula. But rest of India does not have any oil deposit.

(ii) Minerals deposits are mostly available in the peninsular plateau region of Chotanagpur and rock systems of Rajasthan.

(iii) The vast alluvial plains of the North India, mountainous regions and coastal plains do not have any mineral deposits.

**6.** What is the importance of energy resources? Give two examples each of conventional and non-conventional sources of energy.

**Ans.** Energy is required for all activities. Energy resources are needed to cook, to provide light and heat, for agricultural activities, propel vehicles and to drive machinery in industries.

Thus, the sustainable development of energy resources is vital for all human activities.

**Examples**

- Two examples of conventional sources of energy are *coal* and *petroleum*.
- Two examples of non-conventional sources of energy are *solar energy* and *wind energy*.

**7.** Describe the distribution of coal in India.

**Ans.** In India, coal is the most abundantly available fossil fuel. Coal is found in a variety of forms depending on the degress of compression and the depth and time of burial. As per these basis, coal deposits are found mainly of two geological ages. *These are*

(i) **Gondwana Coal Deposits** These are about 200 million years old. The major coal deposit in India are Gondwana coal which are high quality metallurgical coal.

These coal deposits are located in Damodar Valley (West Bengal-Jharkhand). Jharia, Raniganj and Bokaro are important coal deposit fields. Besides, the

Godavari, Mahanadi, Son and Wardha valleys also contain such coal deposits.

(ii) **Tertiary Coal Deposits** These are around 55 million years old. Tertiary coal deposits are found in the North-Eastern states of Meghalaya, Assam, Arunachal Pradesh and Nagaland. This coal is of lower quality than the Gondwana coal.

**8.** State the importance of petroleum as an energy resource. Mention any four oil fields of India.

*Ans.* Importance of petroleum can be seen through the following points

- Petroleum or mineral oil is the next major energy source in India after coal.
- It provides fuel for heating and lighting, lubricants for machinery and raw materials for a number of manufacturing industries.
- It is a fuel used in all the automobiles.

Four major oil fields of India are

(i) Mumbai High
(ii) Ankleshwar and Kalol in Gujarat
(iii) Digboi, Naharkatiya and Moran is Assam
(iv) Rajasthan, Mangala, District Barmer

**9.** Crude oil reserves are limited all over the world. If people continue to extract it at the present rate, the reserves would last only 35-40 years more. Explain any three ways to solve this problem. **(CBSE 2019)**

*Ans.* Crude oil reserves are limited all over the world. If people continue to extract it at the present rate, the reserves would last only 30-40 years more. For energy conservation we can take the following steps

(i) We have to adopt a cautious approach for the judicious use of our limited energy resources.
(ii) We can use public transport systems instead of individual vehicles.
(iii) We can switch off electricity when not in use, using power saving devices. We can use non-conventional energy like solar energy, wind power, biogas etc instead of using petroleum.

**10.** What is natural gas? What is its advantage? Name one region of India where its reserves are found.

*Or* "Natural gas is an important source of energy." Support the statement. **(CBSE 2017)**

*Ans.* Natural gas is an important source of energy. It is an important clean energy resource found in association with or without petroleum. It is also used as an industrial raw material in the petrochemical industry.

Advantages of natural gas are

- Natural gas is an environment friendly fuel.
- It generates low carbon dioxide emission during use.
- It is increasingly replacing pollution causing fuels.

Large reserves of natural gas have been discovered in the Krishna-Godavari basin.

**11.** Mention any three factors that determine the economic viability of a reserve. **(CBSE 2014)**

*Ans.* The three factors that determine the economic viability of a reserve are

(i) The quality and quantity of mineral concentration in the ore. For example, magnetite is regarded better than haematite as it has more concentration of iron.
(ii) The cost of extraction. If the cost of extraction is high than mining is not profitable.
(iii) Location of mines near the industries.

**12.** What are the two main ways of generating electricity? How are they different from each other? Explain. **(CBSE 2014)**

*Or* Make a distinction between hydroelectricity and thermal electricity stating three points of distinction.

*Ans.* The two main ways of generating electricity are by running water (hydro electricity) and by burning fuels (thermal electricity).

Differences between these two are

| Hydro Electricity | Thermal Electricity |
|---|---|
| It is generated from fast flowing water falling on turbines. | It is generated from petroleum, coal and natural gas. |
| Its source is perennial or inexhaustible i.e. water. | Its sources are exhaustible or non-renewable sources i.e. coal and petroleum. |
| It does not cause pollution. | The burning of coal and oil cause a lot of pollution. |
| It is cheaper in the long-run. | It is expensive in the long-run. |
| These plants should be near the sources of fast flowing water. | The thermal plants to generate electricity can be set up any where. |

**13.** "Energy is an indispensable requirement in our modern lives." Explain the statement with three examples.

*Ans.* It is true that Energy is an indispensable requirement in our modern lives.

*It can be understood through the following examples*

(i) Every sector of the national economy requires energy. For example, agriculture, industry, transport, commercial and domestic needs require inputs of energy.
(ii) Implementation of economic development plans necessarily require increasing amounts of energy to remain operational.
(iii) Energy is required for all domestic activities like cooking, lighting and heating and even air-conditioning (cooling).

**14.** Why do you think that solar energy has a bright future in India?

**Ans.** Solar energy has a bright future in India due to the following reasons

(i) Solar energy is an inexhaustible source of energy that is produced from sunlight. India is a tropical country thus, there is enough scope for the development of solar energy.

(ii) Many parts (regions) of the country receive sunlight at least 300 days annually and so, it becomes possible to generate 20 MW solar energy per square kilometer in such areas.

(iii) It is easy to establish solar plants in urban and rural areas.

(iv) By setting up solar plants in rural areas, the dependence of people on fire wood can be reduced.

(v) Solar energy is also becoming popular as it is used for cooking, heating water, lighting, etc.

**15.** How naturally occurring gas is different from biogas?

**Ans.** In the following ways naturally occurring gas (Natural gas) is different from biogas

| Natural Gas | Biogas |
|---|---|
| It is a mixture of hydro-carbons and occur frequently with petroleum in the rocks of the earth's crust. | It is formed by the decomposition of animal, plant and farm wastes with the help of 'Micro organisms in the presence of water'. |
| It occurs naturally. | It undergoes a process of formation under controlled man-made conditions. |
| It is non-renewable. | It is renewable. |
| Natural gas is used as a raw material in the petrochemical. | Biogas is used as a fuel and for lighting purposes. |
| It is mainly used in urban areas. | It is mainly used in the rural areas. |

**16.** "India is highly dependent on coal for meeting its commercial energy requirement." Support this statement with three arguments.

**Ans.** The fact that India is highly dependent on coal for meeting its commercial energy requirement can be supported from the following arguments

(i) The majority of electricity generation plants in India are based on burning of coal for generating steam to power turbines.

(ii) Many industries use coal in the blast furnaces for generating heat for their various operations.

(iii) Coal is an important constituent in steel production, alumina refineries, and in chemical and pharmaceutical industries.

**17.** What is tidal energy? Which regions in India provide ideal conditions for utilising tidal energy?

**Ans.** The electrical energy that can be generated through the oceanic tides is known as tidal energy. This can be done by building flood gate dams in areas that get submerged during high tides.

During high tide when the water flows inside the dam, the gates are closed. After the high tide, the water retained by the flood gate falls back to the sea via a pipe that carries it through a power generating turbine.

The regions in India that provide ideal conditions for utilising tidal energy are the Gulf of Khambhat, the Gulf of Kachchh and Gangetic delta in Sunderban.

**18.** Why India has the potential to develop wind energy? Which places in India are sources of wind energy?

**Ans.** India has a long coastline in which there is scope of developing wind energy. The areas along the coastline are windy and wind mills can be established there.

The places in India having source of wind energy or wind mills are

(i) Wind farm cluster located in Tamil Nadu from Nagercoil to Madurai.

(ii) Wind farms in Gujarat, Kerala, Maharashtra, Lakshadweep and Andhra Pradesh.

(iii) Wind farm in Jaisalmer.

## • Long Answer (LA) Type Questions

**1.** Which is the most abundantly available fossil fuel in India? Assess the important characteristics of its different forms. **(CBSE 2015)**

**Ans.** Coal is the most abundantly available fossil fuel in India.

Important characteristics of its different forms are

(i) **Peat** Decaying plants in swamps produce peat.

- It is burnt as fuel or applied to the soil to improve the texture or raise its water-retaining property.

(ii) **Lignite**

- It has 60-70% carbon. It is soft and brown in colour, and having high moisture content.
- It is used for electricity generation.
- It has lowest heat content per kg.

(iii) **Bituminous**

- It is used for commercial purpose especially ideal for smelting iron in blast furnaces.
- It has 75-90% carbon content, dense sedimentary rock, usually black in colour and has medium heat content per kg.
- It is also used as making coke.

(iv) **Anthracite**

- It is used in the metal smelting and fabrication industries especially used as a reduction agent for various applications i.e. briquetting charcoal, iron-ore pellets and other uses.
- It has more than 90% carbon content per kg and its heating content per kg is highest.
- It is also used in residential and commercial space heating.

**2.** How can biogas solve the energy problem mainly in rural India? Give your suggestion. **(CBSE 2015)**

***Ans.*** Biogas can solve the energy problem in the rural areas due to the reasons mentioned below

(i) It produces gas having higher thermal efficiency than charcoal and kerosene.

(ii) It provides a way for optimum utilisation of animal and plant waste.

(iii) It produces enriched organic manure that can supplement or even replace chemical fertilisers.

(iv) It burns smoothly and does not leave much residue behind.

(v) It is easy to produce and store.

Some suggestions to improve the biogas energy production in rural areas are given below

(i) Government should provide monetary assistance to people in the rural areas to set up biogas plants.

(ii) Awareness must be created for using this alternative sources of energy.

**3.** What are the major sources of energy in rural households of India? Identify the major problems faced due to these sources. Give suggestions to solve these problems.

***Ans.*** Firewood and cattle dung cake are the major sources of energy in rural household of India.

Major problems faced due to these sources are

(i) Using cow dung is discouraged because it consumes most valuable manure which could be used in agriculture.

(ii) Use of firewood as fuel is becoming difficult due to decreasing forest area.

Suggestions to solve these problems are

(i) Awareness must be developed in the rural areas regarding the non-conventional sources of energy like solar energy, wind energy, biogas, etc.

It will minimise the dependence of rural households on fire wood and dung cakes, which in turn will contribute to environmental conservation and adequate supply of manure in agriculture.

(ii) Government should take initiatives in setting up the biogas plants in rural areas.

**4.** Differentiate between metallic and non-metallic minerals with examples. **(CBSE 2013)**

***Ans.*** Differences between metallic and non-metallic minerals are

| Metallic minerals | Non-metallic minerals |
|---|---|
| Minerals containing metals are called metallic minerals. | Minerals which do not contain metals are called non-metallic minerals. |
| These minerals are malleable and ductile. | Non-metallic minerals are non-malleable and non-ductile. |
| These minerals are generally associated with igneous and metamorphic rocks. | These minerals are mostly associated with sedimentary rocks. |
| Metallic minerals show lusture. | Non-metallic minerals do not show lusture. |
| Iron-one, manganese, copper, tin, etc are its examples. | Gypsum, potash, salt, etc are its examples. |

**5** "Minerals are an indispensable part of our lives." Justify this statement with suitable examples. **(CBSE 2016)**

***Ans.*** It is true that minerals are an indispensable part of our lives. This can be understood through the following examples

- Almost everything that we use in our daily life, from a tiny pin to a towering building or a big ship, all are made from minerals.
- The railway lines and the paving of the roads, machinery, implements and tools too are made from minerals.
- Minerals form the basis of all industries.
- Our food contains various minerals that are essential for our body. They are absorbed by the body.
- In conclusion, we can say that in all stages of development, human beings have used minerals for their livelihood, decoration, festivities, religious and ceremonial rites.

**6** "Formation of coal is a long drawn process spread over various periods." Elaborate the statement with examples in Indian context.

***Ans.*** It is true that formation of coal is a long drawn process spread over various periods. Coal is formed due the compression of plant material (containing carbon, the major component of coal) over millions of years.

Thus, coal is found in many forms depending on the degrees of compression, the depth and the time of burial. Indian coal was mainly formed during two geological ages the Gondwana and the Tertiary ages.

The Gondwana coal deposits (called 'metallurgical coal'), which are more than 200 million years old, are located in the Damodar valley (West Bengal – Jharkhand), where Jharia, Raniganj and Bokaro are important coal fields. It is also found in the Godavari,

Mahanadi, Son and Wardha valleys. The tertiary age deposits, only about 55 million years old, are mostly found in North-Eastern India in Meghalaya, Assam, Arunachal Pradesh and Nagaland. Thus, formation of coal is a long drawn process spread over various periods.

**7.** "Nuclear energy is expected to play an increasingly important role in India." Give arguments to support this statement. **(CBSE 2016)**

***Ans.*** Nuclear energy is expected to play an increasingly important role in India due to the following reasons

(*i*) India has limited reserves of coal and petroleum. Nuclear energy minerals like Thorium is found in plenty in India. Hence, nuclear energy can compensate for deficiency of fossil fuels.

(*ii*) Nuclear power stations can be established easily and conveniently in those areas where other sources are not available.

(*iii*) Nuclear power releases tremendous amounts of energy. India can utilise this energy for peaceful purposes such as generation of electricity that can be used to run machines in industries.

(*vi*) Nuclear energy is a non-conventional source of energy. After the initial expenses, it becomes very economical.

**8.** "There is a pressing need for using renewable energy sources in India." Justify the statement. **(CBSE 2017)**

***Ans.*** There is a growing need for increasing the use of renewable energy sources due to the following reasons

(*i*) The conventional or non-renewable sources of energy are depleting very fast and we are dependent on imports of petroleum and natural gas to meet our needs.

(*ii*) Renewable energy sources do not cause environmental pollution with their use and so, to preserve our environment, we must change over to use more of such sources.

(*iii*) Non-conventional or renewable sources of energy are very economical in use as compared to conventional sources. Thus, to save expenses, we should use renewable energy sources.

## • Case Based Questions

**1** Read the case/source given and answer the following questions.

**Source A Biogas**

Shrubs, farm waste, animal and human waste are used to produce biogas for domestic consumption in rural areas. Decomposition of organic matter yields gas, which has higher thermal efficiency in comparison to kerosene, dung cake and charcoal.

(i) To what extent do you think biogas is better than dung cake for fuel?

***Ans.*** Biogas is much better than dung cakes as it produces no smoke and has more thermal efficiency.

**Source B Solar Energy**

India is a tropical country. It has enormous possibilities of tapping solar energy. Photovoltaic technology converts sunlight directly into electricity. Solar energy is fast becoming popular in rural and remote areas.

(ii) Why solar energy has more potential to be developed as major fuel in rural areas?

***Ans.*** There is more potential of developing solar energy in rural areas as there are relatively more open spaces. This will reduce the dependence on firewood and dung cakes fuel.

**Source C Wind Energy**

India has great potential of wind power. The largest wind farm cluster is located in Tamil Nadu from Nagarcoil to Madurai. Apart from these, Andhra Pradesh, Karnataka, Gujarat, Kerala, Maharashtra and Lakshadweep have important wind farms.

(iii) What similarity or trait can be seen in the places idealy suited for setting up wind farm?

***Ans.*** The similarities identified are that the areas should be close to sea where there is lot of potential for blowing of wind or other windy areas.

**2** Read the case/source given and answer the following questions.

Decaying plants in swamps produce peat which has a low carbon and high moisture content and low heating capacity. Lighite is low grade brown coal, which is soft with high moisture content. The principal lignite reserves are in Neyveli in Tamil Nadu and are used for generation of electricity. Coal that has been buried deep and subjected to increased temperatures is bituminous coal. It is the most popular coal in commercial use. Metallurgical coal is high grade bituminous coal which has a special value for smelting iron in blast furnaces. Anthracite is the highest quality hard coal.

In India coal occurs in rock series of two main geological ages, namely Gondwana, a little over 200 million years in age and in tertiary deposits which are only about 55 million years old. The major resources of Gondwana coal, which are metallurgical coal, are located in Damodar valley (West Bengal, Jharkhand). Jharia, Raniganj, Bokaro are important coalfields. The Godavari, Mahanadi, Son and Wardha valleys also contain coal deposits. Tertiary coals occur in the North-Eastern states of Meghalya, Assam, Arunachal Pradesh and Nagaland.

(i) Which reserves are important for lignite in India?

***Ans.*** Neyveli reserves in Tamil Nadu are important lignite reserves in India.

(ii) In what extent do you agree that bituminous coal is metallurgical coal? State its one property.

***Ans.*** Bituminous coal is a high grade coal and thus, is a metallurgical coal. This type of coal has a special value for smelting iron in blast furnaces.

**Important Property of Bituminous Coal.**

Bituminous coal is buried deep under the earth's surface and is subjected to increased temperature. It makes it unique to use in smelting iron-ore in blast furnaces.

(iii) Why is coal associated with geological ages? State where it is found?

***Ans.*** Coal is associated with geological ages because coal is formed due to compression of plant material and takes million of years to come into existence. In India, coal occurs in rock series of two main geological ages, namely Gondwana rock series which is a little over 200 million years in age and in tertiary deposits rock series which are only about 55 million years old.

**Distribution of Coal** Gondwana coal deposits are found in Damodar valley (West Bengal, Jharkhand), Jharia, Raniganj, Bokaro, coalfields. The Godavari, Mahanadi, Son and Wardha valleys also contain coal deposits. Tertiary coal deposits are found in the North-Eastern states of Meghalaya, Assam, Arunachal Pradesh and Nagaland.

## • Map Based Questions

**1.** On the given outline map of India, identify the locations with the help of specified information.

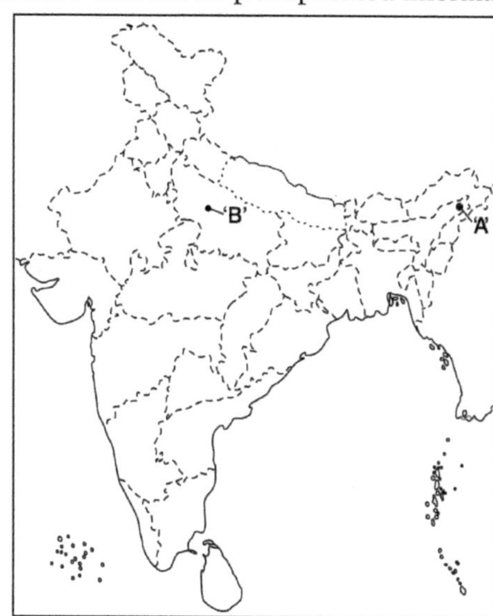


(i) On the political map of India, 'A' is marked as a Thermal Power Plant. Identify it from the following options.

(a) Namrup
(b) Ramagundam
(c) Singrauli
(d) Neyveli

***Ans.*** (a) Naraura

(ii) On the same map, 'B' is also marked as a Nuclear Power Plant. Identify it from the following options.

(a) Naraura (b) Tarapur
(c) Kakrapara (d) Kalpakkam

***Ans.*** (a) Naraura

**2.** On the given outline map of India, identify the locations with the help of specified information.

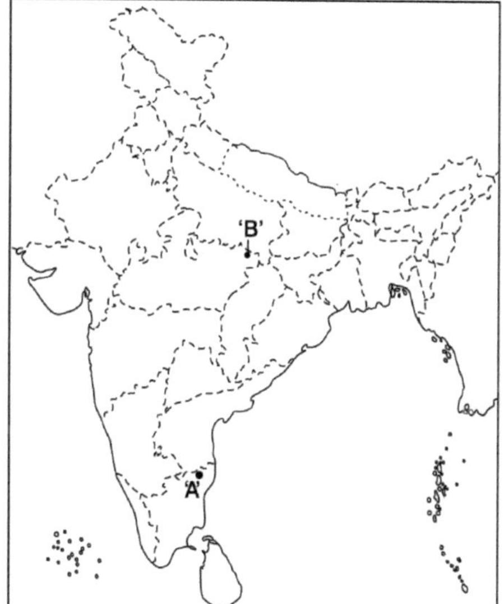


(i) On the political map of India, 'A' is marked as a Nuclear Power Plant. Identify it from the following options.

(a) Tarapur
(b) Kakrapara
(c) Kalpakkam
(d) Naraura

***Ans.*** (c) Kalpakkam

(ii) On the same map, 'B' is also marked as a Thermal Power Plant. Identify it from the following options.

(a) Namrup (b) Ramagundam
(c) Singrauli (d) Neyveli

***Ans.*** (c) Singrauli

**3.** Locate the following on the map of India.

(a) Namrup (b) Kalpakkam

***Ans.***

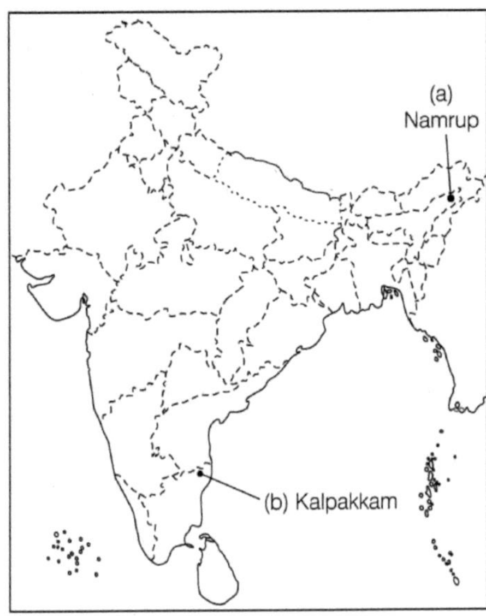


**4.** Identify the following features marked on the given map of India.

(a) A nuclear power plant in Maharashtra

(b) A nuclear power plant in Gujarat

***Ans.***

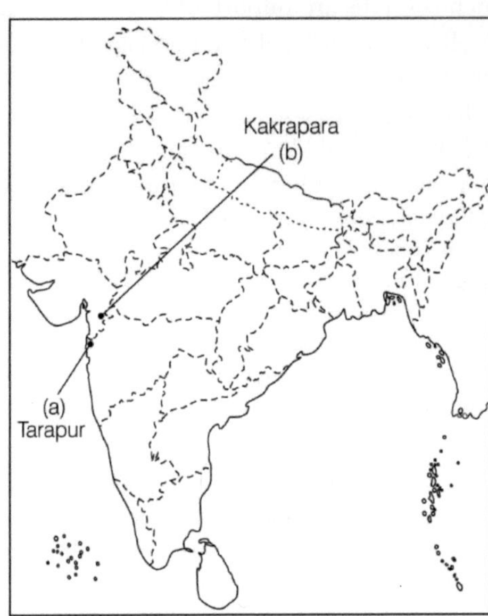


**5.** Locate the following on the map of India.

(a) Singrauli

(b) Ramagundam

***Ans.***

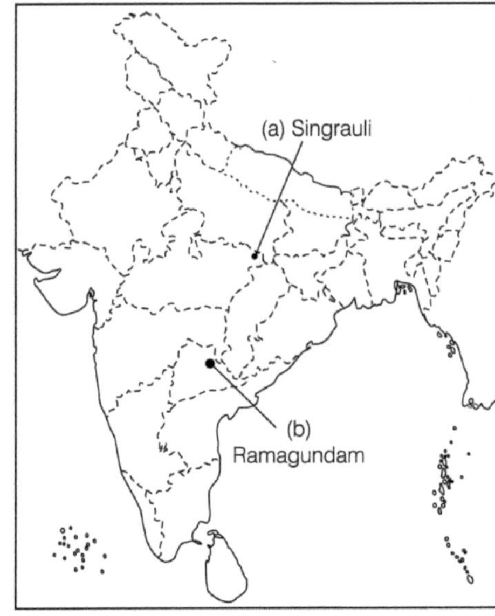

# Chapter Test

## Objective Questions

1. Which of the following minerals is non-ferrous mineral?
   (a) Copper (b) Iron ore
   (c) Nickel (d) Cobalt
2. Which of the following mineral is obtained from veins and loads of igneous and metamorphic rocks?
   (a) Tin (b) Lead
   (c) Zinc (d) All of these
3. Which mineral is used in smaller quantities in the manufacturing of steel?
   (a) Zinc ore (b) Iron ore
   (c) Manganese (d) Tin
4. Which of the following minerals is formed due to compression of plant material over millions of years?
   (a) Coal (b) Lead
   (c) Graphite (d) Marble
5. Gulf of Khambhat and Gulf of Kuchchh are located in which state of India?
   (a) Andhra Pradesh (b) Kerala
   (c) Karnataka (d) Gujarat

## Short Answer Type Questions

6. Which are the types of coal formations based on their geological ages? Where are they found in India?
7. Why should we conserve minerals and energy resources?
8. What is the relevance of non-conventional sources of energy in a country like India? Why do you think so?
9. Why is conservation of resources important? Discuss values associated with it.

## Long Answer Type Questions

10. Why is coal called the most important source of energy even today in India? Explain with reasons.
11. Explain the development of non-conventional sources of energy in India.
12. Examine Tidal energy and Geothermal energy as sources of energy for the future.

## Answers

1. (a) Copper
2. (d) All of these
3. (c) Manganese
4. (a) Coal
5. (d) Gujarat

CHAPTER 02

# Manufacturing Industries

### In this Chapter...


- Importance of Manufacturing
- Contribution of Industry to National Economy
- Industrial Pollution and Environmental Degradation


Production of goods in large quantities by processing raw materials to more valuable products is called **manufacturing**. Manufacturing industries are known as secondary activities, as these industries manufacture primary material (like cotton fibre) into finished goods (like textiles)

## Importance of Manufacturing

Manufacturing sector is very important and is considered as the backbone of economic development because

- Manufacturing industries help in modernising agriculture which form the backbone of our economy.
- Manufacturing also reduces the heavy dependence of people on agricultural income by providing them jobs in secondary and tertiary sectors.
- Industrial development helps in removal of unemployment and poverty as it creates jobs and more income. It also aims at bringing down regional differences by establishing industries in tribal and backward areas.
- Export of manufactured goods expands trade and commerce and brings foreign exchange.

### Agriculture and Industries

Agriculture and industries depend upon each other. On one hand many industries like sugar, textile, etc depend on agricultural products like, cotton is the raw material in cotton textile mills. On the other hand, many industrial products like fertilisers, irrigation pumps, PVC pipes, tractors, machines and tools help in increasing agricultural productivity.

## Contribution of Industry to National Economy

During the last 20 years, the share of the manufacturing sector has stayed at 17 % of GDP. This is much lower than some East Asian economies, where it is 25 to 35 %. The desired growth rate is expected to be 12% in the next decade which has been 7% in the last decade.

To develop the sector of manufacturing industries, government has set-up the **National Manufacturing Competitiveness Council (NMCC)**[1]. The objective is to bring appropriate policy to improve productivity to achieve desired growth rate.

### Industrial Location

The location of an industry is influenced by Government policies, availability of raw material, labour, capital, power and market facilities.

1 **National Manufacturing Competitiveness Council** (NMCC) It has been set up by the Government of India to provide a continuing forum for policy dialogue to energise and sustain the growth of manufacturing industries in India.

The features that influence the ideal location of an industry are

- Decision to locate factory at site.
- Cost of obtaining raw materials at site.
- Cost of Production at site.
- Cost of distribution of production.

### Industry-Market Linkage

Industry and market are closely linked with each other. A number of factors/ components which link these, are

- Money is needed to buy inputs for production. After selling the finished products in the market manufacturers/ industrialists also gain profit in the form of money.
- Inputs (like raw materials/component parts) are needed to produce goods in industries.
- Land, labour, capital, entrepreneur and infrastructure are the factory of production.
- A good network of transport is needed to supply raw materials from source region to factories and finished products to markets.
- Factories are setup to produce different products outputs.
- After manufacturing the finished goods a well developed market is needed to sell these goods.

### Industrialisation and Urbanisation

Industrialisation and **urbanisation**[2] depend upon each other. Industries are located around the cities where there are market of industrial goods and services like banking, insurance, transport, labour, consultants and financial services are available.

During pre-independence era manufacturing units were located near the sea ports for overseas trade such as Mumbai, Kolkata, Chennai. Many industries tends to come together to make use of advantages offered by urban centres known as **Agglomeration Economies**[3].

## Classification of Industries

Industries are classified on the basis of the following criteria

(*i*) On the Basis of Source of Raw Materials used

- **Agro-based industries** e.g., cotton, woollen, jute, silk textile, rubber, sugar, tea, coffee and edible oil.
- **Mineral-based industries** e.g., iron and steel, cement, aluminium, machine tools, petrochemicals.

(*ii*) On the Basis of Role Played by them

- **Basic or key industries** which supply their products as raw materials to other industries to manufacture other goods. For example, iron and steel, copper **smelting**[4], aluminium smelting.
- **Consumer industries** which produce goods for direct consumer use. For example, sugar, paper, toothpaste, sewing machines, fans, etc.

(*iii*) On the Basis of Capital Investment

- **Small scale industries** industries with maximum investment upto 1 crore.
- **Large scale industries** industries with investment above 1 crore.

(*iv*) On the Basis of Ownership

- **Public Sector** which are owned and operated by government agencies, e.g. BHEL, SAIL, etc
- **Private sector** which are owned and operated by individuals or a group of individuals, e.g. TISCO, Bajaj Auto Ltd, Dabur Industries.
- **Joint sector venture** which are jointly run by the state and individuals or a group of individuals e.g. Oil India Ltd.
- **Cooperative sector** which are owned and operated by the producers or suppliers of raw materials, workers or both. They pool in the resources (capital, raw materials, labour) and share the profits or losses proportionately such as the sugar industry in Maharashtra, the coir industry in Kerala.

(*v*) On the Basis of the Bulk and Weight of Raw Material and Finished Goods

- **Heavy industries** in which large machines and heavy or bulky raw materials are used to produce products, including capital goods like automobiles and construction machinery. For example - Iron and steel industry.
- **Light Industries** in which light raw materials are used to produce light utility goods, e.g. electrical industries, toy industry.

### Types of Industries on the Basis of Material Used

On the basis of materials used the industries are classified into agro-based and mineral based industries.

### Agro-Based Industries

Industries that are based on agricultural raw materials belong to this category, e.g. cotton, jute, silk, woollen textiles, sugar and edible oil, etc.

#### Textile Industry

This industry contributes significantly to industrial production. It is the only industry in the country that is self-reliant and complete in the value chain, i.e. from raw material to the highest value added products, everything is done in India.

2 **Urbanisation** The increase in proportion of people living in towns and cities.

3 **Agglomeration Economies** These occur when the larger market, lower transportation costs and other benefits outweigh the added expenses (such as higher rent or taxes) of working in a city.

4 **Smelting** Metal extraction process from an ore.

### Cotton Textiles

In ancient India, cotton textiles were produced with hand spinning and weaving in **handlooms**[5]. The **first textile mill was setup in Mumbai in 1854**, by which the handlooms were replaced by **Powerlooms**[6]. This industry is mainly located in Maharashtra, Gujarat and Tamil Nadu.

**Khadi**[7] handlooms provide large scale employment to weavers and support cottage industries. Cotton goods are exported to Japan, USA, UK, Russia, France, East European countries, Nepal, Singapore, Sri Lanka and several African countries. India has significantly increased its production of good quality long staple cotton.

The challenges related to this industry are

- This industry faces challenges in the form of outdated machinery, irregular power supply, competition from synthetic fibres and low output of labour.
- Exporting of yarn does not provides as much income as exporting of fabrics. Suppose that yarn is sold at ₹ 85 per kg, but if it is sold as trouser it fetches ₹ 800 per kg. Value is added at every stage from fibre to yarn to fabric and to garment.

### Jute Textiles

**India is the largest producer of raw jute and jute goods**. It stands second in the jute export after Bangladesh. After partition in 1947, the jute mills remained in India, but three-fourth of the jute producing area went to Bangladesh (erstwhile East Pakistan). Jute industry is located along the Hugli river in West Bengal.

The **first jute mill was set up near Kolkata in** 1859 at **Rishra**. The factors responsible for the location of jute mills in Hugli basin are

- Proximity of the jute producing areas reduces the cost of transportation.
- Inexpensive water transport and network of railways, roadways to facilitate movement of raw material to the mills.
- Abundant water supply from nearby rivers for processing raw jute.
- Cheap labour from West Bengal and adjoining areas i.e. Bihar, Odisha and Uttar Pradesh.
- Kolkata is a large urban centre which provides banking, insurance and port facilities for export of jute goods from Hugli.

The challenges faced by the industry include less demand and stiff competition in the international market from synthetic fibres and from other jute growing countries like Bangladesh, Philippines, Thailand, Brazil and Egypt.

India has to diversify its jute products to capture the main markets of jute which are USA, UK Canada, Ghana, Saudi Arabia and Australia.

### Sugar Industry

India stands **second** in the world in sugar production and the **first** in the production of *gur* and *khandsari*. Sugar mills are located in Uttar Pradesh, Bihar, Maharashtra, Tamil Nadu, Karnataka, Andhra Pradesh, Gujarat, Punjab, Haryana and Madhya Pradesh sixty per cent sugar mills are in Uttar Pradesh and Bihar.

In recent years, there is a tendency for the mills to concentrate in the Southern and Western states, especially in Maharashtra. This is because the cane produced here has a higher sucrose content and cooler climate also ensures a longer crushing season.

Major challenges to this industry include the seasonal nature of the industry, old and inefficient methods of production, transport delay in reaching cane to factories and the need to maximise the use of by-products like baggase. The raw material is bulky making its transportation difficult and the sucrose content keeps on decreasing with time.

### Mineral Based Industries

Industries that use minerals and metals as raw materials are called mineral based industries.

### Iron and Steel Industry

It is a basic industry as heavy, medium and light industries depend on it for machines and electrical goods. It is also considered heavy industry as raw material and finished goods are both heavy and bulky and involves heavy transportation cost. It is a public sector industry.

This industry manufactures steel which is needed in making of engineering goods, construction material, defence, medical, telephonic and scientific equipments and consumer goods.

India ranked second in the production of crude steel in the world with 111 million tonnes in 2019. **China** is the **world's largest producer** and **consumer of steel** but its production was equal to India in 1950.

---

5 **Handloom** A hand operated machine for producing cloth by weaving.

6 **Powerloom** A textile machine for weaving yarn into cloth which is operated mechanically using electric or other form of power.

7 **Khadi** A coarse handspun cotton cloth made in India. Also called 'Khaddar'.

**India** is the **largest producer of sponge iron**. But its per capita consumption was only 74.3 kg per annum in 2019 against 229.3 kg of world average. India has many integrated steel plants. They are large and handle everything in one complex. India also has many units of mini steel plants. They produce mild and alloy steel.

In India, most of the public sector undertakings trade their steel through Steel Authority of India. Factors which are responsible for location of iron and steel industry at one place are

- Close proximity to the areas where raw materials are found to reduce the transportation cost.
- Availability of cheap labour.
- Regular supply of water and power.
- Nearness to the markets where finished products can be sold.
- Close to sea ports for export facilities.

**Chota Nagpur plateau** region has maximum concentration of iron and steel industries due to having most of these factors.

### Processes of Manufacture of Steel

In order to manufacture steel, iron ore, coking coal and limestone are needed in the ratio of approx. 4 : 2 : 1. Manganese is also required to harden the steel. The processes of manufacture of steel is shown below

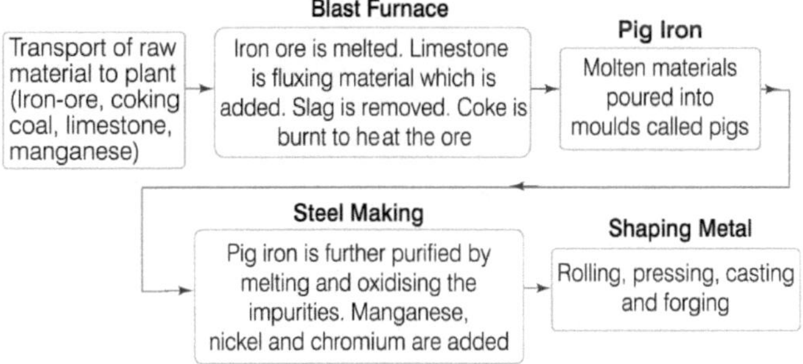


The challenges due to which India is not able to perform to its full potential in this industry are

- Limited availability and high cost of coking coal.
- Poor infrastructure
- Lower labour productivity
- Irregular supply of energy

### Aluminium Smelting

It is the second most important metallurgical industry in India. Bauxite is the basic raw material of this industry which is a very bulky, dark reddish coloured rock. Aluminium is light, resistant to corrosion, a good conductor of heat, malleable and becomes strong when it is mixed with other metals. It is used to manufacture aircraft, utensils and wires. Aluminium has gained popularity as a substitute of steel, copper, zinc and lead in different industries. The factors responsible for the location of this Industry are regular supply of electricity and availability of raw material at minimum cost.

In India, aluminium smelting plants are located in Odisha, West Bengal, Kerala, Uttar Pradesh, Chhattisgarh, Maharashtra and Tamil Nadu.

### Chemical Industries

In India, the chemical industry is fast growing and diversifying in nature. It comprises both large and small scale manufacturing units. Chemical industry has two sectors namely organic and inorganic sectors.

Organic sector produces organic chemicals. These chemicals include petrochemicals. Petrochemicals are used for manufacturing of synthetic fibres, synthetic rubber, plastics, dye-stuffs, drugs and pharmaceuticals.

Organic chemical plants are located near oil refineries or petrochemical plants. Inorganic sector produces inorganic chemicals. These chemicals include sulphuric acid used to manufacture fertilisers, synthetic fibres, plastics, adhesives, paints, dyes stuffs, nitric acid, alkalies, soda ash (used to make glass, soaps and detergents paper) and caustic soda. These chemical plants are located all over the country.

### Fertiliser Industry

This industry produces a number of different fertilisers. These fertilisers include nitrogenous fertilizers (mainly urea), phosphatic fertilisers and Diammonium Phosphate (DAP).

It also produces complex fertilisers which are produced by Nitrogen (N), Phosphate (P) and Potash (K). India imports potash from other countries. It is because the country does not have any reserves of commercially usable potash or potassium compounds in any form.

The Green Revolution provided a boost to this industry in the country. Around half of the fertiliser production is done by Gujarat, Tamil Nadu, Uttar Pradesh, Punjab and Kerala. Other important producers are Andhra Pradesh, Odisha, Rajasthan, Bihar, Maharashtra, Assam, West Bengal, Goa, Delhi, Madhya Pradesh and Karnataka.

### Cement Industry

The **first cement plant was set up in Chennai in 1904**. After independence the industry flourished in India. Cement is the basic requirement for construction activities like building houses, factories, bridges, roads, airports, dams and other commercial establishments. The factors needed to set up cement industry in a place are

- Availability of bulky and heavy raw materials such as limestone, silica and gypsum.
- Availability of coal and electric power to run the Industry and good transport network, such as rail transport.
- The cement industry has established its plants in Gujarat because the state provides access to the market in the Gulf countries.
- Indian cement industry has found its market in East Asia, Middle East, Africa and South Asia. The country also has large domestic demands for cement.

#### Automobile Industry

This industry provides quick transportation vehicles for goods and passengers. In India, there are centers for manufacture of trucks, buses, cars, motor cycles, scooters, three-wheelers and multi-utility vehicles.

The industry is located around Gurugram, Mumbai, Pune, Chennai, Kolkata, Lucknow, Indore, Hyderabad, Jamshedpur, Delhi and Bengaluru.

#### Information Technology (IT) and Electronics Industry

It covers products from transistor sets to televisions, telephones, cellphones, telephone exchanges, radars, computers and other equipment required by the telecommunication and computer industry. **Bengaluru** has emerged as the **electronic capital of India.** Other important centres for electronic goods are Noida, Mumbai, Chennai, Hyderabad, Pune, Delhi, Kolkata, Lucknow and Coimbatore.

## Industrial Pollution and Environmental Degradation

Although industries have contributed significantly to India's economic growth and development but their waste products have caused environmental degradation. Industries are responsible for four types of pollution i.e. air, water, land and noise.

### Air Pollution

It is caused by the presence of high proportion of sulphur dioxide, carbon monoxide, air borne **particulate matter**[8] like dust, sprays mist and smoke. Smoke is emitted by chemical and paper factories, brick klins, refineries and smelting plants and burning of fossil fuels in big and small factories.

It adversely affects human health, animals, plants, buildings and the atmosphere as a whole.

### Water Pollution

It is caused when organic and inorganic untreated industrial wastes and affluents are discharged into rivers. Textile and dyeing, petroleum refineries, tanneries and electroplating industries are the main industries causing water pollution.

It threatens plant, aquatic and human life. Fly ash, phospho-gypsum and iron and steel slags are major solid wastes in India.

### Thermal Pollution

This occurs when hot water from factories and thermal plants is drained into rivers and ponds before cooling. Wastes from nuclear power plants, nuclear and weapon production facilities cause cancer, birth defects and miscarriages.

Soil becomes polluted when harmful chemicals, industrial affluents, glass, packaging salts and garbage are dumped into the soil. Chemicals get absorb in the soil, making the soil useless.

#### NTPC

National Thermal Power Corporation is a major power providing corporation in India. It has ISO certification 14001 for developing Environment Management Systems. Major task of NTPC is to set up power plants by conserving the natural environment and resources like air, water, oil gas, coal and other fuels. This is possible through

- Optimum utilisation of equipments, adopting latest techniques and upgrading old equipment wherever possible.
- Minimising waste generation in thermal power plants by adopting ash utilisation techniques.
- Development of green belts by afforestation to maintain ecological balance.
- Reducing environmental pollution through ash pond management, ash water recycling system and liquid waste management.
- Installing facilities for ecological monitoring, review and online database management in all the power stations.

### Noise Pollution

Noise from industrial and construction activities, machinery, generators, saws and pneumatic and electric drills, etc. contribute to noise pollution.

This type of pollution results in hearing impairment, increased heart rate, blood pressure and physiological effects such as stress and irritation.

8 **Particulate Matter** Solid or liquid matter that remains dispersed in gas or liquid emissions and creates pollution.

## Control of Environmental Degradation

Some suggestions to minimise the industrial pollution of freshwater are

- Minimising water usage by reusing and recycling waste water in two or more successive stages.
- Rainwater harvesting to meet water requirements.
- Treating hot water and industrial wastes before releasing them in rivers and ponds.

This can be done in three phases

(*i*) **Primary treatment** by mechanical means (i.e. **screening**[9], grinding, **flocculation**[10] and sedimentation.)

(*ii*) **Secondary treatment** by biological processes. Such as planting trees, rain water harvesting.

(*iii*) **Tertiary treatment** by chemical, physical and biological processes like recycling of waste water, in sewage treatment plants.

**Note** *Sewage treatment plant under Yamuna Action Plan is located at Faridabad.*

General measures to minimise environmental pollution are

- Overdrawing of groundwater reserves by industries needs to be regulated legally.
- Generators and other machinery should be fitted with silencers and other noise absorbing materials to reduce their sound.
- Particulate matter in the air can be reduced by fitting smoke stacks to factories with **electrostatic precipitators**[11], **fabric filters**[12], **scrubbers**[13] and **inertial separators**[14].
- Use of oil or gas instead of coal to reduce smoke emission from factories.
- Redesigning of machinery to increase their efficiency in using energy.
- Promote sustainable development by integrating economic development goals with environmental construction.

9 **Screening** It is a method to trap solid (large objects) from the waste water.
10 **Flocculation** Particles in waste water sticking to each other thus, increasing in mass.
11 **Electrostatic Precipitator** An air pollution control device for removing fine solid particles from emitted smoke.
12 **Fabric Filter** An air pollution control device that removes particulates out of air by using woven or felted fabric as a filter medium.
13 **Scrubber** Pollution control device which uses liquid spray to wash out particulate matter and neutralises gaseous pollutants.
14 **Inertial Separator** A device that uses centrifugal force to separate waste particles.

# Chapter Practice

## PART 1 Objective Questions

### • Multiple Choice Questions

**1.** Which one of the following groups of states have the largest number of cotton textile centers? Identify the correct option.

(a) Gujarat and Maharashtra
(b) Karnataka and Tamil Nadu
(c) Maharashtra and Madhya Pradesh
(d) Uttar Pradesh and Gujarat

***Ans.*** (a) Cotton textile industry is mainly located in Maharashtra, Gujarat and Tamil Nadu.

**2.** Which one of the following agencies markets steel for the Public Sector plants? **(NCERT)**

(a) HAIL (b) SAIL
(c) TATA Steel (d) MNCC

***Ans.*** (b) SAIL is one of the agencies that markets steel for all the Public Sector Plants.

**3.** Most of the integrated steel plants in India are located in ............ . Choose the correct option.

(a) Malwa Plateau (b) Chota Nagpur Plateau
(c) Bundelkhand Plateau (d) Meghalaya Plateau

***Ans.*** (b) Chota Nagpur Plateau region is the region where most of the integrated steel plants are located in India.

**4.** Which one of the following industries uses bauxite as a raw material? **(NCERT)**

(a) Aluminium Smelting (b) Cement
(c) Paper (d) Steel

***Ans.*** (a) Aluminium Smelting uses bauxite as a raw material.

**5.** Which of the following group of factors is a prime group for the location of aluminium smelting plant? Identify the correct option.

(a) Capital and market (b) Raw material and electricity
(c) Labour and raw material (d) Capital and transport

***Ans.*** (b) Raw material and regular supply of electricity are the prime factors which are responsible for the location of aluminium smelting industry.

**6.** Which one of the following industries manufactures telephones, computer, etc?

(a) Steel (b) Electronic
(c) Aluminium Smelting (d) Information Technology

***Ans.*** (b) Electronic industries manufactures telephones, computer, etc.

**7.** Identify the type of industry with the help of informations given below.

- This industry comprises of both large scale and small scale manufacturing units.
- It consists of two sectors namely organic and inorganic sectors.

(a) Automobile Industry (b) Fertiliser Industry
(c) Chemical Industry (d) Cement Industry

***Ans.*** (c) Chemical Industry comprises of both large and small scale manufacturing units. This industry has two sectors namely organic and inorganic sectors.

**8.** Identify the type of pollution with the help of given information.

- This occurs when hot water from factories and thermal plants is drained into rivers and ponds before cooling,
- Due to this pollution chemicals get absorb in the soil, making the soil useless.

(a) Air Pollution
(b) Water Pollution
(c) Thermal Pollution
(d) Noise Pollution

***Ans.*** (c) Thermal Pollution

**9.** Find the incorrectly matched pair from the given options.

(a) Public Sector – BHEL
(b) Private Sector – SAIl
(c) Joint Sector – Oil India Limited
(d) Manufacturing Sector – NMCC

***Ans.*** (b) SAIL is a public sector industry. Private sector industries are owned and operated by individuals or group of individuals. For example, TISCO, Bajaj Auto Ltd and Dabur Ltd.

**10.** Choose the correctly matched pair about Industries and their challenges.

(a) Cotton Textile Industry – Seasonal Nature of Industry
(b) Jute Textile Industry – Lower Labour Productivity
(c) Iron and Steel Industry- Irregular supply of Energy
(d) Sugar Industry- Less Demand

*Ans.* (c) Irregular supply of energy is a challenge to iron and steel industry.

**11.** Match the following items given in Column A with those in Column B.

| **Column A** (Types of Industries) | **Column B** (Location) |
|---|---|
| A. Aluminium Smelting Plants | 1. Bihar |
| B. Fertiliser Industry | 2. Jamshedpur |
| C. Automobile Industry | 3. Gujarat |
| D. Sugar Industry | 4. Odisha |

**Codes**

| | A | B | C | D | | A | B | C | D |
|---|---|---|---|---|---|---|---|---|---|
| (a) | 2 | 3 | 4 | 1 | (b) | 3 | 4 | 1 | 2 |
| (c) | 4 | 3 | 2 | 1 | (d) | 1 | 4 | 3 | 2 |

*Ans.* (c)

**12.** Match the following items given in Column A with those in Column B.

| **Column A** (Mill/Plant) | **Column B** (Year of Establishment) |
|---|---|
| A. First Textile Mill | 1. 1904 |
| B. First Jute Mill | 2. 1854 |
| C. First Cement Plant | 3. 1859 |

**Codes**

| | A | B | C | | A | B | C |
|---|---|---|---|---|---|---|---|
| (a) | 2 | 3 | 1 | (b) | 1 | 3 | 2 |
| (c) | 3 | 2 | 1 | (d) | 2 | 1 | 3 |

*Ans.* (a)

## • Assertion-Reason MCQs

**Directions** (Q. Nos. 13-17) *Each of these questions contains two statements, **Assertion** (A) and **Reason** (R). Each of these questions also has four alternative choices, any one of which is the correct answer. You have to select one of the codes (a), (b), (c) and (d) given below.*

**Codes**

(a) Both A and R are true and R is the correct explanation of A
(b) Both A and R are true, but R is not the correct explanation of A
(c) A is true, but R is false
(d) A is false, but R is true

**13.** **Assertion** (A) In recent years, there is a tendency for the sugar mills to concentrate in the Southern and Western States, especially in Maharashtra.

**Reason** (R) The cane produced in the Southern and Western states has higher sucrose content and cooler climate also ensures a longer crushing season.

*Ans.* (a) In recent years, there is a tendency for the sugar mills to concentrate in the Southern and Western States, especially in Maharashtra.

This is because the cane produced here has higher sucrose content and cooler climate also ensures a longer crushing season. Hence, both assertion and reason are true and reason is the correct explanation of assertion.

**14.** **Assertion** (A) Aluminium has gained popularity as a substitute of steel, copper, zinc and lead in different industries.

**Reason** (R) Aluminium is the second most important metallurgical industry in India.

*Ans.* (b) Aluminium has gained popularity as a substitute of steel, copper, zinc and lead in different industries. On the other hand, Aluminium is the second most important metallurgical industry in India. Hence, both assertion and reason are true, but reason is not the correct explanation of assertion.

**15.** **Assertion** (A) The Cement Industry has established its plant in Gujarat.

**Reason** (R) After Independence, cement industry has flourished in India.

*Ans.* (b) The Cement Industry has established its plant in Gujarat because the state provides access to the market in the Gulf countries.

On the other hand, after Independence the cement industry has flourished in India as it is the basic requirement for construction activities and other commercial establishments. Hence, both assertion and reason are true, but reason is not the correct explanation of given assertion.

**16.** **Assertion** (A) India imports potash from other countries.

**Reason** (R) India does not have any of the commercially usable potash or potassium compounds in any form.

*Ans.* (a) India imports potash from other countries because the country does not have any reserves of commercially usable potash or potassium compounds in any form. Hence, both assertion and reason are true and reason is the correct explanation of assertion.

**17. Assertion** (A) National Thermal Power Corporation (NTPC) is a major power providing corporation in India.

**Reason** (R) The major task of NTPC is to set up power plants by conserving the natural environment and resources like air, water, oil gas, coal and other fuels.

***Ans.*** (b) National Thermal Power Corporation is a major power producing corporation in India as it has an ISO certification 14001 for developing Environment Management Systems. On the other hand, the major task of NTPC is to set up power plants by conserving the natural environment and resources like air, water, oil gas and other fuels. Hence, both assertion and reason are true, but reason is not the correct explanation of given assertion.

## • Case Based MCQs

**18.** Read the case/source given and answer the questions that follow by choosing the correct option.

India stands second as a world producer of sugar but occupies the first place in the production of gur and khandsari. The raw material used in this industry is bulky, and in haulage its sucrose content reduces. The mills are located in Uttar Pradesh, Bihar, Maharashtra, Karnataka, Tamil Nadu, Andhra Pradesh, Gujarat, Punjab, Haryana and Madhya Pradesh. Sixty per cent mills are in Uttar Pradesh and Bihar. This industry is seasonal in nature so, it is ideally suited to the cooperative sector. Can you explain why this is so?

In recent years, there is a tendency for the mills to shift and concentrate in the southern and western states, especially in Maharashtra; this is because the cane produced here has higher sucrose content. The cooler climate also ensures a longer crushing season. Moreover, the cooperatives are more successful in these states. Major challenges include the seasonal nature of the industry, old and inefficient methods of production, transport delay in reaching cane to factories and the need to maximise the use of bagasse.

(i) Fill in the blank from the given options:

India stands second as a world producer of sugar but occupies the first place in the production of gur and khandsari. Sugar industry comes under .............. group of industries.

(a) Public sector
(b) Cooperative sector
(c) Private sector
(d) Joint sector venture

***Ans.*** (b) Sugar industry comes under cooperative sector of industries.

(ii) Read the following statements about cooperative sector and find the incorrect from the given options.

I. Cooperative Sector is owned and operated by the producers or suppliers of raw materials, workers or both.

II. This sector pools in the resources and share the profits or losses proportionately.

III. This sector is jointly run by the state and individuals or a group of individuals.

**Codes**

(a) Only I
(b) Both I and II
(c) Only III
(d) Both I and III

***Ans.*** (c) Statement III is incorrect regarding the Cooperative Sector. It is the Joint Sector Venture which is run by the state and the individuals or a group of individuals, e.g. Oil India Limited.

(iii) Why sugar mills are perfectly convenient for the sector in which industries owned by suppliers or producers of raw materials, workers or both? With reference to the above context, infer the appropriate option.

(a) Because this industry is seasonal in nature.
(b) Dueto its efficient methods of production.
(c) Due to better transport system.
(d) Because raw material are bulky.

***Ans.*** (a) Sugar mills are perfectly convenient for the sector in which industries owned by suppliers or producers of raw materials, workers or both because this industry is seasonal in nature.

(iv) Why there is a high concentration of sugar mills in Uttar Pradesh? Select the best suitable option from the following in reference to the context.

(a) Because Uttar Pradesh is the largest producer of sugarcane.
(b) Because labour is easily available in Uttar Pradesh.
(c) Due to high consumption in Uttar Pradesh.
(d) All of the above

***Ans.*** (a) There is a high concentration of sugar mills in Uttar Pradesh because it is the largest producer of sugarcane.

(v) Why Sugar industries are shifting to the South and the West? Identify the best suitable reason from the given options.

(a) Due to cooler climate in these areas.
(b) Due to success of cooperative movement in these areas.
(c) Due to higher sucrose content in the sugarcanes cultivated in these areas.
(d) All of the above

***Ans.*** (d) All the given statements are correct.

(vi) Which of the following is not a major challenge for sugar industry? Select the best suitable option from the following.

(a) Traditional methods of production
(b) Need to maximise the use of bagasse
(c) Availability of water
(d) Seasonal nature of this industry

***Ans.*** (c) Availability of water is not a major challenge for sugar industry.

PART 2

# Subjective Questions

## • Short Answer (SA) Type Questions

**1.** What is manufacturing? How does manufacturing lead to value addition of the raw material? Explain with the help of examples. **(CBSE 2013)**

***Ans.*** Production of goods in large quantities by processing of raw materials to more valuable products is called manufacturing.

Manufacturing leads to value addition of the raw material as people employed in the secondary activities manufacture the primary materials into finished goods. These finished goods are more useful, hence more in value. For example, paper is manufactured from wood, sugar from sugarcane, iron and steel from iron ore, aluminium from bauxite, etc.

Thus, raw materials are transformed into a wide variety of finished goods of higher value. Countries that transform in this way are prosperous.

**2.** What is the contribution of industries to national economy of India? Compare this contribution with the East-Asian countries. What is the desired growth and present position of industry in GDP? **(CBSE 2011)**

***Ans.*** The contribution of industries to national economy of India has not been satisfactory for the last two decades. It has stagnated at 17 per cent of GDP out of a total of 27 per cent for the industries which includes 10 per cent of mining, quarrying, electricity and gas. In comparison to India's 17 per cent share in the GDP, the manufacturing sector in East-Asian countries have a contribution of 25 to 35 per cent of their GDP.

The desired growth rate over the next decade is 12 per cent. At present, growth rate is about 9 to 10 per cent and it is expected that we can achieve the growth rate of 12 per cent by some efforts like setting up of the National Manufacturing Competitiveness Council (NMCC).

**3.** "Industrialisation and urbanisation go hand in hand." Justify the statement by giving any three arguments. **(CBSE 2012)**

***Ans.*** Industrialisation and urbanisation go hand in hand. For example,

(i) Industrialisation causes growth in available factory jobs. As a result, employment rate increases which pulls people from various places towards the places where industries are located.

(ii) Many industries tend to come together to make use of advantages offered by the urban centres.

(iii) Cities provide markets and also provide services such as banking, insurance, transport, labour, consultants and financial advice, which are needed by the industry.

**4.** Why was the cotton textile industry concentrated in the cotton growing belt in the early years? Explain. **(CBSE 2015)**

***Ans.*** In the early years, the cotton textile industry was concentrated in the cotton growing belt of Maharashtra and Gujarat due to availability of raw cotton, market, transport including accessible port facilities, labour, moist climate, etc.

This industry has close links with agriculture and provides a living to farmers, cotton ball pluckers and workers engaged in ginning, spinning, weaving, dyeing, designing, packaging, tailoring and sewing.

The industry by creating demands supports many other industries, such as chemicals and dyes, mill stores, packaging materials and engineering works. All these factors determine location of cotton mill in early years.

**5.** Explain any three problems faced by cotton textile industries in India. **(CBSE 2017)**

***Ans.*** Three problems faced by cotton textile industries in India are

(i) Power supply is erratic. Regular power supply without breaks is essential for this industry.

(ii) Output of labour is low because the machinery is outdated. Particularly in the weaving and processing sectors, the machinery needs to be upgraded.

(iii) This industry faces stiff competition from the synthetic fibre industry in terms of cost and convenience of use.

**6.** Mention any six factors responsible for the location of jute mills in the Hugli basin. **(CBSE 2014)**

***Ans.*** Factors responsible for location of jute mills in the Hugli basin are

(i) Proximity of the jute producing areas.

(ii) Inexpensive water transport, supported by a good network of railways and roadways.

(iii) Abundance of water for processing raw jute.

(iv) Availability of cheap labour from nearby areas.

(v) Facilities for export of jute goods.

(vi) Banking, insurance and other commercial facilities to jute industry.

**7.** Mention any two challenges faced by the jute industry in India. State any one step taken by the government to stimulate its demand. **(CBSE 2012, 11)**

***Ans.*** The two challenges faced by the jute industry in India are

(i) Stiff competition in the international market from synthetic substitutes.

(ii) Supply competition from other jute producing nations like Bangladesh, Brazil, Philippines, Egypt and Thailand.

The step taken by the government to stimulate the demand for jute is that it has introduced a policy of mandatory use of jute packaging. The main markets of jute industries are USA, Canada, Ghana, Saudi Arabia, UK and Australia.

**8.** What are mineral based industries? Give four examples. **(CBSE 2013)**

**Ans.** Industries that use minerals and metals as raw materials are called mineral based industries.

Four examples of mineral based industries are

(i) **The Iron and Steel Industry** All other industries depend on it for their machinery.

(ii) **Chemical Industry** It contributes approximately 3 per cent of India's GDP.

(iii) **Fertiliser Industry** It is centered around the production of nitrogenous, phosphatic, ammonium phosphate and complex fertiliser.

(iv) **Cement Industry** This requires limestone, silica, alumina and gypsum as raw materials.

**9.** Why is iron and steel industry called the basic industry? What are the problems faced by this industry? **(CBSE 2013, 12)**

*Or* Explain any three problems faced by Iron and Steel industry in India. **(CBSE 2011)**

**Ans.** Iron and steel industry is known as the basic industry because all the other industries (heavy, medium and light) depend on it for their machinery and products.

Problems faced by this industry are

(i) The finished goods of this industry are heavy and bulky that require heavy transportations costs.

(ii) There is limited availability of coking coal and productivity of labour is low. Other problems are irregular supply of energy and poor infrastructure.

**10.** Mention any two factors that have contributed to a healthy growth of the automobile industry in India. Name two centres where this industry is located.

**Ans.** Two factors contributing to healthy growth of the automobile sector are

(i) Liberalisation is one of the major factors which provided boost in the growth of the automobile industry in India. With the introduction of new and contemporary models of automobiles in the country, the demand for these vehicles increased at a faster pace.

(ii) With the introduction of new technology in this sector, Indian industries are now capable to compete with the global technologies. This could happen by Foreign Direct Investment (FDI).

Two major centres where this industry is located are Gurugram and Indore.

**11.** How do industries create thermal and noise pollution? Mention their consequences.

**Ans.** Industries create thermal and noise pollution in the following ways

- Thermal pollution of water bodies occurs when hot water from factories and thermal power plants is released into them before cooling.
  The consequence of thermal pollution are that aquatic life in the water bodies can be killed. This includes plants as well as fish.
- Noise pollution is generated by the unbearable noise from industrial and construction activities, machinery, generators, pneumatic and electric tools.
  The consequences of noise polutions create irritation, anger, stress, hearing impairment, increased heart rate and blood pressure among other physiological effects.

**12.** Examine how industrial pollution of freshwater can be reduced.

*Or* Suggest any three measures to reduce the industrial pollution of freshwater resources.

**Ans.** The industrial pollution of freshwater resources can be reduced in the following ways

(i) Restructuring the manufacturing processes in various industries to reduce or eliminate pollutants through pollution prevention methods.

(ii) Creating man-made cooling ponds designed to cool heated effluent waters of industries by evaporation, condensation and radiation.

(iii) Filtration of the sewage in water treatment plants before dumping it into water bodies.

**13.** Mention the negative impacts of waste from the nuclear plant. **(CBSE 2013)**

**Ans.** Negative impacts of waste from the nuclear plants are

- Waste from nuclear plants have radioactive properties and may cause cancers, birth defects and miscarriages.
- Nuclear wastes are generally dumped in deep sea-water. In case of their unfortunate leakage, there will be severe threat to aquatic life.
- Radioactive contamination can easily spread throughout the environment and the air, land and water can all become polluted and harm humans and other life forms.

**14.** Explain any five measures to control industrial pollution in India. **(CBSE 2013)**

*Or* Suggest any three steps to minimise environmental degradation caused by industrial development in India. **(CBSE 2017, CBSE 2016)**

*Or* Discuss the steps to be taken to minimise environmental degradation by industry. **(NCERT)**

**Ans.** Five measures or steps to control or minimise industrial pollution in India are

(i) Particulate matter in the air can be reduced by fitting smoke stacks to factories with electrostatic precipitators, fabric filters, scrubbers and inertial separators.

(ii) Smoke can be reduced by using oil or gas instead of coal in factories.

(iii) Updated machinery and equipment should be used that makes less noise and generators should be fitted with silencers.

(iv) Pollution check certificates should be made compulsory.

(v) Machineries used in the industries can be redesigned to increase energy efficiency and reduce noise. Noise absorbing materials may also be used.

**15.** "Sugar industry in India is facing challenges." Analyse the statement with suitable arguments. **(CBSE 2019)**

***Ans.*** Sugar industry in India is facing lot of challenges which are

(i) This industry is seasonal as it is dependent on sugarcane which is an annual crop. Workers get employed only for a short period.

(ii) The machines and ways of producing sugar from sugarcane are old and inefficient.

(iii) The raw material i.e. sugarcane is bulky which increases the transportation cost and difficulty of transporting.

(iv) The sucrose content in sugarcane keeps on decreasing with time so transport delay in reaching sugarcane to factories results in losses.

(v) There is also the challenge of using the byproducts of sugarcane properly like bagasse.

## • Long Answer (LA) Type Questions

**1.** Why is the economic strength of a country measured by the development of manufacturing industries ? Explain with examples. **(CBSE 2018)**

***Ans.*** The economic strength of a country is measured by the development of manufacturing industries because

- Manufacturing industries help in modernising agriculture, which forms the backbone of our economy. For example, these provide tractors, thresher, irrigation pumping machines and other modern machineries for agricultural development.
- Manufacturing also reduces the heavy dependence of people on agricultural income by providing them jobs in secondary and tertiary sectors.
- Industrial development helps in removal of unemployment and poverty. It also aims at bringing down regional differences by establishing industries in backward areas. For example, handloom industries in tribal regions.
- Export of manufactured goods expands trade and commerce and brings much needed foreign exchange.
- Countries that transform their raw materials into a wide variety of finished goods of higher value are prosperous.

**2.** Explain any three physical factors and two human factors for the location of the industry. **(CBSE 2016)**

*Or* Explain with examples any five factors that are responsible for industrial location. **(CBSE 2019)**

*Or* Explain any three factors affecting the localisation of industries with suitable examples. **(CBSE 2012, 11)**

***Ans.*** The physical and human factors that affect the location of industry are

**Physical Factors**

(i) **Availability of Raw Materials** The factory needs to be close to the location of raw material if they are heavy and bulky to transport. For example, iron and steel industry is located near the source of raw material.

(ii) **Water Source** Water is an important factor that determines the location of industries. Water is required for various industrial processes. River water and waterfalls can also be used to generate hydroelectricity.

(iii) **Climate** It plays a significant role in establishment of industries. Harsh climate is not much suitable for industries. Extremely hot, humid, dry or cold climate is not very conducive for industries.

For example, cotton textile industry requires humid climate because thread breaks in dry climate.

**Human Factors**

(i) **Labour** A large and cheap labour force is required for labour-intensive and manufacturing industries. High-tech industries have to be located where suitable skilled workers are available.

(ii) **Capital** This is the money that is invested to start a business. The amount of capital will determine the size and location of the factor.

(iii) **Government Policies** Industrial development is encouraged in some areas and restricted in others. Industries that are located in backward areas may receive financial incentives and assistance from the government in the form of low rent and tax rates.

**3.** Which factor plays the most dominant role in the ideal location of an industry? Explain any three reasons in support of this factor.

***Ans.*** Least cost factor plays the most dominant role for the ideal location of an industry due to the following reasons

(i) Cost of obtaining raw material at the factory site should be minimum i.e. raw materials should be available nearby or may be transported cheaply to the industrial location.

(ii) The factory should be located as such that the manufactured products may easily be distributed or transported to the market at the least cost by rail, road or water transport.

(iii) Cost of manufacturing at the factory site should be low. This means that trained experienced labour should be readily available locally or in nearby areas, electric power supply should be readily available and cheap. Also, land for locating the industry should be available at proper rates.

**4.** Why does the textile industry occupy an important position in the Indian economy ? Explain. **(CBSE 2019)**

***Ans.*** Textile industry occupies unique position in Indian economy because

(i) **Contribution to Industrial Production** This industry is self-reliant and complete in the value chain, which means from production of cotton to processing of textiles, all the procedures are well developed and done in the country.

(ii) **Employment Generation** This industry generates employment for large number of persons directly or indirectly.

(iii) **Demand Creation** Textile industries create demand for other industries such as chemicals, dyes, packaging materials, engineering works, handicrafts industry etc.

(iv) **Foreign Exchange Earnings** By exporting the products of this industry, the country earns foreign exchange.

(v) **Supports Agriculture** This is a major agro-based industry of India and supports agriculture in a big way both by buying agricultural output (cotton) and by providing agricultural inputs (hybrid cotton seeds, implements).

**5.** Which states of India have the maximum extent of cotton textile growth? Give four reasons for its concentration in this state. **(CBSE 2013)**

***Ans.*** Maharashtra and Gujarat states have the maximum extent of cotton textile growth. The reasons for the concentration of cotton textile industry in these states are

(i) **Availability of Raw Materials** Due to favourable soil type and other climatic conditions, cotton is grown in a vast area in these states. So, raw materials are available in plenty.

(ii) **Transport** These states are well connected to the rest of the country by rail and road. Also, they have many large ports from where the finished products can be easily exported.

(iii) **Market** They also enjoy well-developed markets where there is lot of demands for cotton textiles.

(iv) **Labour** Although they have locally available cheap labour force, they are supported by migrant labours from the other states.

(v) **Moist Climate** For cotton cultivation, moist climate is a must. These states have favourable climatic conditions.

**6.** Why does the 'Chota Nagpur Plateau region' have the maximum concentration of iron and steel industries? Analyse the reasons. **(CBSE 2015)**

*Or* Explain the reasons for concentration of iron and steel industries in and around Chotanagpur region. **(CBSE 2019)**

***Ans.*** The reasons/factors responsible for the concentration of iron and steel industries in and around the 'Chotanagpur Plateau Region' are

(i) **Low Cost of Iron Ore** Iron mines are located in the nearby areas. It helps to reduce the transportation cost of iron ore to the industries.

(ii) **High Grade Raw Materials in Proximity** Bulky raw materials like, coking coal, limestone are also available in proximity.

(iii) **Availability of Cheap Labour** From the adjoining areas of Bihar, Jharkhand and Odisha, cheap labour is available in abundance.

(iv) **Dense Transport Network** This region is well connected with roadways and railways that help in the swift movement of raw materials and finished goods to the industry and market areas, respectively.

(v) **Port Facilities** Kolkata is a well developed port that is near to this area.

**7.** How are industries responsible for environmental degradation in India? Explain with examples. **(CBSE 2019)**

***Ans.*** Industries are responsible for environmental degradation in India as they pollute the environment by polluting air, water and land in following ways

(i) **Air Pollution** Industries cause air pollution by the emission of gases from industrial complexes and power generation units. Leakage of poisonous gases and chemicals and smoke from chemical industries also lead to air pollution.

(iii) **Water Pollution** It is caused when industrial effluents both organic and inorganic are discharged into rivers or other water bodies. Industries like paper, pulp, chemical, textile and dyeing, petroleum refineries, tanneries and electroplating industries discharge detergents acids, salts and heavy metals like lead and mercury, pesticides, fertilisers, synthetic chemicals with carbon, plastic and rubber, etc. into water bodies.

(iii) **Thermal Pollution** This pollution occurs when hot water from factories and thermal plants is drained into rivers and ponds before cooling. It badly affects the aquatic life. For example, wastes from nuclear power plants, nuclear and weapon production causes cancers, birth defects, miscarriages etc. Rain water percolates to the soil carrying the pollutants to the ground and thus ground water also gets contaminated.

(iv) **Noise Pollution** Undesirable noise pollution from industries like construction, running of generators to generate power, electrical drills, etc. is responsible for disturbing our environment. Noise pollution not only irritates us, but it also causes hearing impairment, increased heart rate and blood pressure etc.

## • Case Based Questions

**1.** Read the given cases/sources and answer the following questions

**Source A Importance of Manufacturing**

Manufacturing industries not only help in modernising agriculture, which forms the backbone of our economy, they also reduce the heavy dependence of people on agricultural income by providing them jobs in secondary and tertiary sectors.

(i) To what extent do you agree that manufacturing industries are important for people? State only two reasons.

*Ans.* It is true that manufacturing industries are important for people because these industries create jobs for people and reduce heavy dependence of people on agricultural income.

**Source B Contribution of Industry to National Economy**

Over the last two decades, the share of manufacturing sector has stagnated at 17 per cent of GDP - out of a total of 27 per cent for the industry which includes 10 per cent for mining, quarrying, electricity and gas. This is much lower in comparison to some East Asian economies, where it is 25 to 35 per cent.

(ii) Why it is said that manufacturing sector of Indian economy is much lower than the East Asian economics? What initiatives are taken by the government to deal with this situation?

*Ans.* Manufacturing sector of Indian economy is much lower than the East Asian economics because the manufacture sector of India has stagnated at 17% of GDP whereas East Asian economics have 25-35% GDP.

In order to develop the sector of manufacturing industries, government has set up the National manufacturing Competitiveness Council (NMCC). The objective is to bring appropriate policy to improve productivity to achieve desired growth rate.

**Source C Industrial Location**

Industrial locations are complex in nature. These are influenced by availability of raw material, labour, capital, power and market, etc. It is rarely possible to find all these factors available at one place. Consequently, manufacturing activity tends to locate at the most appropriate place where all the factors of industrial location are either available or can be arranged at lower cost.

(iii) Why it is said that it is rarely possible to find all the factors of industrial location available at one place? State only one aspect.

*Ans.* It is rarely possible to find all the factors of industrial location available at one place because these factors are different in nature. For example, some factors are physical in nature like raw materials, water source and climate whereas some are human factors such as labour, capital, power and market places.

**2** Read the given case/source and answer the following questions.

In the early years, the cotton textile industry was concentrated in the cotton growing belt of Maharashtra and Gujarat. Availability of raw cotton, market, transport including accessible port facilities, labour, moist climate, etc. contributed towards its localisation.

This industry has close links with agriculture and provides a living to farmers, cotton ball pluckers and workers engaged in ginning, spinning, weaving, dyeing, designing, packaging, tailoring and sewing. The industry by creating demands supports many other industries, such as, chemicals and dyes, packaging materials and engineering works.

(i) Which two places were important in early years for the concentration of textile industry in India? State any one challenge faced by cotton textile industries in India.

*Ans.* Gujarat and Maharashtra were important in early years for the concentration of textile industry in India.

The challenges faced by cotton textile industries in India is that this industry faces stiff competition from the synthetic fibre in terms of cost and convenience of use.

(ii) To what extent do you agree that these places are suitable for the location of cotton textile industry? State any two reasons.

*Ans.* Gujarat and Maharashtra are suitable for the location of cotton textile industry because

(i) Both states have favourable climate conditions for growing cotton.

(ii) Both states have well developed market, where there is a lot of demand for cotton textiles.

(iii) To what extent do you agree that cotton textile industry has close links with agriculture and also supports other industries as well? State two reasons.

*Ans.* It is true that cotton textile industry has close links with agriculture and also supports industries as

(i) Cotton textile industry provides a living to farmers and cotton ball pluckers because they grow cotton which is the basic raw material of this industry.

(ii) This industry by creating demands supports many other industries. For example, chemicals and dyes, mill stores, packaging materials and engineering works.

## • Map-based Questions

**1.** On the given political map of India, mark and label the following features with appropriate symbols.

(i) Bokaro Steel Plant. **(CBSE 2019)**
(ii) Mumbai Cotton Textile Industry
(iii) Salem Iron and Steel Plant **(CBSE 2019)**
(iv) Indore Cotton Textile Industry

*Ans.*

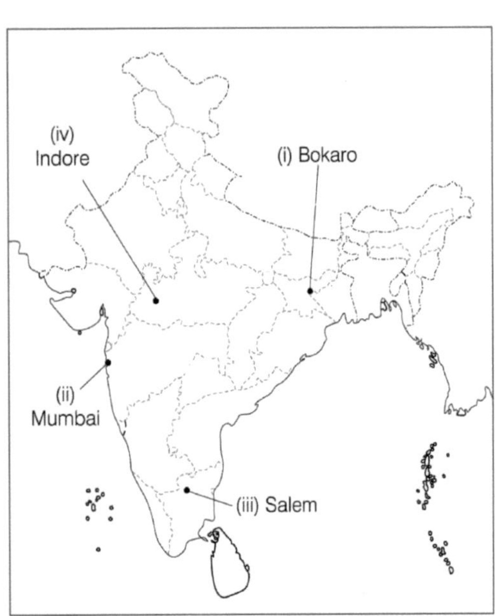


**2** On the given political map of India, locate and label the following features with appropriate symbols. **(CBSE 2015)**

(i) Surat Cotton Textile Industry
(ii) Jamshedpur Iron and Steel Plant
(iii) Gandhinagar Software Technology Park **(CBSE 2019)**
(iv) Noida Software Technology Park
(v) Coimbatore Cotton Textile Industry
(vi) Bengaluru Software Technology Park

*Ans.*

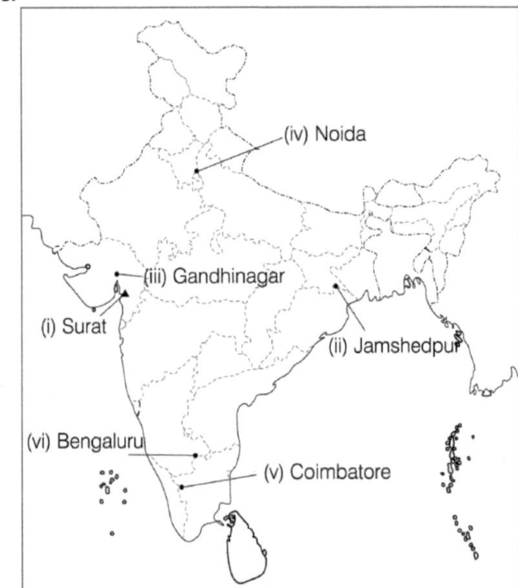

**3** On the following political map of India, locate, mark and label any four of the following with appropriate symbols.

(i) Mumbai– Software Technology Park
(ii) Kanpur–Cotton Textile Industry **(CBSE 2011)**
(iii) Bhilai–Iron and Steel Plant **(CBSE 2016, 12)**
(iv) Chennai Software Technology Park **(CBSE 2019)**
(v) Vijaynagar Iron and Steel Plant **(CBSE 2019)**

***Ans.***

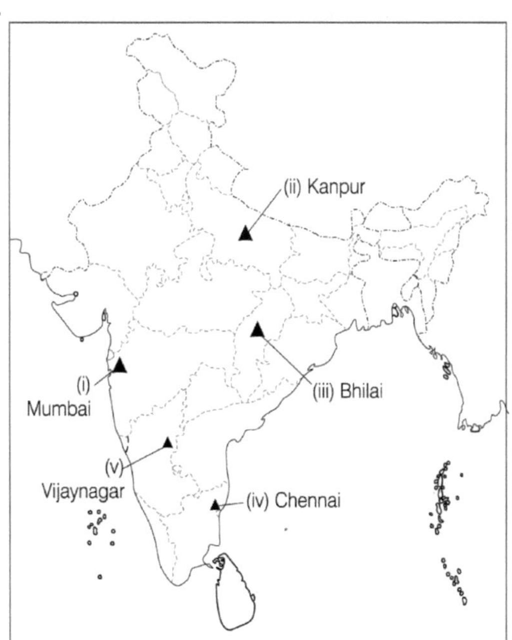


**4** On the given political map of India, locate and label the following features.

(i) Thiruvananthapuram Park
(ii) Durgapur Iron and Steel Plant
(iii) Hyderabad Software Technology Park **(CBSE 2019)**
(iv) Pune Software Technology Park

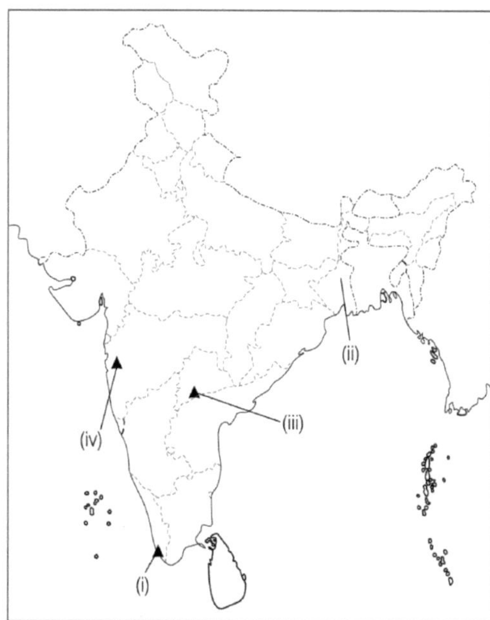


***Ans.***

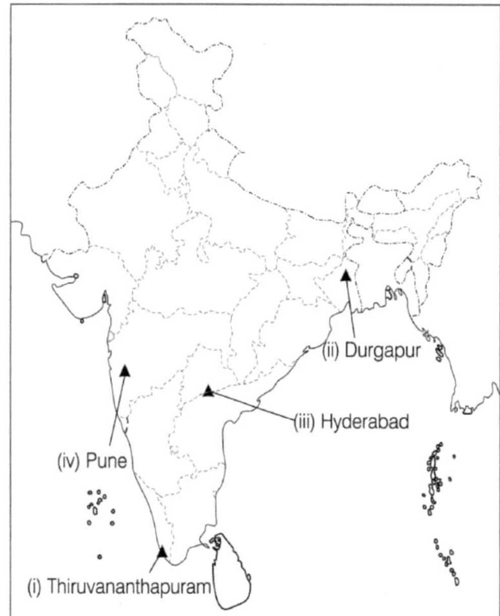

# Chapter Test

## Objective Questions

1. Which of the following is jointly owned by public and private sectors?
   (a) Bajaj Auto Ltd  (b) TISCO
   (c) BHEL  (d) Oil India Ltd

2. Which type of pollution occurs when hot water from factories is drained into rivers and ponds before cooling?
   (a) Thermal pollution  (b) Water pollution
   (c) Air pollution  (d) Noise pollution

3. Reducing environmental pollution through ash pond management, ash water recycling system and liquid relates to
   (a) waste management  (b) work done by NTPC
   (c) providing employment  (d) All of these

4. In which of the following states is Kalpakkam nuclear power plant located?
   (a) Gujarat  (b) Odisha
   (c) Kerala  (d) Tamil Nadu

5. Which of the following is not correct ?
   (a) Agriculture and industries are dependent on each other.
   (b) India is largest producer of raw jute and jute goods
   (c) Sugar and textile industry are examples of mineral industry.
   (d) Chemical industry has two sectors i.e. organic and inorganic.

## Short Answer Type Questions

6. How do industries pollute air and water?
7. Write a short note on sugar industry.
8. Explain three facts about information technology and electronics industry.
9. Compare the different patterns of development of jute and cotton industry.
10. Classify industries on the basis of source of raw material. How are they different from each other?
11. Describe the role of industries in the development of agriculture.

## Long Answer Type Questions

12. Why are jute mills concentrated along the Hugli river?
13. Why is it important for us to improve our weaving sector instead of exporting yarn in large quantities?
14. Explain any four problems faced by cotton textiles industries in India.

## Answers

1. (d) Oil India Ltd
2. (a) Thermal pollution
3. (b) work done by NTPC
4. (d) Tamil Nadu
5. (c) Sugar and textile industry are examples of mineral industry.

CHAPTER 03

# Lifelines of National Economy

### In this Chapter...

- Transport in India
- Communication
- International Trade

The modes of transportation and communication like railways, airways, waterways, newspapers, radio, television, cinema, internet, etc are contributing to India's socio-economic progress by linking India with the world.

## Transport in India

The movement of goods and services from supply locations to demand locations is termed as transportation. The efficient means of transportation is a necessary condition for fast development of a country. There are different means of transport through which movement of these goods and services is done over three important domains of the earth i.e. land, water and air.

## Roadways

India has one of the largest road networks in the world which is about 56 lakh km. Road transport is growing in importance as compared to railways because

- Construction cost of roads is much lower than that of railway lines.
- Roads can be built in uneven surfaces like hills and mountains.
- Roads can be built over higher slopes and can traverse (cross) mountains such as the Himalayas.
- Road transport is economical in transportation of few persons and relatively smaller amount of goods over short distances.
- Road transport also provides door-to-door service, thus, the cost of loading and unloading is much lower.
- Road transport links other modes of transport like between railway stations, air and sea ports.

### Classification of Roads on the Basis of Capacity

In India, roads are classified in six classes according to their capacity as

#### (i) Golden Quadrilateral Super Highways

This is an important road development project which has been launched by the Government of India. These are six lane super highways which connect Delhi-Kolkata, Chennai-Mumbai and Delhi. They have the following corridors

- **North-South corridors**[1] linking Srinagar (Jammu and Kashmir) and Kanniyakumari (Tamil Nadu).
- **East-West corridors**[2] linking Silchar (Assam) and Porbander (Gujarat).

1 **North-South Corridor** An ongoing National Highways project from Srinagar (Jammu and Kashmir) to Kanniyakumari (Tamil Nadu), a distance of about 4000 km, with a spur from Salem (Tamil Nadu) to Kochchi (Kerala).

2 **East-West Corridor** An ongoing National Highways project from Silchar (Assam) to Porbandar (Gujarat), a distance of about 3300 km.

The major objective of these super highways is to save time and reduce distance between the above mega cities in India. National Highway Authority of India (NHAI) is the regulatory which implements these highway projects.

### (ii) National Highways

They link extreme parts of the country. National Highways are the primary road systems and are constructed and maintained by the Central Public Works Department (CPWD) under NHAI's supervision. India has a number of National highways which connect the North-South and East-West parts of the country.

The National Highway No-1 is a historical highway which is known as **Sher Shah Suri Marg**. This highways connects Delhi and Amritsar.

### (iii) State Highways

These are roads linking a state capital with its district headquarters. They are constructed and maintained by the State Public Works Department (SPWD) in States and Union Territories.

### (iv) District Roads

These roads connect the district headquarters with other places of the district. These roads are maintained by the Zila Parishad of the district.

### (v) Other Roads

Rural roads, which link rural areas and villages with towns, are classified under this category. These are constructed under Pradhan Mantri Grameen Sadak Yojana (PMGSY).

Under this scheme, special provisions have been made to link every village to a major town in the country by an all season motorable road.

### (vi) Border Roads

The Border Roads Organisation (BRO) constructs and maintains roads in the border areas of the country. This organisation was established in 1960.

The objective of this organisation is to develop roads of strategic importance in the Northern and North-Eastern border areas. Border roads have improved accessibility in areas of difficult terrain and have helped in the economic development of these areas.

The World's Longest Highway Atal Tunnel (9.02 km) has been built by Border Roads Organisation. It connects Manali to Lahaul-spiti. It is located on Pir Pranjal-range of Himalaya at an altitude of 3000 metres from the mean sea level.

### Classification of Roads on the Basis of Material Used

On this basis of type of material used, roads are of two types

(*i*) **Metalled Roads** They may be made of cement, concrete or even bitumen of coal. Therefore, these are **all weather roads.**

(*ii*) **Unmetalled or Unpaved Roads** They are made of clay, crushed rock and can be used in dry season only. They have no use during rainy season.

## Railways

Railways are the principal mode of transportation for freight (goods) and passengers in India. They carry bulky weight and are excellent for long distances. The Indian Railways network spread over a route length of 68,442 km. Railways provide a number of different activities to people like business, sightseeing, pilgrimage as well as transportation of goods over longer distances.

For the administrative convenience, Indian railways are divided into 16 zones. There are 3 types of guages (railways track) i.e. **broad guage**, **metre guage** and **narrow guage**.

Indian Railways is the largest public sector undertaking in the country. The **first train** started from Mumbai to Thane in 1853, covering a distance of 34 km.

### Challenges for Indian Railway

- It is difficult to lay railway lines in the hilly regions of peninsular India. In these regions railways tracts are laid through low hills, gaps or tunnels.
- The Himalayan mountainous regions too are unfavourable for the construction of railway lines due to high relief, sparse population and lack of economic opportunities.
- It requires construction of bridges over rivers in India.
- It is difficult to lay railway lines on the sandy plain of Western Rajasthan, swamps of Gujarat, forested tracks of Madhya Pradesh, Chhattisgarh, Odisha and Jharkhand.
- There are problems of sinking of railway tracks. For example, Sahyadri or Western Ghats has faced a number of problems such as sinking of track in some stretches and landslides.
- The initial costs of laying the tracks are too high.

### Problems of Indian Railways

- Many passengers travel without tickets.
- Theft and damaging of railway property has not yet stopped completely.
- People stop train by pulling the chain unnecessarily that causes heavy damage to the railway.

## Pipelines

Pipelines are used for transporting crude oil, petroleum products and natural gas and solids like iron ore when converted into **slurry**[3]. Inland locations of refineries like Barauni, Mathura, Panipat are viable because of pipelines.

- Initial cost of laying pipelines is high (especially for underground pipelines), but subsequent running costs are minimal. Pipelines control trans-shipment losses or delays.

### Important Pipeline Networks

Important pipeline transportation networks for oil and gas are

- **Pipeline from Oil Fields in Upper Assam to Kanpur (Uttar Pradesh) *via* Guwahati, Barauni and Allahabad** It has branches from Barauni to Haldia, via Rajbandh, Rajbandh to Maurigram and Guwahati to Siliguri.
- **Pipeline from Salaya in Gujarat to Jalandhar in Punjab, *via* Viramgam, Mathura, Delhi and Sonipat** It has branches to connect Koyali (near Vadodara, Gujarat) Chakshu and other places.
- **Gas Pipeline from Hazira in Gujarat to Jagdishpur (Uttar Pradesh) *via* Vijaipur (Madhya Pradesh)** It has branches to Kota in Rajasthan, Shahajahanpur, Barbala and other places in Uttar Pradesh.

## Waterways

Waterways are the cheapest means of transport. It is fuel-efficient, environment-friendly and suitable for carrying heavy and bulky goods.

### Inland Waterways

India has inland navigation waterways of about 14,500 km in length out of which 5,685 km are navigable by mechanised boats.

The waterways declared as the National Waterways are

| National Waterways | Description |
|---|---|
| NW - 1 | Allahabad to Haldia (1,620 km) on the Ganga river system. |
| NW - 2 | Sadiya to Dhubri (891 km) on the Brahmaputra river. |
| NW - 3 | West-Coast canal in Kerala (205 km), (Kottapuram-Komman, Udyogamandal and Champakkara canals). |
| NW - 4 | Parts of Krishna and Godavari rivers along with Kakinada-Puducherry stretch of canals (1,078 km). |
| NW - 5 | Parts of Brahmani river along with Matai river, delta channels of Mahanadi and Brahmani rivers and East coast canal (588 km). |

There are some other inland waterways on which substantial transportation takes place. These are Mandavi, Zuari and Cumberjua, Sunderbans, Barak and backwaters of Kerala.

### Major Sea Ports

The country's 95% foreign trade is moved by sea that constitute 68% in terms of value. With a long coastline of about 7516.6 km, India has 12 major and 200 intermediate and minor ports. Some prominent sea ports of India are

- **Kandla** It is located in the Gulf of Kuchchh. It was the first port which was developed soon after independence when the Karachi port went to Pakistan due to partition. It was developed to facilitate the volume of trade on the Mumbai port. It is also known as the **Deendayal port**.
  It is a **tidal**[4] **port. It handles exports**[5] and **imports**[6] of highly productive granary and industrial belt stretching across the states of Jammu and Kashmir, Himachal Pradesh, Punjab, Haryana, Rajasthan and Gujarat.
- **Mumbai** It is the **biggest port in India** with **natural harbour**[7]. **Jawahar Lal Nehru** port developed nearby to ease off the decongestion in Mumbai port.
- **Marmagao** (Goa) It is the premier iron ore exporting port in India. This port account for about 50% of India's iron ore export.
- **New Mangalore** It is located in Karnataka. It caters to export of iron-ore from Kudremukh mines.
- **Kochchi** It is the extreme South-Western port located at the entrance of a lagoon with a **natural harbour**.
- **Tuticorin** It is located in Tamil Nadu. It is the extreme South-Eastern port with a natural harbour and **hinterland**[8]. It caters cargoes to Sri Lanka, Maldives etc.
- **Chennai** It is the **oldest artificial port** ranking next to Mumbai in terms of cargo, volume of trade.
- **Vishakhapatnam** It is the deepest landlocked and well protected port for exporting iron-ore.
- **Paradwip** It is located in Odisha and specialises to export iron-ore.

3 **Slurry** A thin mixture of semi solid with liquid, especially water and any of several finely crushed substances, such as cement, clay or mineral ore particles.
4 **Tidal Port** The water levels within tidal port are subjected to change with the ocean tides. Tidal ports are usually in coastal regions.
5 **Export** When goods are sent to another country it is called export.
6 **Import** When goods come from another country be sold in India, it is called import.
7 **Natural Harbour** A landform where a part of a body of water is protected and deep enough to furnish anchorage for ships.
8 **Hinterland** Remote areas of a country away from the coast or the banks of major rivers.

- **Kolkata** It is a **tidal port** and inland **riverine port**[9]. It serves as a very large and rich hinterland of Ganga-Brahmaputra basin.
- **Haldia** It was developed to relieve pressure from Kolkata port.

## Airways

The air travel is the fastest, most comfortable and prestigious mode of transport. It can cover very difficult terrains like high mountains, vast deserts, dense forests and long oceanic stretches with great ease. Air transport was **nationalised** in 1953. Air India provides domestic and international air services.

**Pawanhans Helicopters Limited** provides helicopter services to Oil and Natural Gas Corporation (ONGC) to inaccessible areas and difficult terrains like the North-Eastern states and the interior parts of Jammu and Kashmir, Himachal Pradesh and Uttarakhand.

# Communication

It is an act of exchanging information. Personal communication and mass communication including television, radio, press, films, etc are the major means of communication in the country.

## Personal Communication

It is a process of transferring or transmitting message between two people. Mobile phones, postal letters are the examples of personal communication.

### Indian Postal Network

The Indian Postal Network is the largest in the world. It handles parcels as well as personal written communications. Mails in India are categorised *viz,* **first-class mail** and **second-class mail**.

Post cards and envelopes are considered as **first-class mail**. These mails are airlifted between stations covering both land and air.

**Second-class mail** includes book packets, registered newspapers and periodicals. These mails are carried by surface mails, covering land and water transport.

### Mail Channels

These facilitate quick delivery of mails in large cities. There are six mail channels i.e. Rajdhani Channel, Metro Channel, Green Channel, Business Channel, Bulk Mail Channel and Periodic Channel.

### Telecom Networks

India has **one of the largest telecom networks** in Asia. To improve telephonic communications from the grassroot to the higher level, the government has made special provision to extend 24 hours Subscriber Trunk Dialling (STD) facility to every village in the country.

Excluding urban places more than two-thirds of the villages in India have already been covered with Subscriber Trunk Dialling (STD) telephone facility.

There is a uniform rate of STD facilities all over India. It has been made possible by integrating the development in space technology with communication technology.

### Digital India

It is a programme to prepare India for a knowledge based transformation. The focus of Digital India Programme is on being transformative to realise IT (Indian Talent) + IT (Information Technology) IT (India Tomorrow) and is on making technology central to enabling change.

## Mass Communication

It is a process of transferring or transmitting a message to a large group of people, which requires the use of some forms of media. It provides entertainment and creates awareness among people about various national programmes and policies. It includes radio, television, newspapers, magazines, books and films.

### Television and Radio

All India Radio (Akashwani) broadcasts a variety of programmes in national, regional and local languages for various categories of people.

**Doordarshan, the national television channel of India** is one of the largest terrestrial networks in the world. It broadcasts a variety of programmes from entertainment, educational to sports, etc for people of different age groups.

### Newspapers, Periodicals and Magazines

In India, a large number of periodicals and newspapers are published annually. They are of different types depending upon their periodicity.

Newspaper are published in 100 languages and dialects. The largest number of newspapers published in the country are in Hindi, followed by English and Urdu.

### Films

India is the largest producer of feature films in the world. It produces short films, video feature films and video short films. The **Central Board of Film Certification** is the authority to certify both Indian and foreign films exhibited in India.

9 **Riverine Port** A place on a waterway with facilities for loading and unloading ships.

## International Trade

The exchange of goods among people, states and countries is referred to as **trade**. Trade between two countries is called international trade.

The market is a place where such exchanges take place. The international trade may take place through sea, air or land routes. Local trade is carried in cities, towns and villages. State level trade is carried between two or more states.

International trade is very essential and no country can survive without it. It is because the resources are distributed unevenly over the earth's surface and no country is self-sufficient in every kind of resources.

### Balance of Trade (BOT)

**Export** and **import** are the components of trade. The balance of trade is the difference between export and import of a country.

When the value of export exceeds the value of imports, it is called a **favourable balance of trade.** On the other hand, if the value of imports exceeds the value of exports, it is termed as **unfavourable balance of trade.**

India has trade relations with all the major trading blocks and all geographical regions of the world.

### Exported and Imported Commodities

The commodities exported from India to other countries include gems and jewellery, chemicals and related products, agriculture and allied products, etc.

India has emerged as a software giant at the international level and it is earning large foreign exchange through the export of information technology.

The commodities imported from other countries of India include petroleum crude and products, gems and jewellery, chemicals and related products, base metals, electronic items, machinery, agriculture and allied products.

### Tourism as a Trade

Tourism in India has grown substantially over the last three decades. More than 15 million people are directly engaged in the tourism industry in India.

Tourism promotes national integration and provides support to local handicrafts and cultural pursuits. It also helps in the development of international understanding about our culture and heritage.

Foreign tourists visit India for heritage tourism, eco-tourism, adventure tourism, cultural tourism, medical tourism and business tourism.

# Chapter Practice

## PART 1 Objective Questions

### • Multiple Choice Questions

**1.** Which of the following corridors links Srinagar and Kanniyakumari? Identify the correct option.
(a) North- South Corridor (b) East- West Corridor
(c) North- East Corridor (d) South-West Corridor

***Ans.*** (a) North- South Corridor links Srinagar and Kanniyakumari.

**2.** Which two of the following extreme locations are connected by the East-West Corridor? **(NCERT)**
(a) Mumbai and Nagpur
(b) Silchar and Porbander
(c) Mumbai and Kolkata
(d) Nagpur and Siligudi

***Ans.*** (b) The two extreme locations that are connected by the East-West Corridor are Silchar (Assam) and Porbander (Gujarat).

**3.** Which of the following is an autonomous agency responsible for management of National Highways in India?
(a) Border Roads Organisation
(b) National Highway Authority of India
(c) Central Public Works Department
(d) None of the above

***Ans.*** (b) National Highway Authority of India is an autonomous agency of the Government of India that is responsible for management of a network of National Highways in India.

**4.** Which mode of transportation reduces trans-shipment losses and delays?
(a) Railways (b) Roadways
(c) Pipeline (d) Waterways

***Ans.*** (c) Pipeline is the mode of transportation that reduces or control trans-shipment losses and delays. Pipelines are used for transporting crude oil, petroleum products and natural gas and solids like iron ore when converted into slurry.

**5.** Which of the following was the first port developed soon after Independence to use the volume of trade on the Mumbai Port?
(a) Kandla (b) Kochi
(c) Marmagao (d) Tuticorin

***Ans.*** (a) Kandla was the first port which was developed soon after Independence when the Karachi port went to Pakistan due to partition. It was developed to facilitate the volume of trade on the Mumbai Port. It is also known as Deendayal Port.

**6.** Which of the following is the Northernmost international airport in India?
(a) Raja Sansi International Airport
(b) Indira Gandhi International Airport
(c) Netaji Subhash Chandra Bose International Airport
(d) Meenam Bakkam International Airport

***Ans.*** (a) Raja Sansi International Airport is the Northernmost international airport in India.

**7.** Identify the port through the given features.
- It is the deepest landlock port.
- It is well protected port for exporting iron-ore.
- It is located in Andhra Pradesh.

(a) Tuticorin port (b) Vishakhapatnam port
(c) Paradip port (d) Kandla port

***Ans.*** (b) The given information is about Vishakhapatnam port.

**8.** Identify the name of the National waterways with the help of given clues.
- The total distance of the waterways is 991 km.
- It covers distance between Sadiya to Dhubri.
- It is located on the Brahmaputra river.

(a) NW-1 (b) NW-2 (c) NW-3 (d) NW-4

***Ans.*** (b) The given information is about NW–2.

**9.** Choose the correctly matched pair about the National Waterways and their length.
(a) NW-1 – 1620 km (b) NW-2 – 205 km
(c) NW-3 – 891 km (d) NW-4 – 588 km

***Ans.*** (a) The total distance of National waterways 1 is 1620 km. From Allahabad to Haldia on the Ganga river system.

**10.** Choose the correctly matched pair about the major sea port and their location.

(a) Kandla – Goa (b) Marmagao – Mumbai
(c) Tuticorin – Tamil Nadu (d) Paradwip – West Bengal

*Ans.* (c) Tuticorin is located in Tamil Nadu. It is the extreme South-Eastern port with a natural harbor and hinterland. It provides cargoes services from to Sri Lanka, Maldives, etc.

**11.** Match the following.

| Column A | Column B |
|---|---|
| A. National Highways | 1. Central Public Works Department |
| B. State Highways | 2. Border Roads Organisation |
| C. Rural Roads | 3. State Public Works Department |
| D. Border Roads | 4. Pradhan Mantri Grameen Sadak Yojana |

**Codes**

| | A | B | C | D | | | | | |
|---|---|---|---|---|---|---|---|---|---|
| (a) | 2 | 1 | 4 | 3 | (b) | 1 | 3 | 4 | 2 |
| (c) | 4 | 2 | 3 | 1 | (d) | 3 | 4 | 1 | 2 |

*Ans.* (b)

**12.** Match the following.

| Column A | Column B |
|---|---|
| A. Kolkata Port | 1. Biggest Port |
| B. Visakhapatnam Port | 2. Oldest Artificial Port |
| C. Chennai Port | 3. Deepest Landlocked and well- protected port |
| D. Mumbai Port | 4. Tidal and Inland riverine port |

**Codes**

| | A | B | C | D | | A | B | C | D |
|---|---|---|---|---|---|---|---|---|---|
| (a) | 2 | 4 | 3 | 1 | (b) | 3 | 2 | 1 | 4 |
| (c) | 4 | 3 | 2 | 1 | (d) | 4 | 1 | 2 | 3 |

*Ans.* (c)

## • Assertion-Reason MCQs

**Directions** (Q. Nos. 13-17) *Each of these questions contains two statements,* **Assertion** *(A) and* **Reason** *(R). Each of these questions also has four alternative choices, any one of which is the correct answer. You have to select one of the codes (a), (b), (c) and (d) given below.*

**Codes**

(a) Both A and R are true and R is the correct explanation of A
(b) Both A and R are true, but R is not the correct explanation of A
(c) A is true, but R is false
(d) A is false, but R is true

**13. Assertion** (A) Transport and Communications are called lifelines of our economy.

**Reason** (R) Transport and Communications do not help in easy movement of goods and materials between countries.

*Ans.* (c) Assertion is true as Transport and Communication are called lifelines of our economy as they reduces distances and brings people close to another by promoting interdependence among themselves. Reason is false as transportation helps in easy movement of good and materials between countries.

**14. Assertion** (A) The Himalayan mountainous regions are unfavourable for the construction of railway lines.

**Reason** (R) The Himalayan mountainous regions have high relief, sparse population and lack of economic opportunities.

*Ans.* (a) The Himalayan mountainous regions are unfavourable for the construction of railway lines due to high relief, sparse population and lack of economic opportunities.

**15. Assertion** (A) Waterways are the cheapest means of transport.

**Reason** (R) It is a fuel-efficient and environment friendly mode of transport.

*Ans.* (a) Waterways are the cheapest means of transport as it is fuel-efficient, environment friendly and suitable for carrying heavy and bulky goods. Hence, both assertion and reason statements are true and justify each other.

**16. Assertion** (A) Trade is considered as the economic barometer of the country.

**Reason** (R) Trading helps largely in developing countries like India. Advancement of Trade is an index to its economic prosperity.

*Ans.* (a) Trade is considered as the economic barometer of the country as advancement of trade is an index to economic prosperity. Trade helps largely in developing countries like India. Hence, both assertion and reason statements are true and justify each other.

**17. Assertion** (A) Tourism promotes national integration.

**Reason** (R) Millions of people are directly engaged in tourism industry.

*Ans.* (b) Tourism promotes national integration and helps in the development of understanding among various countries about one's culture and heritage, on the other hand, millions of people are directly engaged in tourism industry. Hence, here reason is not the correct explanation of assertion.

## • Case Based MCQs

**18.** Read the case/source given and answer questions that follow by choosing the correct option.

Railways are the principal mode of transportation for freight and passengers in India. Railways also make it possible for people to conduct multifarious activities like business, sightseeing, pilgrimage along with transportation of goods over longer distances.

Apart from an important means of transport the Indian Railways have been a great integrating force for more than 150 years.

Railways in India bind the economic life of the country as well as accelerate the development of the industry and agriculture. The Indian Railway is now reorganised into 16 zones.

The distribution pattern of the Railway network in the country has been largely influenced by physiographic, economic and administrative factors. The Northern plains with their vast levell and, high population density and rich agricultural resources provided the most favorable condition for their growth.

However, a large number of rivers requiring construction of bridges across their wide beds posed some obstacles. In the hilly terrains of the peninsular region, railway tracts are laid through low hills, gaps or tunnels.

(i) Which of the following factors are responsible for distribution pattern of railways network in the country? Identify the correct option:

(a) Topographical factors
(b) Economic and administrative factors
(c) Social factors
(d) Both (a) and (b)

***Ans.*** (d) The distribution pattern of railway network is influenced by topographical, economic and administrative factors.

(ii) **Assertion** (A) Rail Transport is the most convenient means of transportation in the Northern Plains.

**Reason** (R) The Northern Plains are densely populated, which enables the maximum number of people to utilise this means of transport.

**Codes**

(a) Both A and R are true and R is the correct explanation of A
(b) Both A and Rare true, but R is not the correct explanation of A
(c) A is true, but R is false
(d) A is false, but R is true

***Ans.*** (a) Rail Transport is the most convenient means of transportation in the Northern Plains because the Northern plains are densely populated which enables maximum number of people to utilise this means of transport. Hence, both assertion and reason statements justify each other.

(iii) When was the first railway line opened in India? Choose the correct option from the following.

(a) 1803 (b) 1823
(c) 1853 (d) 1854

***Ans.*** (c) Railways were first introduced to India in 1853, when a line was constructed from Mumbai to Thane covering a distance of 34 km.

(iv) Why Indian railway network is mostly concentrated in Ganga Plains? Choose the most suitable option:

(a) Due to concentration of Industries.
(b) Due to topographical uniformity and high density of population.
(c) Due to high agricultural production.
(d) Due to lack of economic opportunities.

***Ans.*** (b) Indian railway network is mostly concentrated in Ganga Plains due to their topographical uniformity, high population density and rich agricultural resources.

(v) Why is the Indian Railways called the lifeline of the country? With reference to the above context, infer the appropriate option.

(a) Railways in India bind the economic life of the country.
(b) It is the largest public undertaking in the country.
(c) Railways are the principal mode of transportation for freight and passengers in India.
(d) All of the above

***Ans.*** (d)

(vi) Why is it essential to develop a unigauge system of railways in our country? Identify the correct option.

(a) It will lead to reduction in trans-shipment.
(b) Because it has larger capacity.
(c) Both (a) and (b)
(d) It will bring administrative convenience.

***Ans.*** (c) It is essential to develop unigauge system of railways in our country as this system of railways has larger capacity, higher speed, cheaper transportation and reduction in trans-shipment.

PART 2

# Subjective Questions

## • Short Answer (SA) Type Questions

**1.** How has the world been converted into a global village? Explain. **(CBSE 2013)**

**Ans.** The world has been converted into a global village with the help of efficient and fast moving transport and communication facilities in the following ways

- Daily flights to different countries and improved technology to develop fast means of transportation has connected the countries.
- Computer and internet facilities supported by satellite services have made the world a small village wherein an information can be reached at almost instantly.
- Every country is well-linked with the rest of the world through various means of transport and communication.
- Means of transportation such as railways, airways, waterways and means of communication such as newspapers, radio, television, cinema, internet, etc have been contributing to its socio-economic progress in many ways.

**2.** What has necessitated the need for transport? Is it right to say that efficient means of transport are prerequisites for fast development? Justify.

*Or* "Efficient means of transport are pre-requisites for fast development of the country." Support the statement with examples. **(CBSE 2020)**

**Ans.** The need for transport has been necessitated due to the need for movement of goods and services from their supply locations to demand locations or market. Some people are engaged in facilitating these movements. These are known to be traders who make the products come to the consumers by transportation.

Efficient means of transport are prerequisite for fast development because more development of goods and services are not enough. The goods need to be transported from one place to another in proper time for their distribution and consumption.

**3.** State the ways by which means of transport and communication help the growth of industries in India.

**Ans.** The ways by which means of transport and communication help the growth of industries in India are

- Transport facilities are required to transport raw materials from their source region to industrial locations.
- Final products from industries also require transport facilities for their transportation to market.
- Communication lines supply required information about various industries.
- Means of transport and communication also help in reduction of regional imbalances resulting in balanced regional development.

**4.** "Roadways have an edge over Railways." Support the statement with examples. **(CBSE 2020)**

**Ans.** Roadways still have an edge over the railways in India because

- Construction cost of roads is much lower than railway lines.
- Roads can be constructed easily in hilly terrains and undulating topography than railways.
- Roadways act as a feeder to other modes of transport, as they provide a link between railway stations, air and sea ports.
- Road transport is economical in transportation of few persons and relatively smaller amount of goods over short distances.
- Road transport provides door-to-door service thus, the cost of loading and unloading is much lower.

**5.** "Distribution of roads is not uniform in India." Support the statement with examples.

**Ans.** It is true that the distribution of roads is not uniform in India. For example,

- Density of roads (length of roads per 100 square km of area) varies from Jammu and Kashmir (UT), which has the lowest density of road to Kerala, which has the highest density of roads in the country.
- The density of road is high in most of the Northern states and major Southern states. It is low in the Himalayan region, North-Eastern region, Madhya Pradesh and Rajasthan due to their topography.
- Nature of terrain and the level of economic development are the main determinants of density of roads. Construction of roads is easy and cheaper in the plain areas while it is difficult and costly in hilly and plateau areas.

**6.** Why are metalled roads better than unmetalled roads? What is the role of border roads and national highways in transportation?

*Or* Explain the importance of 'Border Roads' for India. **(CBSE 2017)**

**Ans.** Metalled roads are better than unmetalled roads because they have a waterproof coating on their upper surface, this makes them usable in all seasons. On the other hand, unmetalled roads are difficult to use in the rainy season, as their upper surface becomes uneven due to absorption of rain water.

Importance of border roads is

- They have improved accessibility in areas of difficult terrain.
- These roads help in the economic development of the border areas of the country.

Role of National Highways is

- National Highways link important parts of the country like state capitals and commercial centres.
- They enable fast and efficient movement of goods in areas connected to them.

**7.** "Rail transport suffers from certain problems in India." Support the statement with examples. **(CBSE 2020)**

**Ans.** Rail transport suffers from certain problems which are

- The infrastructure of railways is poor. For example, the tracks are old and outdated which cause many serious railway accidents. This also leads speed reduction and cause delay in arrival of trains on stations.
- Another major problem that is being faced in India is that a large number of passengers travel without purchasing tickets. Indian railways have to bear a huge loss every year on account of travelling without tickets.
- The incidence of railway accidents in our country is greater as compared to other countries of the world. Accidents occur due to the errors and negligence of the employees.

**8.** Explain any two merits and two demerits of pipelines transport.

**Ans.** Merits of pipelines transport are

(i) There are no trans-shipment losses or delays in transportation of materials.

(ii) Their construction has made inland locations of refineries like Barauni and Mathura and gas based fertiliser plants viable.

Demerits of pipelines transport are

(i) Initial costs of laying pipelines are very high, particularly oil and gas pipelines which have to be laid underground.

(ii) Leakage in pipes or damage to the pipeline might pollute soil and contaminate ground water, damaging the environment.

**9.** Explain briefly the advantages that result in using waterways as a mode of transport for heavy and bulky goods.

**Ans.** Advantages/features of using waterways as mode of transport for heavy and bulky goods are

- Waterways are the cheapest means of transport and most suitable for carrying heavy and bulky goods.
- They are fuel-efficient and environment-friendly mode of transport.
- Heavy and bulky goods being exported or imported are easier for trans-shipment from waterways to ships on the coast, as the waterways lead to ports.

**10.** Explain any four characteristics of Kandla sea port. **(CBSE 2012, 10)**

**Ans.** The four characteristics of Kandla sea port are

(i) It was the first port developed soon after independence.

(ii) It was developed to reduce the volume of traffic on Mumbai port.

(iii) It is a tidal port.

(iv) It caters to the convenient handling of exports and imports of highly productive granary and industrialised belts including Jammu and Kashmir, Himachal Pradesh, Punjab, Haryana, Rajasthan and Gujarat.

**11.** Distinguish between a major port and a minor port. **(CBSE 2012)**

**Ans.** Differences between a major and a minor port are

| Major Port | Minor Port |
|---|---|
| Major ports are bigger ports compared to minor ports. There are about 12 major ports in India. | In India, there are 200 minor ports in operation. |
| Major ports mostly deal with international trade. | Minor ports, on the other hand, deal with the coastal trade along with fishing. |
| Major ports are controlled and managed by Port Trusts and Central Government. | Minor ports are the responsibility of State Governments. |
| Mumbai, Chennai and Kandla are examples of major ports. | Dwarka, Porbandar and Okha are some of the examples of minor ports. |

**12.** Why is air transport more popular in the North-Eastern part of the country? Give three reasons.

*Or* "Airways is the most preferred mode of transport in North-Eastern states of India." Give three reasons to prove this preference. **(CBSE 2017)**

**Ans.** Air transport or airways is the most preferred mode of transport in the North-Eastern states in India because

(i) Big and wide rivers are present in the North Eastern states, due to which rail or road bridges over them are difficult and costly to construct.

(ii) This area has dissected relief features, preventing durable construction of rail and road links.

(iii) Dense forests in this region create many difficulties in construction of railway lines and roads.

**13.** Explain any four merits and two demerits of air transport. **(CBSE 2016, 2012)**

**Ans.** Merits of air transport are

(i) Air transport is the fastest, most comfortable and prestigious mode of transport.

(ii) It can cover very difficult terrains with great ease.

(iii) It makes access to far-flung and remote or otherwise inaccessible areas easier and quicker.

(iv) It provides transport services to offshore oil and gas exploration activities.

Demerits of air transport are

(i) Air transport is a very costly means of transportation.

(ii) Places not having airports or helipads are not covered by it.

**14.** Classify communication services into two categories? Explain main features of each.

**Ans.** Communication services are classified into personal communication and mass communication.

Features of Personal communication are

- In personal communication, people can express their thoughts and share with others.
- Letters, e-mails, SMSs, telephone and mobile phone facilities including STD and ISD services are examples of personal communication.

Features of mass communication are

- Mass communication provides entertainment and creates awareness among people about various national programmes and policies.
- It includes radio, television, newspapers, magazine, books and films.

## • Long Answer (LA) Type Questions

**1.** Explain the importance of means of transport as a prerequisite for the development of a country. **(CBSE 2019)**

**Ans.** Efficient means of transport are prerequisite for fast development because more development of goods and services are not enough alone.

The importance of means of transport is

- Transportation offers numerous opportunities within the employment sector. Traffic control, pilots, captains, delivery services and drivers are some of the jobs that are provided through this industry. Thus, it also helps the country to reduce unemployment ratio.
- High quality transport links ensure that communities can access basic services, facilities and employment opportunities. The connectivity provided by such links promotes social inclusion. It can also reduce social isolation and enhance quality of life.
- Transport facilities are also required to transport raw materials from their source region to industrial locations such as transportation of coal to iron and steel industry.
- Final products from industries also require transport facilities for their transportation to market so that consumers are able to buy them.
- Availability of transport services i.e. roadways, railways and waterways (wherever there is scope) help in increasing trade, connect the areas and facilitate movement of people. This helps in the development of a country.

**2.** Explain the importance of roadways as a means of transport. **(CBSE 2019)**

**Ans.** The importance of roadways as a means of transport is

- Road transport is economical in transportation of few persons and relatively smaller amount of goods over short distances.
- Road transport also provides door-to-door service, thus, the cost of loading and unloading is much lower.
- Road transport links other modes of transport like between railway stations, air and sea ports.
- National and state highways help in linking the extreme parts of the state and country. Through roads the entire country is connected.
- People can go from one place to another in search of jobs, businesses, tourism etc and goods can be transported due to proper linking of roads. Thus, road ways are a very important means of transportation.

**3.** Classify the roads according to their capacity and describe the role of each. **(CBSE 2012)**

**Ans.** In India, roads are classified in six classes according to their capacity as

- **Golden Quadrilateral Super Highways** This super highway links India's four largest metropolitan cities, i.e. Delhi-Kolkata- Chennai-Mumbai.

  North-South and East-West corridor are part of this. These highways reduce time and distance between mega cities.
- **National Highways** These are primary road systems that link important parts of the country.
- **State Highways** These roads link a state capital with its district headquarters. These are constructed by State Public Works Department.
- **District Roads** These roads connect the district headquarters with other places of the district.
- **Rural Roads** These roads, also known as other roads, link rural areas and villages with towns.
- **Border Roads** These roads are constructed along the international border of India by Border Road Organisation. It has improved accessibility in areas of difficult terrain.

**4.** Explain the importance of railways as a means of transport. **(CBSE 2019)**

**Ans.** The importance of Indian Railways as a means of transport is

- Railways are considered as the principal mode of transportation for freight and passengers in India. Daily a lot of commuters and office goers travel through railways.
- Railways provides cheap mode of transport to all. It is cheaper as compared to other modes of transport like airways.
- Railways help to conduct various activities, viz, business, sightseeing, pilgrimage, transportation of goods over long distances etc. Through these activities railways add more revenue to the economy of a country.
- Railways bind the economic life of our country by accelerating the development of the industry and agriculture.

- The Indian Railways is the largest public sector undertaking in the country which is the biggest employer in India.

**5.** Classify any five ports of India according to their types and main purpose.

***Ans.*** The ports of India according to their types and main purpose are

(i) **Chennai Port (Tamil Nadu)**
- **Type of Port** It is one of the oldest artificial ports in India.
- **Purpose** It is made for trade and cargo

(ii) **Haldia Port (West Bengal)**
- **Type of Port** It is a subsidiary port to relieve pressure on Kolkata port.
- **Purpose** It is made for decongesting Kolkata port.

(iii) **Jawaharlal Nehru Port (Maharashtra)**
- **Type of Port** It is specialised in handling container shipments.
- **Purpose** It is made for decongesting Mumbai port and serve as a hub for the region.

(iv) **Kandla Port (Gujarat)**
- **Type of Port** It is a tidal port.
- **Purpose** It was developed after independence to ease the volume of trade on Mumbai port.

(v) **Kochi Port (Kerala)**
- **Type of Port** It is a natural port located at the entrance of a lagoon.
- **Purpose** It specialised in handling container shipments.

**6.** Describe any five points of importance of mass communication. **(CBSE 2013)**

*Or* Write any three importance of means of mass communication. **(CBSE 2013)**

***Ans.*** Importance of mass communication is

(i) Mass communication is required to spread the flow of information upto the grassroot level. Therefore, government has made special provision to extend 24 hours STD facility to every village in the country.

(ii) All India Radio (Akashwani) broadcasts a variety of programmes in national, regional and local languages for various categories of people spread over different parts of the country.

(iii) Doordarshan broadcasts a variety of programmes for entertainment, educational programmes to sports, etc. for people of different age groups.

(iv) India publishes a large number of newspapers and periodicals annually for providing information.

(v) India is the largest producer of feature films in the world. It produces short films, video feature films and video short films for entertainment.

**7.** "International trade is considered the economic barometer of a country." Justify the statement with arguments. **(CBSE 2019)**

***Ans.*** International trade is considered the economic barometer of a country because

- As the resources are limited no country can survive without international trade.
- Goods or resources possessed by one country are required by other and vice-versa. These differences create conditions for international trade.
- Foreign trade has helped India to improve its productivity of manufactured goods. International trade contributes to India's economic growth, raising income levels of people.
- In recent years, exchange of information and knowledge has benefitted in greater exchange of goods across states and countries.
- India has emerged as a software giant at the international level and it is earning large foreign exchange through the export of information technology.

**8.** The pace of change in the communication sector has been rapid in modern times." Support the statement with examples. **(CBSE 2020)**

***Ans.*** The pace of change in communication sector has been rapid in modern times as a result of which the long distance communication has become easier without physical movement of the communicator or receiver. For example,

- The advanced communication meant to save our time and money as well. Personal communication and mass communication including television, radio, press, films etc, are the major means of communication.
- The Indian postal network handles parcels as well as personal written communication. It also deals with first class mails (e.g. cards, envelopes) and second-class mails (e.g. books packets, periodicals, registered newspapers) which are carried by different means of transport. To facilitate quick delivery of mails in large towns and cities, six mail channels namely Rajdhani Channel, Metro Channel, Green Channel, Business Channel, Bulk Mail Channel and Periodical Channel have been introduced recently.
- The use of mobile phones has also provided boost to the communication sector in the modern times.

## • Case Based Questions

**1.** Read the case/source given and answer the following questions.

The distribution pattern of the Railway network in the country has been largely influenced by Physiographic, economic and administrative factors. The Northern plains with their vast level land, high population density and rich agricultural resources provided the most favourable condition for their growth.

However, a large number of rivers requiring construction of bridges across their wide beds posed some obstacles.

In the hilly terrains of the peninsular region, railway tracts are laid through low hills, gaps or tunnels. The Himalayan mountainous regions too are unfavourable for the construction of railway lines due to high relief, sparse population and lack of economic opportunities.

Likewise, it was difficult to lay railway lines on the sandy plain of Western Rajasthan, swamps of Gujarat, forested tracks of Madhya Pradesh, Chhattisgarh, Odisha and Jharkhand. The contiguous stretch of Sahyadri could be crossed only through gaps or passes (Ghats).

In recent times, the development of the Konkan railway along the West coast has facilitated the movement of passengers and goods in this most important economic region of India. It has also faced a number of problem such as sinking of track in some stretches and landslides.

(i) Which factors are largely responsible to influence the railway network in India? Write any one merit of railways.

(ii) Why is it difficult to construct railway lines in the Peninsular region and Himalayan region?

(iii) Although, the railways have become more important in our national economy still this transport is facing a number of problems. Why? State any two reasons.

**Ans.** Factors which are largely responsible to influence the railway network in India are physiographic, economic and administrative factors.

An advantage or merit of railways is that they make it possible to conduct many activities like business, sightseeing, pilgrimage along with transportation of goods over longer distances.

(ii) It is difficult to construct railway lines in the Peninsular region and Himalayan region because

- The Peninsular region and the Himalayan region are hilly and mountainous regions. Peninsular region has undulating topography where railway tracts are laid through low hills, gaps or tunnels.
- On the other hand the Himalayas have high relief, sparse population and lack of economic opportunities.

(iii) It is true that railways have become more important in our national economy but still this transport is facing a number of problems which are

- Many passengers travel by trains without tickets. This incurs heavy loss of rail budget.
- People stop the trains, pull the chain unnecessarily and this causes heavy damage to the railway.

**2.** Read the cases/sources given and answer the following questions.

**Source A Golden Quadrilateral Super Highways**

The government has launched a major road development project linking Delhi–Kolkata–Chennai–Mumbai and Delhi by six-lane Super Highways. The North–South corridors linking Srinagar (Jammu and Kashmir) and Kanniyakumari (Tamil Nadu), and East-West Corridor connecting Silchar (Assam) and Porbander (Gujarat) are part of this project. The major objective of these Super Highways is to reduce the time and distance between the mega cities of India. These highway projects are being implemented by the National Highway Authority of India (NHAI).

(i) What is the Golden Quadrilateral? To what extent do you agree that Golden Quadrilateral Super Highways are important for our country? Give only one aspect.

**Ans.** Golden Quadrilateral comprises of the National Highways connecting Delhi-Mumbai-Chennai- Kolkata by a 6-lane Super Highway.

I agree with that Golden Quadrilateral Super Highways are important for our country because these highways reduce time and distance between mega cities of India.

**Source B National Highways**

National Highways link extreme parts of the country. These are the primary road systems and are laid and maintained by the Central Public Works Department (CPWD). A number of major National Highways run in North-South and East–West directions. The historical Sher-Shah Suri Marg is called National Highway No. 1, between Delhi and Amritsar.

(ii) To what extent do you agree that India needs a number of National Highways? Give only one reason. Discuss the role of National Highways.

**Ans.** I agree with that India needs a number of National Highways because India is a vast country and National Highways link extreme parts of the country with each other. Role of National Highways is

- National Highways link important parts of the country like state capitals and commercial sectors.
- They enable fast and efficient movement of goods in areas connected to them.

**Source C State Highways**

Roads linking a state capital with different district headquarters are known as State Highways. These roads are constructed and maintained by the State Public Works Department (PWD) in State and Union Territories.

(iii) Evaluate the importance of the State Highways.

*Ans.* Importance of the State Highways is

- State Highways are constructed within a state to provide better connectivity of roads and places.
- These highways link a state capital with different district headquarters.

## • Map based Questions

**1.** On the given political map of India, identify the following by the locations marked and their description given below.

(i) Chennai (Meenam Bakkam) International Airport.

(ii) Tuticorin port **(CBSE 2019)**

(iii) Kolkata International Airport (Netaji Subhash Chandra Bose)

(iv) Mumbai (Chhatrapati Shivaji) International Airport.

(v) Marmagao port

*Ans.*

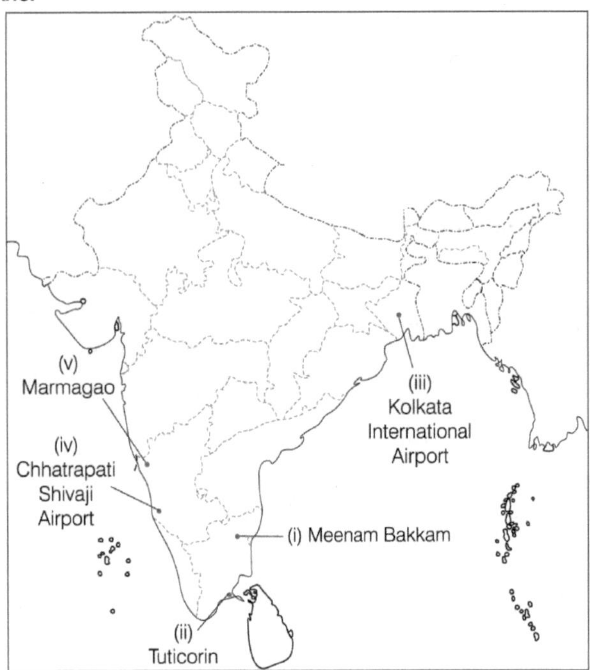


**2.** On the political map of India, locate, mark and label any four of the following with appropriate symbols.

(i) The port developed after independence to ease the volume of trade on Mumbai port. **(CBSE 2010, 11, 12, 14)**

(ii) Rajiv Gandhi International Airport

(iii) Vishakhapatnam port

(iv) Indira Gandhi International Airport

(v) Chennai port

(iv) Raja Sansi International Airport **(CBSE 2018, 2019)**

*Ans.*

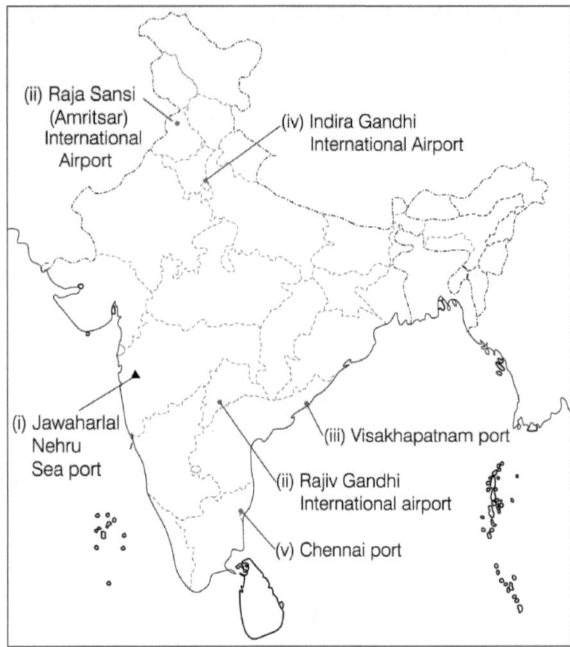


**3.** On the political map of India, locate and label any four of the following features with appropriate symbols.

(i) Kandla Seaport. **(CBSE 2019)**

(ii) Mumbai Seaport (iii) New Mangalore Seaport

(iv) Kochi Seaport **(CBSE 2019)**

(v) Paradip **(CBSE 2019)**

(vi) Haldia Seaport

*Ans.*

# Chapter Test

## Objective Questions

**1.** Which of the following is the largest Public Sector Undertaking in the country?

(a) Airways (b) Roadways
(c) Waterways (d) Railways

**2.** The trade between two countries is called

(a) International trade (b) National trade
(c) Community trade (d) None of these

**3.** What type of trade is carried in cities, towns and villages?

(a) State level trade (b) Local trade
(c) District level trade (d) None of these

**4.** .................... is the type of communication service in India that is largest in the world.

(a) Telecom Network (b) Postal Network
(c) Television Network (d) Radio Network

**5.** Which of the following statements is not correct ?

(a) Roads can be built in uneven surface like hills and mountains.
(b) The National Highway 1 is also known Sher-Shah Suri Marg.
(c) The total distance of Atal Tunnel is 9.02 km.
(d) The first train was started in 1954 in India.

## Short Answer Type Questions

**6.** Where are railways developed in hilly areas and why? Trace their history in the colonial period.

**7.** Why are border roads important for us?

**8.** Explain why road transport still needs to be developed in India. What are the priority areas?

**9.** "Transport routes are called the basic arteries of our economy." Support this statement with relevant examples.

**10.** Describe the significance of tourism as a trade of India.

## Long Answer Type Questions

**11.** What is the importance of railway transport? Describe any three major problems faced by Indian Railways.

**12.** Describe any four features of Indian tourism as a trade.

**13.** What is the importance of waterways in India?

## Answers

**1.** (d) Railways **2.** (a) International trade **3.** (b) Local trade
**4.** (b) Postal Network **5.** (d) The first train was started in 1954 in India

CHAPTER 01

# Political Parties

## In this Chapter...


- Why Do We Need Political Parties ?
- How Many Parties Should We Have ?
- Types of Political Parties
- Challenges to Political Parties
- Reformation of Political Parties


## Why do We Need Political Parties?

Political parties are one of the most visible institutions in a democracy. For the ordinary citizens, democracy is equal to political parties. It is important to know the nature and working of political parties.

### Meaning of Political Parties

A **political party** is a group of people who come together to contest elections and hold power in the government.

All political parties have some policies and programmes for the society with a view to promote the collective good. They try to persuade people why their policies are better than others. They seek to implement their policies by winning popular support through elections.

Political parties reflect fundamental political divisions in a society. All the parties favour certain part of the society and thus they involve **partisanship**[1].

A party is known by which part it stands for, which policies it supports and whose interests it upholds.

A political party has following three components

(i) The leaders (ii) The active members (iii) The followers

### Functions of Political Parties

Political parties performs the following functions

(*i*) Candidates are put forward by political parties to contest elections. These candidates may be chosen by the top leaders or by members of the party. In some countries like USA, members and supporters of a party choose its candidate. In India top party leaders choose candidates for contesting elections.

(*ii*) Parties put forward their policies and programmes for voters to choose from them.

(*iii*) Political parties play a major role in making laws for the country. No law can become a bill unless majority parties support it. Laws are debated and passed in the Legislature.

(*iv*) Political parties form and run governments. The big policy decision taken by political executive come from the political parties. Parties recruit leaders, train them and make them ministers.

(*v*) Parties that lose election, play the role of opposition to the party in power. They criticise government for their wrong policies and mobilise opposition to the government.

1 **Partisanship** Partisanship is marked by a tendency to take a side and inability to take a balanced view on an issue.

(*vi*) Parties shape public opinion. They raise and highlight issues. Parties have large number of members and activists spread all over the country. Many of the pressure groups act as extension of political parties. Parties sometimes also launch movements for the resolution of the problem faced by the people.

(*vii*) Political parties provide people access to government machinery and welfare schemes. It is easy for the public to approach their local party leader than a government officer. The local party leader has to listen to people's need and demands, otherwise people can reject them in the next elections.

## Necessity of Political Parties

Political parties are needed because they perform variety of functions. Modern democracies cannot exist without political parties.

Without existence of parties, following situations may occur

- Every candidate in the elections will be independent. No one will be able to make any promises to the people about any major policy changes.
- The government may be formed, but its utility will remain ever uncertain. Elected representatives will be accountable to their constituency for what they do in the locality. But no one will be responsible for how the country will be run.
- The non-party based elections to the Panchayat occur in many states of India. Here the parties do not contest formally. It is generally noticed that the village gets split into more than one group, each of which puts up a 'panel' of its candidates. This creates need for the political party.
- The rise of political parties is directly linked to the emergence of representative democracies. As societies became large and complex, they needed some agency to gather different views on various issues and to present these to the government.
- Society needs a mechanism to support or restrain the government, make policies, justify or oppose them. Political parties fulfil these needs of every representative government.

# How Many Parties Should We have?

The different countries around the world opt different party systems. Broadly, political party system can be divided into following three categories

(*i*) **One-Party System** In this party system, only one party is allowed to control and run the government. For example, China has one-party system. This system is not a good option for democracy because it does not provide a fair chance for competing parties to gain power.

(*ii*) **Two-Party System** In this party system, two parties have a serious chance to win majority and form government. The power usually changes between two main parties. The United States of America and United Kingdom are the examples of two-party system.

(*iii*) **Multi-Party System** In this party system, more than two political parties contest election to gain power. In India, there is a multi-party system with more than 750 parties registered by the Election Commission of India. It allows a variety of interests and opinions to enjoy political representation.

### Coalition of Parties

In India, government is formed by various parties coming together in a coalition. When several parties in a multi- party system join hands for the purpose of contesting and winning, it is called **alliance** or front.

For example, the National Democratic Alliance (NDA) and the United Progressive Alliance (UPA) in India.

### Ideal Party System

Party system evolves over a long time, depending on the nature of society, its social and regional divisions, and history of politics. The social and geographical diversity of our country is not easily absorbed by two or even three parties. Thus, India has a multiparty system.

### Popular Participation in Political Parties

Political parties are facing crisis of unpopularity and indifference among the citizens.

The evidence, based on a series of large sample surveys conducted over several decades, shows that

- Political parties do not enjoy much trust among the people in South Asia.
- Still the level of participation in the activities of political parties is fairly high.
- The proportion of the members of some political party is higher in India than many advanced countries like Canada, Japan, Spain and South Korea.
- Over the last three decades, the proportion of members close to a political party in India has gone up steadily.

# Types of Political Parties

Democracies that follow a federal system all over the world tend to have two kinds of political parties

(*i*) **State Parties** Parties that are present in only one of the federal units.

(*ii*) **National Parties** Parties that are present in several or all units of the federation.

In India, there are both **National** and **State parties**. Every party in the country has to register with the Election Commission.

## National Parties

A party that secures at least 6% of the total votes in Lok Sabha elections or Assembly elections in 4 states and wins at least 4 seats in the Lok Sabha, is recognised as a National Party. The commission treats all parties equally, but it offers some special facilities to large and established parties. These parties are given a unique symbol. Only the official candidates of that party can use that election symbol.

These parties are called **recognised political parties** due to special privileges and facilities provided to them by the Election Commission.

### Some National Political Parties of India

In 2018, there were seven recognised national political parties in the country. These are

(*i*) **Indian National Congress** (INC) It is popularly known as the Congress Party which is one of the oldest parties of the world founded in 1885. It supports **secularism**[2] and welfare of weaker sections and minorities.

(*ii*) **Communist Party of India** (CPI) It was founded in 1925. It believes in **Marxism-Leninism**[3], secularism and democracy. It opposes the forces of secessionism and communalism. It has significant presence in Kerala, West Bengal, Punjab, Andhra Pradesh and Tamil Nadu.

(*iii*) **Communist Party of India-Marxist** (CPI-M) It was founded in 1964. It believes in Marxism-Leninism. It supports socialism, secularism and democracy and opposes imperialism and communalism. It enjoys strong support in West Bengal, Tripura and Kerala.

(*iv*) **Bharatiya Janata Party** (BJP) It was founded in 1980, by reviving the erstwhile *Bharatiya Jana Sangh*. The aim of the party is to build a strong and modern India by drawing inspiration from India's ancient culture and values. It came to the power in 1998 as the leader of the National Democratic Alliance including several state and regional parties.

(*v*) **Bahujan Samaj Party** (BSP) It was founded in 1984, under the leadership of *Kanshi Ram*. It seeks to represent and secure power for the Bahujan Samaj which includes the Dalits, Adivasis, OBCs and religious minorities. It has its main base in Uttar Pradesh and substantial presence in Madhya Pradesh, Chhattisgarh, Uttaranchal, Delhi and Punjab.

(*vi*) **All India Trinamool Congress** (AITC) It was formed on 1st January, 1998 under the leadership of Mamta Banerjee. This party is recognised as a National Party in 2016. The party symbol is flowers and grass. It has its presence in West Bengal, Arunachal Pradesh, Manipur and Tripura.

(*vii*) **Nationalist Congress Party** (NCP) It was founded in 1999, following a split in the Congress Party. It supports democracy, Gandhian secularism, equity, social justice and federalism. It has its significant presence in Maharashtra, Meghalaya, Manipur and Assam.

***Note :*** Currently (November, 2021) there are eight recognised national parties. The National People's Party (NPP) was accorded the status of nation party on 7th June, 2019. The party symbol is Book.

## State Parties

A party that secures at least 6% of the total votes in an election to the Legislative Assembly of a state and wins at least 2 seats, is recognised as a State party. These are commonly referred to as **regional parties**. Some of the regional parties are all India parties have succeeded only in some states. Parties like the Samajwadi Party, Samata Party and Rashtriya Janata Dal have national level political organisation with units in several states.

Some of these parties like **Biju Janata Dal, Sikkim Democratic Front** and **Mizo National Front** are conscious about their state identity.

### Status of State Parties

Over the last three decades, the number and strength of these parties has expanded. This made the Parliament of India politically more and more diverse. No national party is able to secure on its own a majority in Lok Sabha.

As a result, the national parties are compelled to form alliances with state parties. Since 1996, nearly every state party has got an opportunity to be a part of one or the other national level Coalition Government. This has contributed to the strengthening of federalism and democracy in our country.

# Challenges to Political Parties

Popular dissatisfaction and criticism has focussed on four problem areas in the working of political parties. Political parties need to face and overcome these challenges which are

2 **Secularism** It is the principle of seeking to conduct human affairs based on secular, naturalistic considerations.

3 **Marxism-Leninism** It is a communist ideology and was the main communist movement throughout 20th century.

### Lack of Internal Democracy within Parties

In most of the political parties, the power is concentrated in the hands of one or few leaders at the top. Parties do not keep membership registers, do not hold organisational meetings and do not conduct internal elections regularly. Ordinary members of the party do not get sufficient information about the happenings inside the party.

The leaders assume greater power to make decisions in the name of the party.

### Dynastic Succession

The top positions in many political parties are generally controlled by members of one family. Leaders on the top have unfair chance of favouring their families and friends. This is also bad for democracy, since people who do not have adequate experience or popular support, come to occupy positions of power. This tendency is present in all over the world, including some older democracies.

### Money and Muscle Power

This is a prominent challenge to political parties during elections. Since parties are focussed only on winning elections, they tend to use shortcuts to win elections. Such shortcuts include the following

- They tend to nominate those candidates who have or can raise lots of money. Rich people and companies who give funds to the parties tend to have influence on the policies and decisions of the party.
- In some cases, parties support criminals who can win elections.

### Meaningful Choice to the Voters

It states that very often parties do not seem to offer a meaningful choice to the voters. In order to offer meaningful choice, parties must be significantly different.

Like for instance, sometimes people cannot even elect very different leaders as the same set of leaders keep shifting from one party to another.

## Reformation of Political Parties

In order to face the challenges, political parties need to be reformed. Some of the recent efforts and suggestions in our country to reform the political parties are

- **Anti-Defection Law** According to this law, MLAs or MPs cannot change the party after the election.

  If any MLA or MP changes parties, he or she will lose the seat in the Legislature. This was done because many elected representatives were involved in **defection**[4] in order to become ministers or for cash rewards.
- **Details of Property and Criminal Cases** In order to reduce the influence of money and criminals, the Supreme Court of our country passed an order. Now, it becomes mandatory for every candidate who contest elections to file an **Affidavit**[5] giving details of his property and criminal cases pending against him. But there is no system to check if the information given by the candidate is true or not.
- **File an Income Tax Return** The Election Commission passed an order making it necessary for political parties to hold their organisational elections and file their income tax returns. The parties have started doing so, but sometimes, it is only formality.

Besides these suggestions, many other suggestions are often made to reform political parties which are

- A law should be made to regulate the internal affairs of political parties. It should be made compulsory for political parties to maintain a register of its members, to follow its own Constitution, to have an independent authority, to act as a judge in case of party disputes and to hold open elections to the highest posts.
- It should be made mandatory for political parties to give a minimum number of tickets (about one-third) to women candidates. Similarly, there should be a quota for women in the decision-making bodies of the party.
- There should be state funding of elections. The government should give parties money to support their election expenses.
- We must be very careful about legal solutions to political problems. Over-regulation of political parties can be counter-productive.

There are two other ways in which political parties can be reformed

(*i*) People can put pressure on political parties through petitions, publicity and agitations. If political party feels that it would lose public support, it would become more serious about reforms.

(*ii*) Political parties can improve if those who want this, join political parties. The quality of democracy can be improve by the public participation. If ordinary citizens do not take part in politics then reforming politics is impossible.

4 **Defection** It means changing party allegiance from the party on which a person got elected to a different party.

5 **Affidavit** It is a signed document submitted to an officer, where a person makes a sworn statement regarding her personal information.

# Chapter Practice

## PART 1 Objective Questions

### • Multiple Choice Questions

**1.** Political Parties are the most visible institutions in a democracy. Which among the following options is incorrect about political parties? Identify.

(a) Political Parties play an important role in law making process.
(b) Political Parties form and run governments.
(c) Political Parties do not shape public opinion.
(d) Political Parties reflect fundamental divisions in a society.

***Ans.*** (c) Political Parties are most visible institutions in a democracy as it helps to shape public opinions, plays an important role in law making process, form and run governments and reflects the fundamental divisions in a society.

**2.** What does the term 'Partisan' means? Choose the correct option.

(a) The affair of the state or the science of the governance.
(b) A person who is strongly committed to the party.
(c) The ruling party which runs the government.
(d) A group of people who come together to promote common beliefs.

***Ans.*** (b) In politics, a partisan is a dedicated, loyal and a committed member of a political party or political coalitions. In a multi-party system, the term denotes politicians strongly supporting their party's policies, without compromising to their political opponents.

**3.** Which of the following party system does not provide a fair chance for competing parties to gain power?

(a) One-party system
(b) Two-party system
(c) Multi-party system
(d) Both (a) and (b)

***Ans.*** (a) One-party system does not provide a fair chance for competing political parties to gain power as compared to two-party and multi-party systems.

**4.** What is the guiding philosophy of the Bhartiya Janata Party? **(NCERT)**

(a) Bahujan Samaj
(b) Revolutionary Democracy
(c) Integral Humanism
(d) Modernity

***Ans.*** (c) The guiding philosophy of the Bhartiya Janata Party is based upon the ideas of integral humanism given by Pandit Deendayal Upadhyaya.

**5.** Who among the following is the founder of the Bahujan Samaj Party? **(NCERT)**

(a) Kanshi Ram (b) Sahu Maharaj
(c) B R Ambedkar (d) Jyotibha Phule

***Ans.*** (a) Kanshi Ram is the founder of Bahujan Samaj Party. It was formed in 1984. It seeks to represent and secure power for the Bahujan Samaj which includes the dalits, adivasis, OBCs and religious minorities.

**6.** Identify the political party with the help of the following information.

- It was formed in 1925.
- It believes in Marxism - Leninism, secularism and democracy.
- It opposed the forces of sucessionism and communalism.

Select the appropriate option from the following.

(a) Bhartiya Janata Party (BJP)
(b) Communist Party of India (CPI)
(c) Nationalist Congress Party (NCP)
(d) All India Trinamool Congress (AITC)

***Ans.*** (b) The given information is about Communist Party of India (CPI).

**7.** Identify the Political Party with the help of the following information.

- It was formed in 1999 following a split in the Congress party.
- It wants that high offices in the government be confined to natural born citizens of a country.
- It is a major party in Maharashtra and has a significant presence in Meghalaya, Manipur and Assam.

Select the appropriate option from the following:
(a) Communist Party of India - Marxist (CPIM)
(b) All India Trinamool Congress (AITC)
(c) Nationalist Congress Party (NCP)
(d) Bahujan Samaj Party

**Ans.** (c) The given information is about Nationalist Congress Party (NCP) .

**8.** Choose the correctly matched pair about the political parties and their year of formation.

| | List I | | List II |
|---|---|---|---|
| (a) | Bharatiya Janata Party | – | 1885 |
| (b) | Indian National Congress | – | 1980 |
| (c) | All India Trinamool Congress | – | 1998 |
| (d) | Nationalist Congress Party | – | 1997 |

**Ans.** (c) All India Trinamool Congress was formed in 1998. Bharatiya Janata Party was formed in 1980, Indian National Congress was formed in 1885 and Nationalist Congress Party was formed in 1999.

**9.** Choose the correctly matched pair about the political parties and their ideology:
(a) Communist Party of India - Social Justice
(b) Nationalist Congress Party - Gandhian Secularism
(c) Indian National Congress - Modernity
(d) Bahujan Samaj Party - Revolutionary Democracy

**Ans.** (b) Nationalist Congress Party supports the ideology of Gandhian secularism, democracy, equity, social justice and federalism. Since 2004, it is a member of the United Progressive Alliance.

**10.** Match the following items given in List 1 with those in List 2:

| List I (Political Parties) | List II (Election Symbols) |
|---|---|
| A. All India Trinamool Congress | 1. |
| B. Nationalist Congress Party | 2. |
| C. Bahujan Samaj Party | 3. |
| D. Communist Party of India | 4. |

**Codes**

| | A | B | C | D | | A | B | C | D |
|---|---|---|---|---|---|---|---|---|---|
| (a) | 1 | 2 | 3 | 4 | (b) | 2 | 3 | 1 | 4 |
| (c) | 3 | 4 | 2 | 1 | (d) | 4 | 1 | 3 | 2 |

**Ans.** (c)

**11.** Match the following: **(NCERT)**

| List I | List II |
|---|---|
| A. Congress Party | 1. National Democratic Alliance |
| B. Bhartiya Janata Party | 2. State Party |
| C. Communist Party of India (Marxist) | 3. United Progressive Alliance |
| D. Telugu Desam Party | 4. Left Front |

**Codes**

| | A | B | C | D | | A | B | C | D |
|---|---|---|---|---|---|---|---|---|---|
| (a) | 3 | 1 | 2 | 4 | (b) | 3 | 4 | 1 | 2 |
| (c) | 3 | 1 | 4 | 2 | (d) | 4 | 3 | 1 | 2 |

**Ans.** (c)

**12.** In the given cartoon what kind of Political reform has been discussed? Identify from the given options.

(a) The Election Commission of India has issued a code of conduct which needs to be strictly followed before and during the elections.
(b) Minimising the number of non-serious electoral candidates.
(c) Internal democracy in political parties.
(d) Compulsory voting for all the citizens.

**Ans.** (a) The Election Commission of India has issued a code of conduct which needs to be strictly followed before and during the elections.

**13.** Following cartoon was drawn during the Presidency of George Bush of the Republican Party in the USA. Here the party symbol is Elephant. What does the cartoon seems to suggest? Identify from the given options:

(a) Two party system is ignored
(b) Republican Party is the only party
(c) Corporate American dictates all major institutions of the country.
(d) Republican Party faces many problems.

**Ans.** (c) Corporate American dictates all major institutions of the country.

## • Assertion-Reason MCQs

**Direction** (Q. Nos. 14-18) *Each of these questions contains two statements, **Assertion** (A) and **Reason** (R). Each of these questions also has four alternative choices, any one of which is the correct answer. You have to select one of the codes (a), (b), (c) and (d) given below.*

**Codes**

(a) Both A and R are true and R is the correct explanation of A
(b) Both A and R are true, but R is not the correct explanation of A
(c) A is true, but R is false
(d) A is false, but R is true

**14. Assertion** (A) Political Parties play a major role in making laws for the country.

**Reason** (R) No law can become a bill unless majority parties support it.

**Ans.** (a) Political Parties plays a major role in making laws for the country as no law can become a bill unless majority parties support it. Laws are debated and passed in the Parliament which consists of members of different political parties. Thus, both Assertion and Reason are true and Reason is the correct explanation of Assertion.

**15. Assertion** (A) Political Parties do not enjoy much trust among the people in South Asia.

**Reason** (R) Political Parties are one of the least trusted institutions all over the world.

**Ans.** (a) As per the large sample surveys conducted over several decades, it shows that political parties do not enjoy much trust among the people in South Asia. Most of the other democracies as political parties are one of the least trusted institutions all over the world. Thus, reason is not the correct explanation of Assertion.

**16. Assertion** (A) Nationalist Congress Party was formed in 1999.

**Reason** (R) It is a major party in Maharashtra and demands for Gandhian Secularism.

**Ans.** (b) Nationalist Congress Party was formed in 1999 following a split in the Congress Party. It supports democracy, Gandhian Secularism, equity, social justice and Federalism. It has its significant presence in Maharashtra, Meghalaya, Manipur and Assam. Thus, both Assertion and Reason are true but Reason is not the correct explanation of Assertion.

**17. Assertion** (A) The Constitution was amended to prevent elected MLA's and MP's from changing parties.

**Reason** (R) It should be made mandatory for political parties to give one-third tickets to women candidates.

**Ans.** (b) The Constitution was amended to prevent elected MLA's and MP's from changing parties. This was done because many elected representatives were indulging themselves in defection in order to become ministers or for cash rewards. To reform the political parties, it was suggested that minimum number of tickets (about one-third) should be given to the woman candidates.

Thus, reason is not the correct explanation of assertion.

**18. Assertion** (A) Only those parties that are recognised as national parties can contest elections for the Union level.

**Reason** (R) Recognition to a political party as a national party is accorded by the Election Commission.

**Ans.** (d) A is false as political parties whether it is State or National can contest elections for the Union level.

R is true as the Election Commission treats all parties equally, but it offers some special facilities to large and established parties like National Parties. These parties are given unique symbol. Only the official candidates of that party can use election symbol.

## • Case Based MCQs

**19.** Read the given case/source and answer the questions that follow by choosing the correct option.

We can understand the necessity of political parties by imagining a situation without parties. Every candidate in the elections will be independent. So no one will be able to make any promises to the people about any major policy changes. The government may be formed, but its utility will remain ever uncertain. Elected representatives will be accountable to their locality. But no one will be responsible for how the country will be run.

We can also think about it by looking at the non-party based elections to the Panchayat in many states. Although, the parties do not contest formally, it is generally noticed that the village gets split into more than one faction, each of which puts up a panel of its candidates. Thus it exactly what the party does. That is the reason we find political parties in almost all countries of the world whether these countries are big or small, old or new, developed or developing.

The rise of political parties is directly linked to the emergence of representative democracies. As we have seen, large societies need representatives democracy. As societies became large and complex, they also need some agency to gather different views on various issues and to present these to the government.

(i) Why is the existence of Political Party necessary for a democracy? Choose the correct options from the following.
(a) Political Parties helps to develop public opinion.
(b) No independent candidate can make any promise to the people.
(c) Independent elected representatives are only responsible for their own constituency.
(d) Political Parties helps to inculcate insecurity among the people.

**Ans.** (a) Political Parties are necessary as they, helps to develop public opinion.

(ii) 'Political Faction' means a group of individuals within a political party that share a ................ . Identify.
(a) Balanced view
(b) Common political purpose
(c) Regional and communal diversities
(d) Ideal political structure

**Ans.** (b) A political faction is a group of individuals that share a common political purpose but differs in some respect to the rest of the entity. Factions are not limited only to political parties as they can be formed within in a group with a political aim or purpose.

(iii) Consider the following statements about political parties and choose the correct option.
I. Political Parties are a necessary condition for a democracy.
II. Political Parties help the government to make policies.
III. Political Parties justify or oppose the representative governments.

**Options**
(a) Only I (b) Both I and II
(c) Both II and III (d) All of these

**Ans.** (d) All the given statements are correct.

(iv) Which of the following describes representative democracy? Identify the best suitable option depicting the same from the following.
(a) It is not a common form of democracy in the modern age.
(b) It involves direct participation.
(c) It involves indirect participation through elected representatives.
(d) It was the most prevalent form of democracy in the Colonial era.

**Ans.** (c) Representative democracy involves indirect participation through elected representatives. It is also known as indirect democracy. It is a type of democracy founded on the principle of elected persons representing a group of people.

(v) Why does large society need representative democracies? With reference to the above context, infer the appropriate option.
(a) To form a responsible government.
(b) To form an ideal form of government.
(c) To gather public opinions.
(d) To resolve issues of minority communities.

**Ans.** (a) Large society need representative democracies to form a responsible government.

(vi) Why can't modern democracies exist without political parties? Identify the reason from the given options.
(a) As the utility of government will remain uncertain in nature.
(b) Loss of Accountability towards people.
(c) State responsibility will lead to national integration.
(d) Both (a) and (b)

**Ans.** (d) Modern democracies cannot be exist without political parties as the utility of government will remain uncertain in nature and there will be loss of accountability towards people.

## PART 2
# Subjective Questions

## • Short Answer (SA) Type Questions

**1.** Expain the three components of 'political party'.

**Ans.** A political party is a group of people who come together to contest elections and hold power in the government.

The three components of political party are

(i) **The Leaders** Every political party has some prominent leaders who formulate policies and programmes of the party and choose candidates for contesting elections.

(ii) **The Active Members** They are involved in different committees of the party and participate directly in their activity.

(iii) **The Followers** They believe in the party's ideology and support the party by casting their votes in favour of the party at the time of the elections.

**2.** What is the role of the opposition party in a democracy? (CBSE 2020)

**Ans.** The opposition party plays a very important role in a democracy as

- It acts as pressure group.
- It mobilises the government.
- It keeps a check on the working of the ruling party.
- It puts different views in the Parliament and criticise the government for its failures or wrong policies.
- It watches over the ruling party to prevent the government from being authoritarian and restrict its powers.
- It also have the right to audit the government's spending.
- The opposition parties outside the legislature draw media's attention and publish their criticism of government policy in the newspapers.

**3.** Give any two merits and demerits of one-party system.

**Ans.** Merits of one-party system are

(i) **Strong and Stable Government** Since there is no opposition party, government is strong and cannot be removed or voted out of power.

(ii) **Less Expensive** Since there is only one party and one candidate of the party, not much money is spent on the election.

Demerits of one-party system are

(i) **Undemocratic** Government can become dictatorial.

(ii) **No Choice** It gives no choice to the voters.

**4.** State any two advantages of the multi-party system. In what way is an alliance different from a coalition government?

**Ans.** The advantages of multi-party system are

(i) This system allows a variety of interests and opinions to enjoy political representation.

(ii) Under this system, the choice of the voter is not limited to two candidates only. It gives a voter enough scope to make intelligent choice.

In the following ways, alliance is different from coalition

| Alliance | Coalition Government |
|---|---|
| When several parties join hands for the purpose of contesting elections, it is called an alliance or a front, e.g. the National Democratic Alliance. | When no single party gets a majority in the election and the government is formed by two or more parties coming together, it is referred to as a coalition government. |

**5.** Why has India adopted a Multi-party system? Explain. (CBSE 2015)

**Ans.** India adopted a Multi-party system because

- As India is a vast and diverse country, the multi-party system was needed to accommodate the vast population.
- The social and geographical diversity of India could not be represented by two or three parties.
- The multi-party system in India evolved over a long time, depending on the nature of society, its social, regional division, its history of politics and its system of elections.
- Multi-party system ensures a healthy competition between different parties and prevents dictatorship of a single party. Indian Constitution declares India as a democratic country. Multi-party system fulfils this criteria and provides chance for proper growth of the nation.

**6.** Write a short note on Bahujan Samaj Party (BSP).

**Ans.** Bahujan Samaj Party (BSP) was founded by Kanshi Ram in 1984. It seeks to represent Bahujan Samaj, which includes Scheduled Castes (SCs), Scheduled Tribes (STs), OBCs and religious minorities.

It gets inspiration from the ideas and teachings of Sahu Maharaj, Mahatma Phule, Periyar Ramaswami Naicker and BR Ambedkar. It stands for the cause of securing the interests and welfare of the dalits and oppressed people. It has its main base in Uttar Pradesh and substantial presence in neighbouring states like Madhya Pradesh, Chhattisgarh, Uttarakhand, Delhi and Punjab.

**7.** When was the Communist Party of India (Marxist) formed? Mention the ideologies of the party.

**Ans.** The Communist Party of India (Marxist) Party was formed in 1964.

Ideologies of Communist Party of India (Marxist) are

- The party believes in Marxism-Leninism. It supports socialism, secularism and democracy and opposes imperialism and communalism.
- The party accepts democratic elections as a useful and helpful means for securing the objective of socio-economic justice in India.
- The party is critical of the new economic policies that allow free flow of foreign capital and goods into the country.

**8.** What do you know about Communist Party of India?

**Ans.** The Communist Party of India (CPI) was formed in 1925 and believes in Marxism, Leninism, Secularism and Democracy. It opposed the forces of secessionism and communalism. It accepts parliamentary democracy as a means of promoting the interests of working class, farmers and the poor.

It became weak after the split in the party in 1964 that led to the formation of Communist Party of India (Marxist). It had significant presence in Kerala, West Bengal, Punjab, Andhra Pradesh and Tamil Nadu. Its support base had gradually declined over the years.

**9.** How are political parties recognised as regional and national parties in India? Explain with examples. **(CBSE 2019)**

***Ans.*** In India, there are both national and regional parties. The parties that are present in only one of the federal units are called regional or state parties. On the other hand parties that are present in several or all units of the federation are known as national parties.

Hence, the political parties are recognised as regional and national parties on the following basis

- A party that secures at least 6% of the total votes in an election to the Legislative Assembly of a state and wins at least two seats, is recognised as a State or Regional party. For example, Janata Dal (Secular), Telugu Desam Party.
- A party that secures at least 6% of the total votes in Lok Sabha elections or Assembly elections in four states and wins at least four seats in the Lok Sabha , is recognised as a National party. For example, India National Congress, Bharatiya Janata Party etc.

**10.** "Nearly every one of the state partes wants to get an opportunity to be a part of one or the other national level coalition." Support this statement with arguments.

***Ans.*** Nearly every one of the state parties wants to get an opportunity to be a part of one or the other national level coalition because

- The members of the state party get a chance of being included in the cabinet or the council of ministers.
- State parties get an opportunity and a platform to express their views and ideology at the national level.
- It helps in strengthening of federalism and democracy, and thus bringing diversity in the parliament.

**11.** What is the difference between national and regional party? **(CBSE 2020)**

***Ans.*** The differences between national and regional party are

| National Party | Regional Party |
|---|---|
| It influences the whole country. | Its influence is limited and region-based. |
| It takes national as well as international issues. | It is interested in promoting regional/state interest only. |
| It has to secure at least 6% of the total votes in the Lok Sabha elections or Assembly elections in 4 states and win at least 4 seats in the Lok Sabha. | It has to secure at least 6% of the total votes in an election to the Legislative Assembly of a state and win at least 2 seats in the State Assembly. |

**12.** How do money and muscle power play an important role in elections? Explain.

***Ans.*** Money and muscle power play an important role in elections in the following ways

- Role of money and muscle power in parties especially during elections is growing. Parties tend to nominate those candidates who have or can raise money.
- Rich people and compaines who give funds to the parties tend to have influence on the policies and decisions of the party.
- In some cases, parties support criminals who can win elections due to their power.

**13.** It is true that meaningful choice is not given to the voters? Discuss.

***Ans.*** Yes, it is true that meaningful choice is not given to the voters as often political parties do not offer them. In order to offer meaningful choice, parties must be significantly different from each other. In recent years, there has been a decline in the ideological differences among parties in most parts of the world. In our country, the differences among all the major parties on the economic policies have reduced. Those who actually want different policies, have no option available to them. Sometimes, people can't even elect very different leader either because the same set of leaders keep shifting from one party to another.

**14.** What is meant by 'defection' in democracy? Explain. **(CBSE 2014)**

***Ans.*** Defection in democracy is a political phenomena. It means moving of a person from one party to another party for some personal benefit. It happens when a legislature, after having been elected from a particular party leaves it and joins in other party.

Anti-Defection Law was formulated to prevent elected MLA's and MP's from changing parties. Now the law states that if any MLA or MP changes parties, he or she will lose seat in the legislature. The new law has brought percentage of defection down and has made dissent even more difficult.

## • Long Answer (LA) Type Questions

**1.** Describe any five functions of political party. **(CBSE 2020)**

*Or* Describe the role of political parties in modern democracy. **(CBSE 2020)**

***Ans.*** The functions and role of political parties in modern democracy are

(i) Political parties put forward different policies and programmes and the voters choose from them.

(ii) Political parties play a decisive role in making laws for our country by making debate and passing law for people.

(iii) Political parties form and run government by recruiting leaders, train them and make them ministers to run the government.

(iv) Political parties shape public opinion by raising and highlighting important issues.

(v) Political parties provide people access to government machinery and welfare schemes implemented by governments. Parties have to be responsive to people's needs and demands otherwise people can reject those parties in the next elections.

**2.** Define the Two-Party system. Explain its advantages and disadvantages. **(CBSE 2019)**

***Ans.*** When two major parties exist in the country and the power generally changes between them (as in USA and England), the system is known as the two-party system.

Advantages of Two-Party system are

- It provides political stability to the country.
- This kind of party system discourages radical minor parties.
- This kind of party system is better than multi-party system as it is easier to govern.
- It is easier for voters to choose between only two political parties.

Disadvantages of Two-Party system are

- Two-party system offers limited options to the people.
- This system creates inconsistent governing.
- These systems donot effectively tackle the issues faced by the minority or other sections of the society.

**3.** "The political parties are necessary for democracy." Justify the statement.

*Or* What is the necessity of a political party for a democracy? **(CBSE 2015, 2019)**

***Ans.*** The political parties are necessary as modern democracies cannot exist without political parties. Without existence of parties, following situations may occur

- Every candidate in the elections will be independent. No one will be able to make any promises to the people about any major policy changes.
- The government may be formed, but its utility will remain ever uncertain. Elected representatives will be accountable to their constituency for what they do in the locality. But no one will be responsible for how the country will be run.
- The Panchayat elections are non-party based elections to the Panchayat in many states of India. Although, the parties do not contest formally, it is generally noticed that the village gets split into more than one group, each of which puts up a 'panel' of its candidates. This creates need for the political party.
- The rise of political parties is directly linked to the emergence of representatives democracies. As societies became large and complex, they needed some agency to gather different views on various issues and to present these to the government.
- Society needs a mechanism to support or restrain the government, make policies, justify or oppose them. Political parties fulfil these needs of every representative government.

**4.** Describe any five features of Bharatiya Janata Party.

***Ans.*** Bharatiya Janata Party was formed in 1980. This party has originated from the Bharatiya Jana Sangh, which was formed in 1951 by Shyama Prasad Mukherjee.

The main features of this party are

- It wants to build a strong modern India by drawing inspiration from India's ancient culture and values and Deendayal Upadhyaya's ideas of integral humanism and Antyodaya.
- Cultural nationalism or Hindutva is an important element in BJP's conception of Indian nationhood and politics.
- It has passed law for full territorial and political integration of Jammu and Kashmir with India.
- It claims a uniform civil code for all people living in the country irrespective of religion.
- It wants to ban on religious conversions. The party wants to get an anti-conversion law to stop religious conversion in the country.

**5.** Identify and list the symbols of the following political parties with their states. **(CBSE 2019)**

(i) Shiromani Akali Dal (ii) Samajwadi Party
(iii) AIADMK
(iv) All India Trinamool Congress
(v) Rashtriya Janata Dal

***Ans.***

| Party | Place | Symbol |
|---|---|---|
| (i) Shiromani Akali Dal | Punjab | Balanced Scales or Weighing Balance |
| (ii) Samajwadi Party | Uttar Pradesh | Bicycle |
| (iii) AIADMK | Tamil Nadu | Two Leaves |
| (iv) All India Trinamool Congress | West Bengal | Flower and Grass |
| (v) Rashtriya Janata Dal | Bihar | Lantern |

**6.** Define 'Political Party'. Describe any four main challenges faced by the Indian political parties. **(CBSE 2020)**

***Ans.*** A political party is a group of people who come together to contest elections and hold power in the government. The four challenges faced by the Indian political parties are

(i) The first challenge is lack of democracy within parties. All over the world, there is a tendency in political parties towards the concentration of powers in one or few leaders at the top.

Parties do not keep membership registers, do not hold organisational meetings and do not conduct internal elections regularly.

(ii) The second challenge is dynastic succession where the top positions of a party are always enjoyed by members of one particular family. This trend is harmful for other members of the party as well as for democracy. This tendency is present in some measures all over the world.

(iii) The third challenge is about the growing role of money and muscle power in parties which is specially observed during elections. Rich people and companies who give funds to the parties always dominate the policies and decisions of the party.

(iv) The fourth challenge is that usually parties do not seem to offer a meaningful choice to the voters. In our country, the difference among all the major parties on the economic policies have reduced. Sometimes, the same set of leaders keep shifting from one party to another, thus people have no option available to them.

**7.** Describe the efforts to reform political parties in India. **(CBSE 2020)**

***Ans.*** The efforts that have been made to reform political parties in India are

- The Constitution was amended to prevent elected MLAs and MPs from changing parties by introducing Anti Defection law. Defection is changing party allegiance from the party on which a person got elected to a different party. The law says that if any MLA or MP changes parties he will lose the seat in the legislature. This new law has helped bring defection down.
- The Supreme Court passed an order to reduce the influence at money and criminal. Now, it is mandatory for every candidate who contests elections to file an affidavit giving details of his property and criminal cases pending against him.
- The Election Commission passed an order making it necessary for political parties to hold their organisational elections and file their income tax returns.

Some effort that have to be made to reform political parties are

- A law should be made to regulate the internal affairs of political parties. It should be made compulsory for political parties to maintain a register of its members to hold open elections to follow its own Constitution, etc.
- It should be made mandatory for political parties to give a minimum number of tickets, about one-third to women candidates.
- There should be state fundings for elections. The government should give parties money to support their election expenses.

## • Case Based Questions

**1** Read the cases/sources and answer the following questions.

**Source A Dissatisfaction with Political Parties**

Political parties need to face and overcome these challenges in order to remain effective instruments of democracy. The first challenge is lack of internal democracy within parties.

All over the world there is a tendency in political parties towards the concentration of power in one or few leaders at the top. Parties do not keep membership registers, do not hold organisational meetings and do not conduct internal elections regularly. Ordinary members of the party do not get sufficient information on what happens inside the party.

(i) Evaluate the reasons for lack of internal democracy within political parties.

***Ans.*** The reason for lack of internal democracy within political parties arises due to the concentration of power in one or few leaders in the party. As a result these leaders take all the important decisions regarding the party's activity. Personal loyalty to these leaders becomes necessary for all the party workers.

**Source B Dynastic Succession Money and Muscle Power**

The second challenge of dynastic succession is related to the first one. Since most political parties do not practice open and transparent procedures for their functioning, there are very few ways for an ordinary worker to rise to the top in a party. Those who happen to be the leaders are in a position of unfair advantage to favour people close to them or even their family members. In many parties, the top positions are always controlled by members of one family.

(ii) To what extent dynastic succession control democracy?

***Ans.*** Dynastic succession controls democracy in the following ways

- Sometimes top positions in a political party is controlled by a family members of a particular family. Even the people who doesn't have adequate experience and popular support becomes the leader.
- Most political parties do not practice open and transparent procedures for their functioning, etc.

This is not good for democracy and hampers the basic idea that citizens should be able to participate in decision making.

**Source C Minimal Choice for Voters**

The fourth challenge is that very often parties do not seem to offer a **meaningful choice** to the voters. In order to offer meaningful choice, parties must be significantly different. In recent years there has been a decline in the ideological differences among parties in most parts of the world.

For example, the difference between the Labour Party and the Conservative Party in Britain is very little. They agree on more fundamental aspects but differ only in details on how policies are to be framed and implemented.

(iii) To what extent political parties are different in our country?

*Ans.* In our country the difference among all major parties has reduced remarkably. In economic field the different parties have little choice to differ. People even can not find better candidate to vote for, as leaders keep shifting from one party to another.

**2.** Read the case/source given and answer the following questions.

Muhammad Yunus is a famous economist of Bangladesh. He received several International honours for his efforts to promote economic and social development for the benefit of the poor. He and the Grameen Bank started, jointly received the Nobel Peace Prize for the year 2006.

In February 2007, he decided to launch a political party and contest in the parliamentary elections. His objective was to foster proper leadership, good governance and build a new Bangladesh. He felt that only a political party different from the traditional ones would bring about new political culture.

His party would be democratic from the grassroots level. The launching of the New party, called Nagarik Shakti (Citizens' Power), has caused a stir among the Bangladeshis. While many welcomed his decision, some did not like it.

"Now I think Bangladesh will have a chance to choose between good and bad and eventually have a good government," said Shahedul Islam, a government official. "That government, we hope, would not only keep itself away from corruption but also make fighting corruption and black money a top priority."

But leaders of traditional political parties who dominated the country's politics for decades were apprehensive. "There was no debate (over him) winning the Nobel, but politics is different—very challenging and often controversial," said a senior leader of the Bangladesh Nationalist Party. Some others were highly critical. They asked why he was rushing into politics. "Is he being planted in politics by mentors from outside the country," asked one political observer. **(NCERT)**

(i) Do you agree with the statements and fears expressed by various people?

(ii) How do you want this new party organised to make it different from other parties?

(iii) If you were the one to begin this political party, how would you defend it?

*Ans.* (i) I agree with the statement of a government official, Shahedul Islam that the launch of the new party may change the political culture of the country. But I do not agree with the view points of a senior leader of the Bangladesh Nationalist Party. He expressed his fear about the capability of Muhammad Yunus in the field of politics.

(ii) I think, people like Muhammad Yunus when established a political party, it should be democratic from very grassroots level. This party should fight against corruption and the problem of black money in the country which dominated the country, as H. Yunus is a respected personality with a great vision.

(iii) If I were one of them to begin this political party, I would try to develop direct interaction with the people living in the countryside and in towns. Regular meetings of the party members, seminars, workshops, etc would have been adopted to win the confidence of the people. I would bring about a totally new political culture, more democratic and more transparent.

# Chapter Test

## Objective Questions

**1.** Which one of the following facilities does the Election Commission offer to a recognised political party?

(a) Election funds
(b) Election symbol
(c) Party name
(d) Manifesto

**2.** In which form of government, rulers are always elected by people?

(a) In democracy
(b) In federalism
(c) In monarchical system
(d) None of the above

**3.** Consider the following statements about recognised political party.

I. A party that is present in only one of the federal units.
II. A party that is based on regional and communal diversities.
III. A party that is present in several or all units of the federation.

Which of the following statement is correct ?

**Codes**

(a) Only I
(b) Only II
(c) Both I and II
(d) Only III

**4.** Choose the correctly matched pair about the political parties and its strong presence within states.

(a) All India Trinamool Congress — Madhya pradesh
(b) Bahujan Samaj Party — Uttar Pradesh
(c) Nationalist Congress Party — Bihar
(d) Communist Party of India (Marxist) — Punjab

## Short Answer Type Questions

**7.** Explain different forms of party system in brief.

**8.** Why are symbols allotted to political parties in India? Explain the reasons.

**9.** How will you define a regional political party? State the conditions required to be recognised as a regional political party.

**10.** What is an alternative political formation?

**11.** Suggest some reforms to strengthen parties so that they perform their functions well.

## Long Answer Type Questions

**12.** What measures have been taken to curb problem of defection?

**13.** What is the guiding philosophy of Communist Party of India (Marxist)?

**14.** What is meant by lack of internal democracy within parties? Explain.

**15.** 'Political parties are necessary condition for a democracy'-Analyse the statement with example.

## Answers

**1.** (b) Election symbol
**2.** (a) In democracy
**3.** (d) Only III
**4.** (b) (b) Bahujan Samaj Party — Uttar Pradesh

CHAPTER 02

# Outcomes of Democracy

## In this Chapter...


- Assessment of Outcomes of Democracy
- Political Outcomes
- Economic Outcomes
- Social Outcomes


The most basic outcome of democracy is to provide political and social quality to the citizens. The democracy is expected to produce a government that works according to the needs and expectations of citizens.

## Assessment of Outcomes of Democracy

The expected and actual outcomes of democracy can be assessed by quality of government, economic well-being, inequality, social differences, freedom and dignity. After assessing outcomes of democracy, it can be recognised that democracy is a form of government which can create conditions for achieving its goal. The citizens can take advantage of those conditions and achieve their goals.

Democracy has been considered a better form of government than other alternatives because it

- promotes equality among citizens
- enhances the dignity of an individual
- improves the quality of decision-making
- provides a method to resolve conflicts
- allows room to correct mistakes

## Political Outcomes

The political outcomes of democracy are to produce accountable, responsive and legitimate government.

### Accountable, Responsive and Legitimate Government

In a democracy, accountable and responsive government is the one that is answerable to its citizens. It is responsible for making all decisions on behalf of its citizens and according to their needs and expectations. Before taking any decision, it is the responsibility of the government to follow procedures. If the government has made wrong decision then it has to accept and correct it immediately.

On the other hand, non-democratic governments do not care about complains of citizens. They are also not worried about public opinions. It takes decision very fast and decisions which are not acceptable to the citizens. Therefore, the outcome of democracy is to produce a government that follows procedure and is accountable to the people.

### Transparency and Decision-Making

Transparency means openness, communication and accountability of the government. It means that government should be operated in such a way that it is easy for citizens to see what actions are performed while decision-making.

The democratic government should develop mechanisms for citizens to hold the government accountable and mechanism for citizens to take part in decision making whenever they think it is possible.

Transparency is considered missing in non-democratic government. But in reality, democratic governments also do not have very good record to share information of decision-making with its citizens.

Democracy can be measured by the regular, free and fair elections, open public debate on major policies and the legislation. Most democracies do not have regular elections that provide a fair chance to all in participating in public debate.

Moreover, it is believed that democracy is attentive to the needs and demands of the people and is largely free of corruption. But there is nothing to prove that these two are available in democracy.

### Legitimate Government

In democracy, a legitimate government is a government where all the laws of the country are equally applicable to all its citizens. In this government, people are governed without fear or favour as well. A legitimate government should be attentive to the needs and demands of the people.

A democratic government may be slow, less efficient and not always responsive but it is people's own government. That is why, there is an overwhelming support for the idea of democracy all over the world. Thus, it is certainly a better and more legitimate form of government.

## Economic Outcomes

Economic growth, development, reduction of poverty and inequality are the prominent economic outcomes of democracy.

### Economic Growth and Development

It is expected from a government that it should bring economic growth and development. However, many democracies of the world are unable to fulfil this expectation. It is because of population size, global situation, cooperation from other countries, economic priorities, etc.

There are some significant differences between rates of economic growth among countries which are under dictatorship and democracy.

### Reduction of Inequality and Poverty

Democracy is based on political equality and all individuals have equal right to choose their representative. Along with political equality there is a growing economic inequality among the individuals.

A small number of ultra-rich enjoy a highly disproportionate share of wealth and incomes. Due to this reason, their share in total income of the country is increasing. On the other hand, the income of poor is declining.

Sometimes the poor find it difficult to meet their basic needs of life, such as food, clothing, house, education and health. Poor constitute a large proportion of voters, but still the democratic governments are not serious enough to improve their conditions.

The situation is much worse in some countries. In Bangladesh, more than half of its population lives in poverty. People of poor countries are now dependent on the rich countries for food supplies.

## Social Outcomes

The social outcomes of a democracy should be accommodating social diversity and providing dignity and freedom to the citizens.

### Accommodation of Social Diversity

Democracies usually develop a procedure to accommodate various social divisions. This reduces the possibility of social tensions becoming explosive or violent. No society can fully and permanently resolve conflicts among different groups. But democracy is best to handle social differences, divisions and conflicts.

A democracy must fulfil the following two conditions in order to achieve its goal

(*i*) It is necessary to understand that democracy is not simply ruled by majority opinion. The majority always needs to protect the interest of the minority, thus the government's function is regarded as representation of general interest.

(*ii*) It is also necessary that rule by majority does not become rule by majority community in terms of religion or race or linguistic group, etc. Rule by majority means that in case of every decision or in case of every election, different persons and groups may and can form a majority.

Thus, democracy remains only as long as every citizen has a chance of being in majority at some point of time. If someone is barred from being in majority on the basis of birth, then the democratic rule ceases to be accommodative for that person or group. Non-democratic regimes often suppress internal social differences.

### Dignity and Freedom of the Citizens

Democracy stands much superior to any other form of government for promoting dignity and freedom of the individual. Every individual wants to receive respect from fellow beings. Sometimes conflict arises among individual as they feel that they are not treated with due respect.

The passion for respect and freedom are the basis of democracy. Democracies throughout the world have recognised and achieved this (respect and freedom) in various degrees. But it is not a simple matter to recognise that all individuals are equal.

### Dignity and Freedom of Women

The long struggles by women have created some sensitivity today that respect and equal treatment of women are necessary for democratic societies.

But women are not always treated with respect. Once the 'respect' is recognised, it becomes easier for women to struggle for it. In a non-democratic set-up, the principle of individual freedom and dignity sometimes have no legal force.

### Dignity and Freedom of Disadvantaged Groups

Democracy in India has strengthened the claims of the disadvantaged and discriminated castes for equal status and equal opportunity.

There are still cases of caste-based inequalities and atrocities, but these lack the moral and legal foundations. It is the recognition that makes ordinary citizens to value their democratic rights.

## Conclusion

The most distinctive feature about democracy is that, its examination never ends. As people get some benefits, they ask for more and want to make democracy even better. Thus, people always come up with more expectations and many complaints. It shows that people have developed awareness and the ability to expect.

Democracy transforms people from the status of a subject into that of a citizen. Today most of the individuals believe that their vote definitely makes a difference to the way the government is run and to their own self-interest.

# Chapter Practice

## PART 1

## Objective Questions

### • Multiple Choice Questions

**1.** Which one of the following is not the feature of Democracy? Identify.

(a) Election

(b) Rule of law

(c) Independent Judiciary

(d) Preference to a particular religion

***Ans.*** (d) Preference to a particular religion is not the feature of democracy.

**2.** Identify the correct statement about democracy.

(a) It is a good form of government due to lesser corruption.

(b) It ensures higher rate of economic growth.

(c) It is rule by majority; therefore it's a good government.

(d) It respects the individual dignity of citizens.

***Ans.*** (d) Democracy respects the individual dignity of citizens.

**3.** Why is the democratic government regarded as a better choice?

(a) It promotes equality among citizens

(b) It ensures economic development

(c) It provides a method to resolve conflict

(d) Both (a) and (c)

***Ans.*** (d) The Democratic government is regarded as a better choice as it promotes equality among citizens as well as it provides a method to resolve conflicts.

**4.** To measure democracies on the basis of expected outcomes, which of the following practices and institutions would one look for?

(a) Regular, free and fair elections

(b) Open public debate on major policies

(c) Citizens' right to information about the government

(d) All of the above

***Ans.*** (d) All the given practices and institutions are looked to measure democracies on the basis of expected outcomes.

**5.** If a government is providing its citizens a right and means to examine the process of decision, then we get which type of government?

(a) A unstable government

(b) An accountable government

(c) A stable government

(d) A transparent government

***Ans.*** (b) If a government is providing its citizens a right and means to examine the process of decision, then it is an accountable government.

**6.** Which factor is often missing from a non-democratic government? Identify.

(a) Efficiency

(b) Effectiveness

(c) Transparency

(d) All of these

***Ans.*** (c) Transparency is one of the major factors which is missing from a Non-democratic government.

**7.** In the context of democracies, which of the following ideas is correct?

Democracies have successfully ............ .

(a) Eliminated conflicts among people

(b) Eliminated economic inequalities among people

(c) Eliminated differences of opinion about how marginalized sections are to be treated

(d) Rejected the idea of political inequality

***Ans.*** (d) Democracies have successfully rejected the idea of political inequality.

**8.** Match the following:

| | List-1 | List-2 |
|---|---|---|
| A. | Democracy is preferable | 1. Pakistan |
| B. | Sometimes dictatorship exists | 2. Brazil |
| C. | High degree of economic inequality | 3. India |

**Codes**

| | A | B | C | | A | B | C |
|---|---|---|---|---|---|---|---|
| (a) | 3 | 1 | 2 | (b) | 2 | 1 | 3 |
| (c) | 3 | 2 | 1 | (d) | 1 | 3 | 2 |

***Ans.*** (a)

**9.** Choose the correctly matched pair from the following

(a) Belgium — Here majority has suppressed the internal social differences with dictatorship.

(b) Sri Lanka — Here majority worked with the minority to produce a harmonious social life.

(c) India — Democracy has strengthened the claims of the disadvantaged and discriminated castes for equal status and opportunities.

(d) Bangladesh — More that half of its population is rich and prosperous.

***Ans.*** (c) In, India, democracy has strengthened the claims of the disadvantaged castes for equal status and opportunities.

**10.** In the following image diverse demands are shown in a democracy. Which of the following options best signifies this cartoon? Identify.

(a) Demand for separate state from Democratic Government.

(b) Democratic Government is facing territorial issues with the bordering states.

(c) Democratic Government is coping with multiple pressures through accommodation.

(d) Democratic Government accepts demands based on separate state.

***Ans.*** (c) Democratic Government is coping with multiple pressures through accommodation.

**11.** Following image shows that world's wealth is owned by few people. Which options are more appropriate in context of democracy?

(a) It is reasonable to expect democracies to reduce economic disparities.

(b) In democracy all citizens have a share in wealth and lead a better life.

(c) Democracy leads to a just distribution of goods and opportunities.

(d) Democracies do not appear to be very successful in reducing economic inequalities.

***Ans.*** (d) Democracies do not appear to be very successful in reducing economic inequalities.

## • Assertion-Reason MCQs

**Direction** (Q. Nos. 12-16) *Each of these questions contains two statements,* **Assertion** *(A) and* **Reason** *(R). Each of these questions also has four alternative choices, any one of which is the correct answer. You have to select one of the codes (a), (b), (c) and (d) given below.*

**Codes**

(a) Both A and R are true and R is the correct explanation of A

(b) Both A and R are true, but R is not the correct explanation of A

(c) A is true, but R is false

(d) A is false, but R is true

**12. Assertion** (A) Democracy stands much superior to any other form of government in promoting dignity and freedom to the individuals.

**Reason** (R) Democracies have successfully reduced economic disparities.

***Ans.*** (c) A is true as democracy stands much superior to any other form of government in promoting dignity and freedom of the individual. R is false as democracies in actual life are unable to reduce economic disparities in the society.

**13. Assertion** (A) Democracy transforms people from the status of a subject into that of a citizen.

**Reason** (R) Most individuals believe that their vote makes a difference to the way the governments run and to their own self-interest.

***Ans.*** (a) Democracy transforms people from the status of a subject into that of a citizen. Thus, most of the individuals believe in a democracy that their vote makes a difference to the way the governments run and their own self-interest. Hence, both A and R statements justify each other.

**14. Assertion** (A) Democracy ensures that decision-making will be based on norms and procedures.

**Reason** (R) A citizen in a democracy who wants to know if a decision was taken through correct procedures can find this out easily.

***Ans.*** (a) Democracy ensures that decision-making will be based on norms and procedures. Thus a citizen can find out easily if in a democracy a decision was taken through correct procedures or not. Hence, both Assertion and Reason statements justify each other.

**15. Assertion** (A) Democracy is not simply a rule by majority of opinion.

**Reason** (R) In a democracy, majority always need to work with the minority so that governments can function to represent the general view.

**Ans.** (a) Democracy is not simply a rule by majority of opinion because in a democracy, majority always need to work with the minority so that governments can function on the general view to reduce social conflicts. Hence, Both A and R statements justify each other.

**16. Assertion** (A) The democratic government will take more time to follow procedures before arriving at a decision.

**Reason** (R) Democratic government has followed procedures, its decisions may be both more acceptable to the people and more effective.

**Codes**

(a) Both A and R are true and R is the correct explanation of A
(b) Both A and R are true, but R is not the correct explanation of A
(c) A is true, but R is false
(d) A is false, but R is true

**Ans.** (a) The democratic government will take more time to follow procedures before arriving at a decision. The reason behind is that democratic government has to follow certain procedures so that its decisions should be more acceptable to the people and becomes more effective. Hence, Both A and R statements justify each other.

## • Case Based MCQs

**1.** Read the case/source given and answer the questions that follow by choosing the correct option.

If democracies are expected to produce good governments, then is it not fair to expect that they would also produce development? Evidence shows that in practice many democracies did not fulfil this expectation. If you consider all democracies and all dictatorships for the fifty years between 1950 and 2000, dictatorships have slightly higher rate of economic growth. The inability of democracy to achieve higher economic development worries us. But this alone cannot be reason to reject democracy.

As you have already studied in economics, economic development depends on several factors: country's population size, global situation, cooperation from other countries, economic priorities adopted by the country, etc. However, the difference in the rates of economic development between less developed countries with dictatorships and democracies is negligible. Overall, we cannot say that democracy is a guarantee of economic development. But we can expect democracy not to lag behind dictatorships in this respect. When we find such significant difference in the rates of economic growth between countries under dictatorship and democracy, it is better to prefer democracy as it has several other positive outcomes.

(i) How can the poor get a voice for a better share in a nation? Identify the correct option.

(a) When they will be given proper representation.
(b) When they will get a chance to participate in decision-making process.
(c) Both (a) and (b)
(d) When they will be given adequate resources and facilities.

**Ans.** (c) The poor will get their voice heard for a better share in a nation if they are provided with proper representation and get a chance to participate in decision-making process.

(ii) On which of the following factors the economic growth of a country depends? Identify from the given options.

(a) Territory or area of the country
(b) Global Scenario
(c) Size of the country's population
(d) Cooperation among the various nations

**Ans.** (d) The economic growth of a country depends on cooperation among the various nations.

(iii) Why should the gains of economic growth be evenly distributed? Identify the reason from the given options.

(a) To make an economically even society
(b) To promote the idea of social justice
(c) To reduce inequality in the society
(d) All of the above

**Ans.** (a) The gains of economic growth should be evenly distributed to make an economically even society.

(iv) What can poor countries do to receive a greater share in the world's wealth? Choose the correct option with reference to the above context.

(a) They should take initiatives to strengthen their internal democracy.
(b) They should get united to fight for the cause.
(c) They should exploit their own available natural resources.
(d) Both (a) and (b)

**Ans.** (d) To receive a greater share in the world's wealth, poor countries should take initiatives to strengthen their internal democracy and they should get united to fight for the cause.

(v) Democracy appeals to some of our deep values. Why democracy is favored more than any other form of government?

(a) It strives to promote equality and social justice.
(b) It provides solutions to all problems.
(c) It provides scope for correction of mistakes.
(d) Both (a) and (c)

**Ans.** (d) Democracy is favoured more than any other form of government because it strives to promote equality and social justice and it provides solutions to all problems.

(vi) Why economic growth is essential for a country? Choose the correct option:

(a) As it increases state capacity and the supply of public goods.
(b) As it benefits the marginal sections of the society.
(c) Help in reduction of economic disparities in a country.
(d) All of the above

**Ans.** (a) Economic growth is essential for a country as it increases state capacity and the supply of public goods.

## PART 2

# Subjective Questions

## • Short Answer (SA) Type Questions

**1.** "There is an overwhelming support for the idea of democracy all over the world." Support the statement. **(CBSE 2015, 12)**

**Ans.** There is an overwhelming support for the idea of democracy all over the world because

- Democracy can address all socio-economic and political problems.
- In democracy, there are regular and free election and there is always a scope for open public debate.
- Democracy is a people's own government where rulers are elected by the people. People wish to be ruled by the representatives elected by them.
- Democracy is a legitimate government.

**2.** "Democracies have had greater success in setting regular free and fair elections." Analyse the Statement. **(CBSE 2019)**

**Ans.** Democracies have had a greater success in setting regular free and fair elections in the following ways

- Every democracy holds elections and it has different political parties and guarantees the voting right of its citizens.
- Every citizen in democracy has the right to elect his leader and has the control over the rulers.
- In democracy whenever possible and necessary citizens participate in decision making that affects them.
- Democracy should practice regular, free and fair election. This differentiates democracy from other form of governments.

**3.** How do democratic governments ensure transparency? Explain. **(CBSE 2019)**

**Ans.** Democratic Governments ensures transparency through the following ways

- In a Democracy, people have the right to choose their representatives and exercise control over them. People have the right to participate in the process of decision making that affects them all. A democratic form of governance, thus, produces a government that is accountable and responsive to the needs of its citizens.
- Democracy allows discussion, which may delay the process of implementation, but in the long run, it serves as a healthy and productive way of decision making.
- Democracy also ensures that decision making is based on a set of norms and procedures. Therefore, in case, a citizen wishes to know if a decision was taken through correct and unbiased procedures, he/she has the opportunity to discover and find it out by examining the procedure in detail, thus, ensuring transparency.

**4.** "Democratic government is a legitimate government." Explain. **(CBSE 2016)**

**Ans.** Legitimate government is a government under which law and action of the government are revealed to the people and government function in a transparent manner.

The features of a democratic government that make it a legitimate government are

- In a democracy, the laws are applicable to all the citizen whether rich or poor.
- In a democracy, there is a political equality i.e. every vote counts equally.
- People have the right to challenge the government policies and actions. If the people are not satisfied with the working of the government they have the right to change it.

**5.** When is democracy considered successful? Explain. **(CBSE 2016)**

**Ans.** The democracy is considered successful when

- the rulers are elected by the people and take all major decision in favour of all people.

- elections offer a free choice and opportunity to the people.
- choice available to all the people is based on political equality.

**6.** List the various aspects and qualifications which help in giving a clear definition of democracy.

***Ans.*** The various aspects and qualifications which help in giving a clear definition of democracy are

- The rulers elected by the people must take all the major decisions.
- Elections must offer a choice and fair opportunity to the people to change the existing rulers.
- Choice and opportunity should be available to all on an equal basis.

**7.** List out some of the merits of democracy.

***Ans.*** Democracy is considered to be the best form of government. The merits of democracy are

- It safeguards the social, economic and political interests of the individuals.
- It assures equality in all social, political and economic rights of the citizens.
- It improves the quality of decision making as decisions are taken by following a procedure.

**8.** "Non-democratic rulers can be very quick and efficient in decision-making and implementation." Do you think with this feature of non-democratic government is a better government than other government? Explain.

***Ans.*** Non-democratic rulers can be very quick and efficient in decision–making and implementation. But it is not a better government than other government. For example,

- A democratic government can take more time to take a decision as compared to other forms of government. The non-democratic governments can take decisions quickly. But there is a possibility that it is not accepted by all, as no procedure has been followed here.
- In democracy 'transparency' is very necessary. Here, the citizens has the rights to know the process of decision-making. This factor would often be missing from a non-democratic government. Thus, non-democratic government is not regarded as a better government than others.

**9.** Differentiate between Democratic and Non-Democratic form of Government.

| Democratic Government | Non-Democratic Government |
|---|---|
| Democracy is based on the ideas of deliberations and negotiations. | In non-democratic government, no such deliberations and negotiations are held. |
| Democratic government takes into account the public opinion before reaching a decision. | Non-democratic governments do not care about public opinions. |
| In this type of governments, there is some delay in taking a decision due to deliberations and negotiations but these decisions are effective in nature. | In this type of governments, they can take quick decision, but these are sometimes less effective and forced on people. |

**10.** How is poverty a major challenge to Democracy? Explain.

***Ans.*** Poverty is a major challenge to democracy as the democracies could not produce expected development. The inability of democracy to achieve higher economic development is one of the major challenges. If we consider all democracies and dictatorships for the fifty years between 1950 and 2000, dictatorships have a slightly higher rate of economic growth.

Within democracies, there is a very high degree of inequalities. A small number of ultra-rich enjoy a highly disproportionate share of wealth and incomes. Those at the bottom of the society have very little to depend upon. Yet, democratically elected governments do not appear to address the question of poverty.

**11.** "Some people think that democracy produces a less effective government." Analyse the statement.

***Ans.*** Some people think that democracy produces a less effective government because

- Democracies often frustrate the needs of the people and often ignore the demands of majority of a population.
- Most democracies fall short of elections that provide a fair chance to everyone and is subjecting every decision to public debate.
- Democratic governments do not have a very good record when it comes to sharing of information with citizens.
- Democracy is unable to achieve higher economic development.
- Democratically elected governments do not appear to address the question of poverty as expected by the citizens.

**12.** "Democracies accommodate various social divisions." Support the statement. **(CBSE 2019)**

***Ans.*** Democracies accommodate various social divisions in the following ways

- Various disadvantaged and marginal social groups can express their grievances by which the government know about the injustice faced by these groups and can initiate some necessary steps to rectify it.

- Expressing various kinds of social division in politics can reduce the intensity of the differences. This leads to strengthen the democracy.
- Marginalised people can express their demands in a peaceful and constitutional way. In this way, they seek a fair position through elections. Thus, democracy becomes a best way to fight for recognition and accommodates diversity.

**13.** Explain any four ways in which democracies have been able to reduce inequality and poverty.

***Ans.*** The ways in which democracies have been able to reduce inequality and poverty are

(i) Women have been given equal rights as those of men in most of the democratic countries like India.

(ii) Special efforts have been made to uplift the weaker sections of the society (like the Scheduled Castes and Scheduled Tribes), so that they could live with dignity and honour.

(iii) Democracies everywhere try to provide a fair share to every citizen in the natural resources of the country.

(iv) In almost all democratic countries of the world, poor people are given many concessions but richer classes are made to pay more income tax.

## • Long Answer (LA) Type Questions

**1.** "Democratic system is better than any other form of government." Support the statement with examples. **(CBSE 2020)**

***Ans.*** Democracy or democratic system is a better form of government when compared with any other form of government because

- Democracy promotes equality among citizens. Every citizen of the country has equal rights before the law. All individuals have equal rights in electing their representatives.
- Democracy enhances the dignity of the individual. By giving its citizens equal rights, it enhances dignity and freedom of the individual. Democracy gives equal treatment and respect to women, disadvantaged and discriminated castes in our society.
- Democracy improves the quality of decision making. As there is open debate in major issues in democracy, quality of decisions is improved.
- Democracy provides a method to resolve conflicts. Democracy reduces the possibility of social tension which leads to peaceful social life. It allows room to correct mistakes.
- Democracy is a legitimate government. Democracy gets the popular support of the people by regular, free and fair elections.

**2.** How does democracy produce an accountable, responsive and legitimate government? **(CBSE 2016, 14, 2012)**

*Or* "Democracies produce an accountable, responsive and legitimate governments." Support the statement with suitable examples. **(CBSE 2011)**

***Ans.*** Democracies produce an accountable, responsive and legitimate governments in the following ways

- **Accountable Government** Democracy produces an accountable government as the people have the right to choose their representatives through the electoral process. These elected representatives form the government and participate in the decision-making process on behalf of the people. This is known as transparency. If these elected representatives do not work in a proper way, people have a chance to not elect them in next election.
- **Responsive Government** Democracy produces a responsive government. As democratic government is elected by the people, it is people's own government. It promotes the formation of public opinion and take care of the needs and expectation of the people.
- **Legitimate Government** Further, democratic government is a legitimate government because regular election after a fixed time is its key feature. It may be slow, less efficient but it is the people's own legitimate government.

**3.** Why is democracy not considered simply a rule of majority? **(CBSE 2013)**

***Ans.*** The democracy is not considered simply a rule of majority because

- In democratic set-up, the majority always needs to work with the minority, so that governments represent the general view.
- Majority and minority opinions are not permanent in democracy.
- The rule by majority does not become rule by majority community in terms of religion, race, linguistic groups, etc.
- Democracy remains democracy only when every citizen of a country has a chance of being majority at some point of time.
- If someone is barred from being in majority on the basis of birth, i.e. on the basis of caste and religion then the democratic rules are not applicable for that persons or groups.

**4.** What are the demerits of democracy. Explain in detail.

**Ans.** The demerits of democracy are

- **Unstable Government** Lots of political parties are allowed to criticise the government and its policies. Sometimes, it leads to the downfall of the ruling party and re-elections in the country. This gives instability to the government.
- **Slow and Inefficient Government** The most common demerit of democracy is that, it is slow in its functioning. The decision-making process involves long debates and deliberations in the Parliament. This takes a lot of time before the decisions are actually taken.
- **Incompetence** Democracy gives every individual the right to voice his concern. As a result, everybody focusses on his personal interests and not the collective interests. This sometimes leads to incompetent and wrong selections of the candidates in the government.
- **Role of Money in a Democracy** Money plays an important role at the time of the elections. A lot of money is needed to organise demonstrations, public meetings and speeches. Those candidates are chosen in the elections, who can raise lot of money for the party.

**5.** "Democracies lead to peaceful and harmonious life among citizens." Justify this statement. **(CBSE 2018)**

**Ans.** Democracies lead to peaceful and harmonious life among citizens in the following ways

- It is expected from democracy that it should produce a harmonious social life. Country like Beligium successfully negotiated difference among its ethnic populations. Democracy develops a procedure to conduct the competition which reduces the possibility of tensions becoming violent.
- Democracy tries to handle social differences, divisions and conflicts. Non-democratic regimes often neglects these problems and tries to suppress internal social differences.
- Democracy is not simply rule by majority opinion. Majority and minority opinions are not permanent things. The majority needs to work with the minority which is performed in democracy.
- In democracy every citizen has the freedom in terms of religion, race or linguistic group etc. Here rule by the majority does not denote rule by the majority community.
- In democracy every citizen has a chance of being in majority at some point of time. Nobody can be barred from being in majority on the basis of birth in democracy.

**6.** "In actual life, democracies do not appear to be very successful in reducing economic inequalities." Explain the statement giving an example. **(CBSE 2019)**

**Ans.** In actual life, democracies do not appear to be very successful in reducing economic inequalities because the democracy does not guarantee economic development. In most of the democracies, a small number of ultra-rich enjoy a highly disproportionate share of wealth and income. For example,

- In countries like South Africa and Brazil, the top 20% people take away more than 60 % of the national income. Unfortunately, those who are at the bottom of the society have a very little share (less than 3 %) to depend upon.
- In India, the elected government looks reluctant to take necessary steps for the upliftment of the large section of poor in our society.
- In Bangladesh, more than half of its population lives in poverty. People in several poor countries are now dependent on the rich countries even for food supplies.

**7.** "Democracy stands much superior to any other form of government in promoting dignity and freedom of the individual." Justify this statement. **(CBSE 2018)**

**Ans.** A democratic form of government stands much superior to any other form of government in promoting dignity and freedom of the individual in the following ways

(i) Often conflict arises among individuals because some feel that they are not treated with equal respect in comparison to others. It is very common in non-democratic countries. However, in democratic countries such conflicts are recognized and resolved atleast in principle.

(ii) Most societies were historically male dominating. The status of women was not satisfactory. After long struggles by women, democracy throughout the world has recognised equal treatment and respect to women at least in principles. Thus in democracy, it becomes easier for women to wage a struggle against what is now unacceptable legally and morally for them.

(iii) Democracy in India strengtened the claims of the disadvantaged and discriminated castes for equal status and opportunity, which is not possible in any non-democratic country.

Thus, it can be concluded that democracy stands much superior to any other form of government in promoting dignity and freedom of the individual.

**8.** Should democracy be judged by its outcome?

***Ans.*** Democracy should be judged by its outcome because it opens the path of expectations, which is one of the criteria for judging any democratic country. The examination procedure of democracy is eternal, as it passes one test, it produces another test. It automatically gives rise to expectations as well as complaints by the people when they want to know about the functioning of democracy. The fact that people also complaint about democracy indicates the awareness and the ability of people to expect and to look critically at power holders and the high and the mighty. It transforms people from the status of a subject into that of a citizen. Most individuals today believe that their vote makes a difference to the way the government is run and to their own self-interest.

## • Case Based Questions

**1.** Read the cases/sources given and answer the following questions.

**Source A Democracy is Accountable**

There are some things that democracy must provide. In a democracy, we are most concerned with ensuring that people will have the right to choose their rulers and people will have control over the rulers. Whenever possible and necessary, citizens should be able to participate in decision making, that affects them all. Therefore, the most basic outcome of democracy should be that it produces a government that is accountable to the citizens, and responsive to the needs and expectations of the citizens.

(i) Evaluate the effectiveness of accountability of democracy.

***Ans.*** Democracy produces a government that is accountable to its citizenas as in democracy people have the right to choose their rulers and have control over them. In this way, citizen are able to participate in decision making procedure.

**Source B Transparency in Democracy**

Let us think in terms of costs. Imagine a government that may take decisions very fast. But it may take decisions that are not accepted by the people and may therefore face problems. In contrast, the democratic government will take more time to follow procedures before arriving at a decision. But because it has followed procedures, its decisions may be both more acceptable to the people and more effective.

So, a citizen who wants to know if a decision was taken through the correct procedures can find this out. She has the right and the means to examine the process of decision making. This is known as transparency. This factor is often missing from a non-democratic government. Therefore, when we are trying to find out the outcomes of democracy, it is right to expect democracy to produce a government that follows procedures and is accountable to the people.

(ii) To what extent democracy is transparent? Give reasons.

***Ans.*** Democracy is transparent as it provide citizen the rights and means to examine the process of decision making. This is not available in non-democratic state. In democracy, government develops mechanism for citizens to take part in decision making when it is possible.

**Source C Democracy is Better than Non-Democracy**

Democracies have had greater success in setting up regular and free elections and in setting up conditions for open public debate. But most democracies fall short of elections that provide a fair chance to everyone and in subjecting every decision to public debate.

Democratic governments do not have a very good record when it comes to sharing information with citizens. All one can say in favour of democratic regimes is that they are much better than any non-democratic regime in these respects.

(iii) To what extent democracy is better than non-democracy?

***Ans.*** Democracy is better than the non-democratic government as in democracy people get free and fair elections through which they apply their rights to choose their leaders.

**2.** Read the case/source given and answer the following questions.

Perhaps more than development, it is reasonable to expect democracies to reduce economic disparities. Even when a country achieves economic growth, will wealth be distributed in such a way that all citizens of the country will have a share and lead a better life? Is economic growth in democracies accompanied by increased inequalities among the people? Or do democracies lead to a just distribution of goods and opportunities?

Democracies are based on political equality. All individuals have equal weight in electing representatives. Parallel to the process of bringing individuals into the political arena on an equal footing, we find growing economic inequalities. A small number of ultra-rich enjoy a highly disproportionate share of wealth and incomes. Not only that, their share in the total income of the country has been increasing.

Those at the bottom of the society have very little to depend upon. Their incomes have been declining. Sometimes they find it difficult to meet their basic needs of life, such as food, clothing, house, education and health.

In actual life, democracies do not appear to be very successful in reducing economic inequalities. The poor constitute a large proportion of our voters and no party will like to lose their votes. Yet democratically elected governments do not appear to be as keen to address the question of poverty as you would expect them to. The situation is much worse in some other countries. In Bangladesh, more than half of its population lives in poverty. People in several poor countries are now dependent on the rich countries even for food supplies.

(i) Why it is expected that democracy will reduce the economic disparities?

***Ans.*** It is expected that democracy will reduce the economic disparity among its citizens as it is a rule of majority and is based on political equality.

(ii) Infer the reason of inability of democracy to achieve higher economic development.

***Ans.*** Democracy is unable to achieve higher economic development as economic development of a country depends on several factors like country's population size, global situation, economic priorities, cooperation from other countries etc and democracy can not control all these factors.

(iii) Why do some poor countries depend on the rich countries ?

***Ans.*** People in poor countries depends on the grants of rich countries as democratically elected government`is not interested to remove the disparity between the rich and poor in the society. Sometimes the poor find it difficult to meet their basic needs, like, food, clothing, house, etc. Poor people in some countries are even dependent on the rich countries for food supplies.

# Chapter Test

## Objective Questions

**1.** What is the most basic outcome of democracy?

(a) Significant decision-making
(b) Answerability to the citizens
(c) Powerful, repressive governance
(d) None of these

**2.** Which feature of democracy is common in most countries of the world?

(a) They have a formal constitution.
(b) They hold elections regularly.
(c) They guarantee the rights of citizens.
(d) All of these

**3.** On which of the following factors does economic development of a country depend?

(a) Cooperation from other countries
(b) The number of rich citizens in the country
(c) Political priorities adopted by the country
(d) All of these

**4.** Democracy is based on the ideas of ......... .

(a) Freedom and Rights
(b) Negotiation
(c) Deliberation
(d) Both (b) and (c)

**5.** Which of these statement is incorrect regarding the non-democratic regimes?

(a) These do not have to bother about public opinion.
(b) These take less time to arrive at a decision.
(c) Principle of individual dignity has a legal force.
(d) These often suppress internal social differences.

## Short Answer Type Questions

**6.** Explain the relationship between democracy and development.

**7.** How can we measure democracy on the basis of its expected outcomes?

**8.** What are the issues in which democracies have failed?

**9.** Examine the political outcomes of democracy.

**10.** What are the features of a good democracy?

## Long Answer Type Questions

**11.** How do democratic governments ensure transparency? Explain any three points.

**12.** Explain how democracies lead to peaceful and harmonious life among citizens.

**13.** What are the factors which are responsible for the economic development of the country? Does democracy provide guarantee of economic development?

## Answers

1. (b) Answerability to the citizens
2. (d) All of these
3. (a) Cooperation from other countries
4. (d) Both (b) and (c)
5. (c) Principle of individual dignity has a legal force.

CHAPTER 01

# Money and Credit

## In this Chapter...


- Money as a Medium of Exchange
- Modern Forms of Money
- Loan Activities of Banks
- Self Help Groups for the Poor


## Money as a Medium of Exchange

Money is used for several transactions. It is considered as a means of exchange, as it acts as intermediate in the exchange process.

### Barter System of Exchange

Before the use of money, people followed barter system of exchange. In this system, goods are directly exchanged (without use of money) between two or more people who agree to exchange each other's goods.

For example, farmer exchanging wheat for shoes and vice versa. In this case, the farmer and shoes manufacturer should be in need of each other's goods. This is called **double coincidence of wants**[1].

The major drawback of this system was the lack of double coincidence of wants, as without it, exchange was not possible. The use of money eliminated the need of double coincidence of wants. Money was accepted as a common **medium of exchange**[2].

## Modern Forms of Money

Modern forms of money include currency (paper notes and coins). Before the introduction of coins, a variety of objects like grains and cattle were used as money. Further, the use of metallic coins of gold, silver, copper, etc started.

### Currency

It is a generally accepted form of money, that includes coins and paper notes. It is authorised by the government and circulated within an economy. The modern currency has no use of its own except as a medium of exchange.

In India, **Reserve Bank of India**[3] can only issue currency notes on behalf of the Government of India. The rupee is widely accepted as a medium of exchange as it is legalised by law.

### Deposits with Banks

It means the amount that people keep in their bank accounts. People deposit their extra money in banks by opening a bank account in their name. The money in bank account are deposits with banks. Banks accept the deposits and also pay an interest on the deposits. People can also withdraw the money when they require. Deposit with banks are called **Demand Deposits**.

#### Cheque Facility

Cheque is basically a paper instructing the bank to pay a specific amount from the person's account to that person in whose name the cheque has been issued. Payments can be made with the use of cheque instead of cash.

1 **Double Coincidence of Wants** A situation where the supplier of goods A wants goods B and the supplier of goods B wants goods A.

2 **Medium of Exchange** Any item that is widely accepted in exchange for the goods and services offered to consumers in a given market, like currency.

3 **Reserve Bank of India** (RBI) The RBI or Central Bank of India, founded in 1935, which maintains the national currency, the rupee and the nation's currency reserves. Its primary function is to regulate the issuing of bank notes.

## Modern Banking System

The modern forms of money i.e. currency and deposits are closely linked to the working of the modern banking system.

# Loan Activities of Banks

Banks accept deposits of the people. In this way, they collect large amount as deposits. They keep only a small portion of deposits (in India, it is 15%) as cash.

This is kept for those depositors who wish to withdraw money from their accounts. Rest of the deposits are given as loans by the banks.

When banks give loans, they charge higher **rate of interest**[4] from the people who have taken loans. This becomes the income of the banks. In this way, banks act as mediator between those who have surplus funds (the depositors) and those who are in need of funds (the **borrowers**).

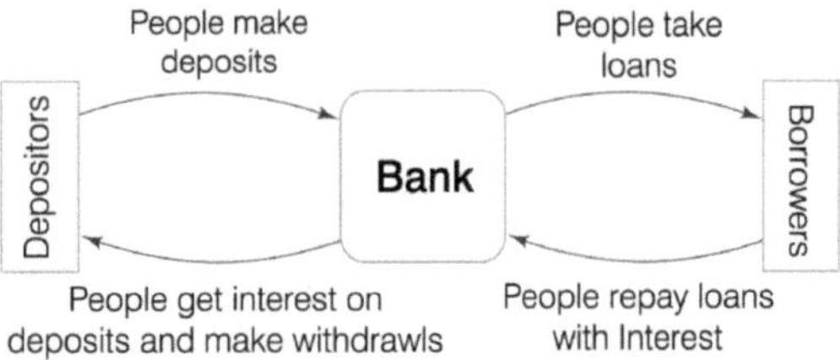


## Credit

Credit or loan refers to an agreement in which the lender supplies money, goods or services to **borrower**[5] with the promise of future payment. A large number of transactions in our day-to-day activities involve credit in some form or the other.

### Two Different Credit Situations

(*i*) In the **first situation**, credit is used to meet the production expenses. When the production is complete then it increases earnings. Here, credit plays a positive role.

For example, Salim a manufacturer takes credit for his business. During the festival season, he receive large orders from traders. To complete production on time, he ask the raw material suppliers to supply material on credit. He also obtains loan in cash from the trader as some of the advance payment for the goods to be supplied.

At the end of the manufacturing cycle, Salim is able to deliver the order, make a good profit and repay the money that he had borrowed. This helps to increase earnings and therefore, the person is better off than before.

(*ii*) In the **second situation**, credit pushes the borrower into a situation from which recovery is very difficult and painful.

For example, Swapna takes loan from moneylender to grow groundnut, hoping that her harvest would help repay the loan.

Midway through the season the crop is hit by pests and the crop fails. She is unable to repay the moneylender and the debt grows over the year into a large amount.

Next year, Swapna takes a fresh loan for cultivation. It is a normal crop this year but the earnings are not enough to cover the old loan. She is caught in debt. She has to sell a part of the land to pay off the debt.

In this situation, credit pushes Swapna into a **debt-trap**. Her condition becomes worse than before.

### Interpretation of Both Situations

- From both the examples, we see that in one situation credit helps to increase earnings and therefore, the condition of a person is better than before.
- In other situation, because of the crop failure credit pushes the person into a debt-trap. Whether credit would be useful or not, it depends on the risks in the situation and whether there is some support, in case of loss.

### Terms of Credit

It is a set of conditions under which a loan is given. It may include method of payment, rate of interest, duration of credit and other related conditions like, collateral, **documentation requirement**[6] and the mode of repayment.

The terms of credit may vary according to the situation of the lender and the borrower.

### Collateral

It is a security against loans. It is an **asset**[7] that the borrower owns and uses this as a guarantee to a lender until the loan is repaid. If the borrower fails to repay the loan, the lender has the right to sell the asset or collateral to obtain payment.

Some examples of collateral security used for borrowing are land titles, deposits with banks, livestock, etc.

### Variety of Credit Arrangements

There may be different credit arrangements for different categories of borrowers. These are

- **Loan from Moneylenders** Small farmers borrow money from the village moneylender at high rate of interest. Due to high interest rate they fell in debt-trap.

---

4 **Rate of Interest** Proportion of amount charged on the principal amount taken by the borrower.
5 **Borrower** An individual, organisation or company that is taking funds, materials or services on credit/loans.
6 **Documentation Requirement** The documents that record the loan agreement between a borrower and a lender, including all necessary evidence regarding collateral.
7 **Asset** Property owned by a person or organisation, regarded as having value and available to meet debts, commitments or legacies.

- **Loan from Traders** Farmers get loans from agricultural traders at a lower rate of interest. But the traders also get the promise of the farmers to sell their crops to him only. In this way, trader ensures that the money is repaid besides making profit. He buys crop from farmers at low price and sell it later, when price is high.
- **Loan from Banks** Some farmers take loan for cultivation from banks, at very low interest rate and at easy repayment terms. Banks also provide other facilities to such borrowers.
- **Loan from Employers** Landless agricultural labourers and workers depend on their employers for loan. The landowner may charge interest rate upto 5% per month. The workers work for landowners in order to repay the loan.
- **Loan from Cooperatives** This is the major source of cheap credit in rural areas. Loans to member of cooperative societies can be provided for the purchase of agricultural implements, cultivation and agricultural trade, fisheries, construction of houses and other expenses.

### Credit Sources in India

The two categories of sources of credit are formal sector credit or loans and informal sector credit or loans.

The formal sector comprises banks and **cooperative societies**. The informal sector may consist of moneylenders, friends and relatives, traders, landowners, large farmers, etc.

### Features of Formal Sector Credit

- It provides loans comparatively at a lower rate of interest and collateral security is required to obtain loans.
- This sector is mainly supervised by the RBI (Reserve Bank of India).
- It includes banks and cooperatives.

### Role of RBI in Formal Sector

RBI has major role in providing formal sector credit. Its role is

- The RBI (Reserve Bank of India) ensures that the banks give loans not just to profit-making businesses and traders, but also to small cultivators, small scale industries, small borrowers, etc.
- Periodically, banks have to submit information to the RBI on how much they are lending, to whom and at what interest rate they are lending to borrowers, etc.
- The banks maintain a minimum cash balance out of the deposits they receive. The RBI monitors the banks in actually maintaining cash balance.

### Features of Informal Sector Credit

- This sector charges higher interest rates on the loans that are given as there is no organisation to supervise this sector.
- This sector could lead to increasing debt as the borrower finds difficulty in paying back.
- People who might wish to start an enterprise by borrowing from the informal sector may not do so because of the high cost of borrowing. However, still poor households in urban and rural areas depend upon informal sources for their borrowing needs as they don't require any collateral.

## Self Help Groups (SHGs) for the Poor

Self Help Group is a group of people usually belonging to one neighbourhood having same social and economic backgrounds. They meet and save money regularly as per their ability.

Members of the group (usually 15-20) can take small loans from the group itself to meet their needs. The group charges interest less than moneylenders on these loans.

After one or two years, if the group is regular in savings, it becomes eligible for availing loan from the bank. Loan is sanctioned in the name of group and is meant to create self-employment opportunities by providing money to buy raw materials, seeds, assets like sewing machines, handlooms, cattle, etc.

### SHGs : A Helping Hand for Women

SHGs are the building blocks of organisation of the rural poor. The SHGs help women to become financially self-reliant and regular meetings of the group provide a platform for women to discuss and act on a variety of social issues such as health, nutrition, domestic violence, etc.

#### Grameen Bank of Bangladesh

**Professor Muhammad Yunus, the founder of Grameen Bank** and recipient of 2006 Nobel Prize for Peace, started the bank as a small project in the 1970s. He provided small credit on reasonable terms and conditions to millions of poor people with different occupations.

# Chapter Practice

## PART 1
## Objective Questions

### • Multiple Choice Questions

**1.** Why money is called a 'medium of exchange' ? Choose the best suitable option:

(a) Because money act as an intermediate in the process of exchange.
(b) Because money adds to the value of a commodity.
(c) Because money is portable.
(d) Because money is used fo several transactions.

***Ans.*** (a) Money is called medium of exchange because money acts as an intermediate in the process of exchange.

**2.** Identify the system where goods were exchanged without using money from the given options.

(a) Goods system (b) Exchange system
(c) Barter system (d) Both (a) and (b)

***Ans.*** (c) In Barter system, the goods were exchanged without using money.

**3.** Modern currency is not made up of any precious metals and does not have any use of its own. Still, it is accepted as money because

(a) it is made up of some metal or paper.
(b) it is authorised by the government of the country.
(c) it can be issued by any legal authority.
(d) All of the above

***Ans.*** (b) Modern currency is not made up of precious metal such as gold, silver and copper. Still, it is accepted as a medium of exchange because the currency is authorised by the government of the country.

**4.** Raghav has surplus money so he open a bank account and deposits in it. Whenever, he needs money, he can go to his bank and withdraw from there. This kind of deposit' with the banks is known as

(a) Fixed Deposit (b) Term Deposit
(c) Demand Deposit (d) Surplus Deposit

***Ans.*** (c) The kind of deposit in the given case is Demand Deposit. Deposits with the bank which can be withdrawn on demand is called Demand Deposits.

**5.** In which of the following situations debt trap occurs? Identify from the given options.

(a) Inability of the poor to repay back the loans at higher rate of interest to money lenders.
(b) In case of crop failure, when the farmer get no return for the capital invested in buying agricultural inputs.
(c) Farmer has to sell a part of his land to repay his loan and has no resources to generate income in the next year.
(d) All of the above

***Ans.*** (d) In all the given situations, debt trap can occurs. Debt trap is a situation where the debtor will not be able to repay the debt incurred.

**6.** Ram and Shyam are small-farmers who have taken loans of ₹ 20,000 from different parties. Ram has taken credit at 1.5% per month interest from a trader while Shyam has taken credit at 8% per annum from a cooperative. Analyse the loan information given above, consider the correct option from the following.

(a) Shyam is better because he receives more interest.
(b) Ram is better as he does no paper work.
(c) Shyam is worse off as he pays more interest.
(d) Ram is worse off as he pays more interest.

***Ans.*** (d) Ram is worse off as he pays more interest.

**7.** Sunil works in a private company, Anil works as a daily wage earner. Both want a credit of ₹ 30,000. The Bank is more likely to give credit to whom?

(a) Anil as he is more needy.
(b) Sunil as he has regular employment.
(c) Neither Sunil nor Anil will be provided credit from bank.
(d) Both Anil and Sunil will be provided credit from bank.

***Ans.*** (b) The bank would likely to give credit to Sunil as he has regular employment.

**8.** Which one of the following options describes 'Collateral'?

(a) Double coincidence of wants
(b) Certain products for barter
(c) Trade in barter (d) Asset as guarantee for loan

***Ans.*** (d) Collateral is an asset as guarantee for loan.

**9.** Sunita owns a small flower shop near a temple. She wants to expand her shop by keeping exotic flowers and flower bouquets. To whom she should approach for a very short term credit?

(a) Moneylenders as they provide short term credit.
(b) Banks as they charge low interest.
(c) Cooperatives as they do not require collateral.
(d) Any of the above

*Ans.* (c) Sunita should approach cooperatives for a very short term credit as they do not require collateral.

**10.** Which of the following is not a formal source of credit from the given options?

(a) Banks (b) Cooperative (c) Employer (d) All of these

*Ans.* (c) Employers do not fall under formal sources of credit lenders in our country.

**11.** Match the following:

| List I (Terms) | List II (Description) |
|---|---|
| A. Double Coincidence of Wants | 1. An individual or organisation taking funds on credit. |
| B. Cheque | 2. Proportion of amount charged on the principal amount taken by the borrower. |
| C. Rate of Interest | 3. A paper instructing the bank to pay a specific amount from one account to another account. |
| D. Borrower | 4. A situation where the supplier of goods A wants goods B and the supplier of goods B wants goods A. |

**Codes**

| | A | B | C | D | | A | B | C | D |
|---|---|---|---|---|---|---|---|---|---|
| (a) | 2 | 3 | 4 | 1 | (b) | 4 | 3 | 2 | 1 |
| (c) | 3 | 4 | 1 | 2 | (d) | 1 | 2 | 4 | 3 |

*Ans.* (b)

**12.** Read the given information carefully and select the most appropriate answer from the given options.

A shoe manufacturer, M.Salim has to make a payment to the leather supplier and writes a cheque for a specific amount. This means that the shoe manufacturer instructs the bank to pay this amount to the leather supplier. The leather supplier takes this cheque and deposits it in his own bank account in the bank. The money is transferred from one bank to another account in a couple of days. The transaction is complete without any payment of cash. After the transaction between Salim and Prem .......... .

(a) Salim's balance in his bank, account increases and Prem's balance also increases
(b) Salim's balance in his bank account decreases and Prem's balance increases
(c) Salim's balance in his bank account increases and Prem's balance decreases
(d) Salim's balance in his bank account decreases and Prem's balance also decreases

*Ans.* (b)

## • Assertion-Reason MCQs

**Directions** (Q. Nos. 13-17) *Each of these questions contains two statements, **Assertion** (A) and **Reason** (R). Each of these questions also has four alternative choices, any one of which is the correct answer. You have to select one of the codes (a), (b), (c) and (d) given below.*

**Codes**

(a) Both A and R are true and R is the correct explanation of A
(b) Both A and R are true, but R is not the correct explanation of A
(c) A is true, but R is false (d) A is false, but R is true

**13.** **Assertion** (A) Modern currency is used as a medium of exchange, however, it does not have a use of its own.

**Reason** (R) Modern currency is easy to carry.

*Ans.* (b) Modern currency is used as a medium of exchange because it is accepted and authorised as a medium of exchange by a country's government. Modern currency is easy to carry as it includes paper notes and coins. Hence, both assertion and reason are true but reason is not the correct explanation of assertion.

**14.** **Assertion** (A) Banks keep only a small proportion of their deposits as cash with themselves.

**Reason** (R) Banks in India these days hold about 15 per cent of their deposits as cash.

*Ans.* (b) Banks only keep a small proportion of their deposits as cash with themselves because they use the major portion of the deposits to extend loans. Banks in India these days hold about 15 pre cent of their deposits as cash. It is kept as a provision to pay the depositors who might come to withdraw money from the bank on any given day. Hence, both assertion and reason are true but reason is not the correct explanation of assertion.

**15.** **Assertion** (A) Banks charge a higher interest rate on loans than what they offer on deposits.
**Reason** (R) The difference between what is charged from borrowers and what is paid to depositors is their main source of income.

*Ans.* (a) The interest charged on loans is higher than the interest paid on deposits because the difference between the two interest rates is the major source of income for banks. Hence, both assertion and reason are true and reason is the correct explanation of assertion.

**16.** **Assertion** (A) Credit would be useful or not depends on the risk involved in a situation.
**Reason** (R) The chance of benefitting from credit is highest in agricultural sector.

**Ans.** (c) A is true as whether credit would be useful or not, depends on the risks involved in the situation. R is false because in the agricultural sector there are high risks of crop failure which can further lead to high debts. Thus, there are low chances of benefit from credit in agricultural sector.

**17.** **Assertion** (A) Collateral is an asset that the borrower owns and use this as a guarantee to a lender until the loan is repaid.

**Reason** (R) Collateral is given as the lender can sell the collateral to recover the loan amount if the borrower fails to repay the loan.

**Ans.** (a) Collateral is an asset that the borrower owns and use as a guarantee to a lender until the loan is repaid. In case of failure of repayment of loan, the lender can sell the collateral to recover the amount. Hence, assertion and reason are true and reason is the correct explanation of assertion.

## • Case Based MCQs

**18.** Read the case given and answer the questions that follow by choosing the correct option.

In recent years, people have tried out some newer ways of providing loans to the poor. The idea is to organise rural poor, in particular women, into small Self Help Groups (SHGs) and pool (collect) their savings. A typical SHG has 15-20 members, usually belonging to one neighbourhood, who meet and save regularly. Saving per member varies from ₹ 25 to ₹ 100 or more depending on the ability of the people to save. Members can take small loans from the group itself to meet their needs. The group charges interest on these loans but this is still less than what the moneylender charges. After a year or two, if the group is regular in savings, it becomes eligible for availing loan from the bank. Loan is sanctioned in the name; of the group and is meant to create self-employment opportunities for the members. For instance, small loans are provided to the members for releasing mortgaged land, for meeting working capital needs (e.g. buying seeds, fertilisers, raw materials like bamboo and cloth), for housing materials, for acquiring assets like sewing machine, handlooms, cattle, etc.

(i) Fill in the blanks from the given options:
In Self Help Groups, ........ decide the savings and loan activity option.

(a) Reserve Bank of India (b) Members
(c) Co-operatives (d) Rural Banks

**Ans.** (b) In Self Help Groups, group members decide the savings and loan activity options.

(ii) 85% of the loans taken by the poor households in the rural areas are from which of the following sources? Identify the source from the given options.

(a) Cooperatives (b) Government Bank
(c) Informal Sources (d) Local bank

**Ans.** (c) 85% of loans taken by the poor households in rural areas are from informal sources.

(iii) Which of the following aspect is correct regarding the Self Help Groups? Identify the correct option.

(a) They have mainly encouraged rural women to obtain credit.
(b) They have helped women to become self-reliant.
(c) They have helped women to discuss on relevant issues like health.
(d) All of the above

**Ans.** (d) All the given statements are correct.

(iv) Why Self Help Groups (SHG) are growing in popularity? With reference to the above context, infer the appropriate option.

(a) As they provide loans at a nominal rate of interest.
(b) They create self-employment opportunities for its members.
(c) Both (a) and (b)
(d) As members of SHG's require collateral to get loans.

**Ans.** (c) Self Help Groups are growing in popularity as they provide loans as at nominal rate of interest and they create self-employment opportunities for its members.

(v) **Assertion** (A) Members can take small loans from the group itself to meet their needs through Self-Help Groups.

**Reason** (R) SHGs are the building blocks of organisation of the rural poor.

**Codes**

(a) Both A and R are true and R is the correct explanation of A
(b) Both A and R are true, but R is not the correct explanation of A
(c) A is true, but R is false (d) A is false, but R is true

**Ans.** (b) Members can take small loans from the group itself to meet their needs as the group charges interest on these loans but this is still less than what the moneylender charges. On the other hand, Self Help Groups are generally considered the building blocks of organisation of the rural poor. Hence, both assertion and reason are true but reason is not the correct explanation of assertion.

(vi) Which is one of the major reasons that prevent the poor from getting bank loans? Choose the best suitable option:

(a) Absence of collateral
(b) Lack of availability of banks in rural areas
(c) Lack of approach towards formal organisations.
(d) All of the above

**Ans.** (a) Absence of collateral is the major reason which prevent poor from getting bank loans.

PART 2

# Subjective Questions

## • Short Answer (SA) Type Questions

**1.** How is money used as a medium of exchange? Explain with examples. **(CBSE 2013)**

***Ans.*** Money is used as a medium of exchange in the following ways

- In day-to-day transactions, goods are being bought and sold with the use of money.
- The transactions are made in money as a person holding money can easily exchange it for any commodity or services.
- Use of money has made it easier to exchange services such as the service of a doctor, teacher etc.

**2.** How do demand deposits have the essential features of money? Explain. **(CBSE 2020)**

***Ans.*** Demand deposits have the essential features of money in the following ways

- Demand deposits can be withdrawn from the bank whenever it is required.
- Demand deposits are widely accepted as a means of payment, along with the currency, thus they are considered as money.
- Demand deposits are also accepted widely as means of payment by way of a cheque instead of cash.

**3.** Examine any three situations in which credit helps in the development of agriculturists. **(CBSE 2019)**

***Ans.*** Three situations in which credit helps in the development of agriculturists are

(i) Farmers can buy farm machinery and equipments along with fertilisers for better crop production by taking cheap loans.

(ii) Farmers can buy other agricultural inputs like hybrid seeds, raw materials or undertake irrigational activities in their farms to get better crop yields.

(iii) Farmers can buy farm animals and other livestock to raise their secondary income with the help of credit facilities.

**4.** Examine any three situations in which credit pushes the borrower into a debt-trap. **(CBSE 2019)**

***Ans.*** Three situations in which credit pushes the borrower into a debt-trap are

(i) When a borrower sells the agricultural produce to repay a loan but it may not be enough. Then more credit is taken to repay the entire amount which pushes the borrower into debt-trap.

(ii) When borrowers depend on informal sources of credit who charge a high rate of interest. This increases the repayment amount and new loans have to be taken to repay the earlier ones.

(iii) In high risk situations, for example, farmers taking credit before sowing of crops. If harvest fails then fresh loans are taken to repay the existing loans leading to debt-trap.

**5.** Explain the three important terms of credit. **(CBSE 2019)**

***Ans.*** Terms of credit is a set of conditions under which a loan is given. Three important terms of credit are

(i) **Collateral** A borrower has to offer a collateral to the lender. It is a security to use as a guarantee till the loan is paid such as land title, bank deposits, livestock, house, factory etc.

(ii) **Rate of Interest** It is the proportion of amount at which the lender lends money to the borrower. The rate at which loan is given is decided by the RBI.

(iii) **Time Period** It is duration of the loan till which the amount will be repayed along with interest.

**6.** Why do lenders ask for collateral while lending? Explain. **(CBSE 2020)**

***Ans.*** The lenders ask for collateral before lending because it is an asset that the borrower owns and uses this as a guarantee to the lender, until the loan is repaid. A collateral is an asset such as land, building, livestock, vehicle or deposits with banks that the borrower owns and uses this as a guarantee to the lender until the loan is repaid.

Collateral with the lender acts as a proof that the borrower will return the money. By keeping a collateral with the lender the borrower is bound to be regular in paying the interest because the borrower does not want to lose the collateral. In case of default i.e. borrower is unable to pay the loan, the lender has the right to sell the collateral or use it.

**7.** Explain the role of credit for economic development. **(CBSE 2020)**

***Ans.*** The role of credit for economic development is

- A country's growth and economic development is greatly dependent on cheap and affordable credit system. Different kinds of economic activities need credit like to set up business for investment purpose, and also buying new house, cars and so on.

- Mostly manufacturing units need a huge amount of money to buy raw materials for their production process. Thus, credit here helps to make such manufacturing works easy.
- Cheap, affordable and fast credit system helps farmers to buy new and advanced technology for agricultural practices, e.g. tractors, threshers, fertilisers, new and advanced seeds (HYVs) and so on.

**8.** "Credit can play a negative role." Justify the statement with arguments. **(CBSE 2019)**

***Ans.*** Credit can play a negative role in the following ways

- In situations where credit is taken to repay the earlier loans then it will increase the burden of repayment.
- In high risk situations when the future is uncertain, there credit plays a negative role. For example, farmers taking credit before sowing but their harvest may not be good and they may not be able to repay their loans.
- Rural borrowers normally depend on informal sources of credit who charge a high rate of interest. This repayment of larger amounts may sometimes be larger then their income. In that case, credit plays a negative role.

**9.** Why is cheap and affordable credit important for the country's development ? Explain any three reasons. **(CBSE 2018)**

***Ans.*** Cheap and affordable credit is important for the country's development because

(i) More lending would lead to higher income and encourage people to invest in agriculture, engage in business and set up small scale industries.

(ii) Cheap credit will allow weaker sections of society to get rid of the exploitation at the hands of money lenders and come out of debt trap.

(iii) Affordable credit would lead to sustainable economic activity that would allow borrowers to invest in better technology to make their business more competitive.

**10.** Why are service conditions of formal sector loans better than informal sector ? Explain. **(CBSE 2019)**

***Ans.*** Service conditions provided by formal sector loans are better than informal sector loans because

- Formal sources of credit provide cheap and affordable credit without any undue exploitation.
- People in rural areas take credit from moneylenders and traders (informal sector) who charge very high rate of interest.
- Informal sector exploit the borrowers leading to debt traps.
- Formal sector is mainly supervised by the Reserve Bank of India. So, every clause is in writing and clear to comprehend. Whereas, no external organisation supervises informal sector. So, there is no such written clause.

**11.** Explain any three reasons for the banks and cooperative societies to increase their lending facilities in rural areas. **(CBSE 2019)**

***Ans.*** Banks and cooperatives are needed to increase their lending facilities in rural areas because

(i) People in rural areas take credit from moneylenders and traders who charge very high rate of interest. These people must be aware about the role of banks and cooperatives so that they can be provided by cheap credit facilities.

(ii) Rural people are exploited by using unfair means thus, leading them to debt traps. To reduce the dependence of informal sector in rural areas, there is need for setting up of more banks.

- (iii)Formal sources of credit provide cheap and affordable credit in rural areas without any undue exploitation. These formal sources will serve as a building block for rural households. This will help the people to start up their small business or trade in certain goods.

**12.** The credit activities of the informal sector should be discouraged." Support the statement with arguments. **(CBSE 2018)**

***Ans.*** The credit activities of the informal sector should be discouraged because

- It is seen that around 85% of the loans taken by the poor households in the urban areas are from informal sources. There is no monitoring system that supervises the credit activities of the lenders in the informal sector.
- High cost of borrowing leads to a major share of earnings going into payment of interest on the loan so formal source of credit is needed.
- Sometimes the higher interest rate leads to the requirement to pay more than the earnings, thus falling into a debt trap. To eliminate this, formal sources are needed.
- Borrowers falling into debt-traps discourage more people from borrowing, which ultimately reduces development of the country.

**13.** Compare and contrast the role of formal and informal source of credit.

***Ans.*** The comparison between the role of formal and informal source of credit is

| Formal sector | Informal sector |
|---|---|
| It consists of banks and cooperatives, which are supervised by the Reserve Bank of India. | It consists of moneylenders, traders, employers, landowners etc. which are not supervised by any organisation. |
| They give loans on low interest rates. | They usually give loans at a high interest rate, which means that the cost of the loan is very high to the borrower. |
| Usually the loans require extensive documentation and some property to be kept as collateral or security against any default in payment. | Usually the informal sources do not require extensive documentation for giving the loan. |

**14.** Explain the features of Self Help Groups.

***Ans.*** The features of the Self Help Groups (SHGs) are

- SHGs typically consist of 15-20 members and each member is required to save and pool (collect) in their resources.
- The SHGs are constituted to provide loans to its members at a reasonable rate.
- After a year or two and with regular savings, the group is eligible to take loans from banks.
- SHGs seek loans from banks for its member collectively and meet the needs of buying assets, machinery, raw materials, construction or repair.
- SHGs also meet regularly to discuss and act on various social issues like dowry, domestic violence, child marriage, health, nutrition, etc.

## • Long Answer (LA) Type Questions

**1.** "Bank plays an important role in the economic development of the country." Support the statement with examples. **(CBSE 2020)**

***Ans.*** Bank plays an important role in the economic development of the country in the following ways

(i) **Bank Accepts the Deposits** Bank accepts the deposits and also pay an amount as interest on the deposits. In this way, people's money is safe with the banks and it earns an amount as interest.

People also have the provision to withdraw the money as and when they require. Since the deposits in the bank account can be withdrawn on demand, these deposits are called demand deposits.

(ii) **Bank Provides Loans** Bank keep only a small portion of their deposits as cash with themselves. Banks use the major portion of the deposits to give loans. There is a huge demand for loans for various economic activities. Banks make use of the deposits to meet the loan requirements of the people.

(iii) **Bank Provides Credit** A large number of transactions in our day-to-day activities involve credits in some form or the other. Many industries are provided credit by the Banks which further helps in the economic development of the country. This generates more employment and raises income the people.

**2.** Which government body supervises the functioning of formal sources of loans in India? Explain its functioning.

*Or* Describe the functions of the Reserve Bank of India. **(CBSE 2019)**

*Or* Describe the significiance of the Reserve Bank of India. **(CBSE 2020)**

***Ans.*** The Reserve Bank of India (RBI) supervises the functioning of formal sources of loans in India. Functions or significance of Reserve Bank of India are

- The RBI monitors that the banks actually maintain the cash balance and do not give all the deposits as loans.
- The RBI ensures that the banks give loans not just to profit-making businesses and rich traders, but also to small cultivators, small scale industries, small borrowers, etc.
- Periodically, banks have to submit information to the RBI on how much they are lending, to whom, etc.
- The rate of interest charged on loans given by the banks is decided by the Reserve bank.
- In this way, the RBI keeps a check on all the activities of banks and checks the flow of credit also.

**3.** How can the formal sector loans be made beneficial for poor farmers and workers? Suggest any five measures. **(CBSE 2016)**

***Ans.*** The measures to make formal sector loan beneficial for poor farmers and workers are

(i) The formal sector like banks and cooperatives should lend more to poor people and workers, particularly in rural areas.

(ii) The formal sector should provide cheap and affordable credit to the poor people so that repayment is easy.

(iii) Formal sector should work out other ways of arranging collateral from the poor people.

(iv) By providing linkage between Self Help Groups and banks, formal sector of credit can be increased.

(v) There should be more number of cooperatives and banks in rural areas and people should be made aware of their presence.

**4.** Mohan works at a construction site in a sub-urban area while Sudhir is a marketing manager in a company. Both want credit to buy a home. Create a list of arguments explaining who has more possibility of getting a home loan from formal sector.

**Ans.** Sudhir has more possibility of getting a home loan from the formal sector due to the following arguments

- Formal sector consists of banks and cooperatives. Banks require proper documentation and collateral. In the above case, Sudhir will be able to provide the necessary documents like salary slip, employment record and other documents that are needed by the banks.
- Banks also require collateral security which can be provided by Sudhir since his economic condition is better. Even if he is not able to provide collateral security then bank can retain the ownership papers of the house as collateral security.
- Since Sudhir has a regular source of income, he is in a better position to repay the loan amount in future. But Mohan will not be able to provide proper documents or collateral security so he has to depend on informal sector for credit needs.

**5.** Name two formal and two informal sources of credit in India. State advantages of formal and informal sources of credit. **(CBSE 2016)**

**Ans.** Two formal sources of credit are bank and cooperatives and two informal sources of credit are moneylenders and traders. The advantages of formal sources of credit are

- It provides loans at a fixed rate and terms.
- It gives loans not just to profit-making businesses and traders but also to small cultivators, small-scale industries and small borrowers etc.
- Cost of borrowing is less and hence promote borrowing and more economic growth.
- There is no exploitation as in the case with the informal sectors.

The advantages of informal sources of credit are

- There is no external control over the lending practices.
- It is suitable for poor households as they didn't have to follow a certain kind of procedure which is required in formal sources of credit.

## • Case Based Questions

**1.** Read the following case and answer the questions that follow

**Source A Informal Credit**

Compared to the formal lenders, most of the informal lenders charge a much higher interest on loans. Thus, the cost to the borrower of informal loans is much higher. Higher cost of borrowing means a larger part of the earnings of the borrowers is used to repay the loan.

(i) To what extent, do you agree that credit from informal sector is not good for borrowers?

**Ans.** Yes, credit from informal sector is not good for the borrowers as the rate of interest charged by the informal lenders is so high that a larger part of income of the borrowers goes to interest payment which results in debt-trap or more poverty.

**Source B Currency**

Unlike the things that were used as money earlier, modern currency is not made of precious metal such as gold, silver and copper. And unlike grain and cattle, they are neither of everyday use. The modern currency is without any use of its own.

(ii) Why modern currency is not like the earlier forms of currency like grain or cattle?

**Ans.** Modern form of currency is unlike earlier forms of currency as Grain and cattle even when they were not used as currency had value of its own. On the other hand, modern currency if not authorised by Reserve Bank of India, becomes an ordinary piece of paper as it has no value of its own.

**Source C Loan Activities of Bank**

There is an interesting mechanism at work here. Banks keep only a small proportion of their deposits as cash with themselves. For example, banks in India these days hold about 15 per cent of their deposits as cash.

(iii) In the above lines, which function of the bank is highlighted?

**Ans.** The function of giving loans is highlighted here. Banks after keeping 15% of their deposits as cash, extend the rest of the deposits to people as loans.

**2.** Read the case given below and answer the questions that follow.

In India, the Reserve Bank of India issues currency notes on behalf of the Central Government. As per Indian Law, no other individual or organisation is allowed to issue currency. Moreover, the law legalises the use of rupee as a medium of payment that cannot be refused in setting transactions in India.

No individual in India can legally refuse a payment made in rupees. Hence, the rupee is widely accepted as a medium of exchange.

The other form in which people hold money is as deposits with banks. At a point of time, people need only some currency for their day-to-day needs. For instance, workers who receive their salaries at the end of each month have extra cash at the beginning of the month.

What do people do with this extra cash? They deposit it with the banks by opening a bank account in their name. Banks accept the deposits and also pay an amount as interest on the deposits.

In this way people's money is safe with the banks and it earns an amount as interest. People also have the provision to withdraw the money as and when they require. Since the deposits in the bank accounts can be withdrawn on demand, these deposits are called demand deposits.

(i) Why is there a need to legalise rupee as a medium of exchange? What monentary system does India follows?

(ii) Mention two uses of opening a bank account by the people.

(iii) How demand deposits are useful for the banks as well as for the people?

***Ans.*** (i) There is a need to legalise rupee as a medium of exchange so that all payments can be made and no one can refuse rupee in settling of transactions. India has adopted a representative paper currency or we can say that managed currency standard.

(ii) Two uses of opening a bank account are

(a) To deposit surplus cash into the bank account.

(b) To earn interest given by the banks on deposits.

(iii) Demand deposits are useful for the banks as well as for the people in the following ways

- For the banks, demand deposits provide an opportunity to extend them as loans.
- For the people, demand deposits are like near money that can be easily withdrawn from the bank.

# Chapter Test

## Objective Questions

**1.** Which of the following is not included in the terms of credit in a bank loan?
(a) The rate of interest
(b) The lender's land
(c) The borrower's land
(d) The time period of the loan

**2.** Which of the following are not modern forms of money?
(a) Currency notes
(b) Deposits with banks
(c) Coins
(d) None of these

**3.** Which among the following is not a feature of informal sources of credit?
(a) It is supervised by the Reserve Bank of India
(b) Rate of interest is not fixed
(c) Terms of credit are very flexible
(d) Traders, employers, friends, etc provides informal credit source.

**4.** Which among the following option will be the cheapest source of credit in rural areas?
(a) Bank
(b) Cooperative Society
(c) Moneylender
(d) Finance Company

**5.** Choose the correctly matched pair from the given options.
(a) Formal Sector — Provides loans at lower rate of interest
(b) Informal Sector — Includes bank and cooperatives
(c) RBI — Didn't monitor the banks
(d) Moneylenders — Provides loans to industry owners

## Short Answer Type Questions

**7.** Write a short note on terms of credit.
**8.** Explain loans from cooperatives.
**9.** Why is it important to have a control over the formal sector loans by the Government of India? Explain.
**10.** Explain the role of Self Help Groups in empowering women.
**11.** Why bank might not be willing to lend certain borrowers? Explain.
**12.** In what ways does the Reserve Bank of India supervise the functions of Banks? Why is this necessary?

## Long Answer Type Questions

**13.** How does a Self Help Group function?
**14.** How can rural poor be encouraged to take loans from the formal sector of credit? Explain.
**15.** Describe four major sources of credit for rural house holds in India.

## Answers

1. (b) The lender's land
2. (d) None of these
3. (a) It is supervised by the Reserve Bank of India
4. (b) Cooperative Society
5. (a) Formal Sector – Provides loans at lower rate of interest

CHAPTER 02

# Globalisation and the Indian Economy

### In this Chapter...


- Production Across Countries
- Foreign Trade and Integration of Markets
- Globalisation
- World Trade Organisation
- Impact of Globalisation on India
- The Struggle for a Fair Globalisation


Globalisation is the integration between countries through **foreign trade** and **foreign investment** by Multinational Companies (MNCs). In recent years, markets in India have transformed due to globalisation.

## Production Across Countries

The early phase of globalisation involved export of raw materials from colonial countries such as India and import of finished products from industrially developed European countries and the USA. But from the middle of the 20th century, things began to change. Some companies became Multinational Corporations (MNCs) as they spread their economic activities to various parts of the world.

### Multinational Corporations (MNCs)

An MNC is a company that owns or controls production in more than one country. MNCs set-up offices and factories for production in regions where they can get cheap labour and other resources, to minimise cost and maximise profit. They sell their finished products globally and also produce the goods and services globally. The production process is divided into small parts and spread out across the globe.

### Advantage of Spreading Out

By spreading out production across different countries, the MNCs get the best quality resources at cheap prices. This increases their profit. By spreading the production, the MNCs generate employment opportunities in **underdeveloped countries.**

## Interlinking Production Across Countries

Some ways of interlinking production across countries are

- **Foreign Investment** It means investment made by a company based in one country (usually an MNC), into a company based in another country. MNCs set-up the production units by setting up factories or offices in the foreign country.
- **Partnerships/Joint Venture** Sometimes MNCs merged with local companies and produce jointly. In this way, MNCs provide money for additional investments like buying new machines for faster production and bring latest technology for production.
- **Local Companies/Mergers/ Takeover** MNCs buy local production units or merge with local companies to expand production. For example, Cargill Foods of USA has taken over Parakh Foods in India and has become the largest producer of edible oil in India.

- **Contracts to Local Companies** MNCs also place orders with small producers for production. The MNC determines the price, quality, delivery and labour conditions for these distant producers, etc.

# Foreign Trade and Integration of Markets

Foreign trade is a trade between different countries of the world. It is also called **international trade, external trade** or **inter-regional** trade. It consists of imports and exports.

Foreign trade helps in the integration (connection) of markets in the following ways

- Facilitate movement of goods and services between countries.
- Facilitate movement of people, ideas and technology.
- Gives opportunity to producers to sell their products beyond local/domestic markets.
- Buyers get more choice of goods.
- Increased competition among producers so better quality of goods and services can be provided.

An example of foreign trade in India is that how the cheap and better quality of Chinese toys replaced the Indian toys.

# Globalisation

It is the process of rapid integration or interconnection between countries by greater foreign investment and great foreign trade. Globalisation causes integration of markets as well as production centres.

In the process of globalisation, MNCs are playing major role. More and more goods and services, investments and technology are moving among different countries.

Besides the movements of goods, services, investments and technology, countries are connected through the movement of people between them, i.e. **migration**. This is because people usually move from one country to another in search of a better life, higher income, better jobs or better education.

### Role of IT in Globalisation

Fast improvement in technology during the last 50 years, such as improvements in transportation technology have resulted in much faster delivery of goods across long distances at lower costs. Information and Communication Technology (**ICT** or **IT**[1]) has speed up the communication services across the globe.

Telecommunication facilities (telegraph, telephone, mobile phones, fax) and internet through satellite communication is used to contact one another around the world, to access information instantly and to communicate from remote areas.

An example of this one is a news magazine published for readers in London, which is designed and printed in Delhi by using telecommunication facilities and internet.

## Foreign Investment Policy

The policy of foreign investment adopted by the government also affects globalisation to a large extent. It restricts or encourages foreign investment seeing the situation in the country. Trade barrier is one such foreign investment policy.

### Trade Barrier

It is a restriction on the free international exchange of goods or services. Tax on imports (called import duty) is an example of a trade barrier. It is called a barrier because some restriction has been set-up. Governments use trade barriers to regulate foreign trade and to decide what kinds of goods and how much of each, should come into the country.

Similarly **Quotas**[2] are a way of restriction on volume or quantity of goods to be imported or exported.

### Restrictions on Foreign Trade

After independence, the Government of India had put barriers on foreign trade and foreign investment, to protect the **domestic producers**[3] from foreign competition, as the industries were just coming up in 1950s and 1960s. At that time, India allowed imports of only essential items such as machinery, fertilisers, petroleum, etc.

### New Economic Policy, 1991

Around 1991, it was felt that Indian producers must compete with producers around the globe, so that they can improve their production and quality of goods and services. Therefore, Government of India in 1991 made some major changes in its foreign investment policy. Liberalisation was one such change. This decision was supported by powerful international organisations like World Trade Organisation (WTO).

# Liberalisation

Removing barriers or restrictions set earlier by the government on foreign trade is known as liberalisation. In India, it refers to the decision to reduce restrictions on imports undertaken by the Government of India in 1991.

1 **ICT/IT** Information and Communication Technology (ICT) or Information Technology (IT) means the business of developing and using technology to process information and aid communications.

2 **Quotas** These are government-imposed trade restrictions that limit the number or value of goods and services that can be imported or exported during a particular time period. Quotas are used in international trade to help regulate the volume of trade between countries.

3 **Domestic Producers** Producers operating or producing within the territory or a country.

With liberalisation of trade, businesses are allowed to make decisions freely about what they wish to import or export. Now, the government imposes less restrictions than before and is therefore considered to be more liberal.

# World Trade Organisation (WTO)

It is an international organisation dealing with the global rules of trade between nations. Its main function is to ensure that trade flows as smoothly, predictably and as freely as possible. It supported the liberalisation of foreign trade and investment in India.

WTO was started at the initiative of the developed countries. Its objective is to liberalise international trade and ensure that its members obey its rules. Though WTO is supposed to allow free trade for all the countries, but it is found that the developed countries have unfairly implemented some rules. They have forced the developing countries to remove barriers from their countries. At the same time, they themselves have restricted imports to their countries or used unfair trade practice to manipulate the market.

An example of this is the trade in agricultural products. **Agriculturists in the USA** are heavily subsidised by their government, so that they can export products like wheat and cotton at very low prices to developing countries. This increase competition and adversely affects farmers in these countries.

# Impact of Globalisation in India

- Globalisation resulted in more competition among producers (both local and foreign). It gives greater choice of goods with improved quality at lower prices.
- MNCs have increased their investments in India in cell phones, automobiles, electronics, soft drinks, fast food and services such as banking in urban areas.
- Many new jobs have been created and local companies supplying raw materials and services to these industries have prospered.
- Globalisation brings in new and improved technology by which even the local companies benefit.
- Some large Indian compaines like Infosys, Tata Motors, Asian Paints, Ranbaxy Infosys (IT), Sundaram Fasteners have emerged as MNCs and set up companies in other countries.
- New companies that provide **call centres**[4], IT related services, accounts and administrative jobs have established.
- Globalisation has threatened small producers as their production has decreased considerably. Producers of small industries like battery, capacitors, plastic toys, tyres, dairy products and vegetable oil are affected due to competition.

### Government Steps to Attract Foreign Investment

In recent years, the Central and State Governments in India are taking special steps to attract foreign companies to invest in India. These are

- They have set-up industrial zones, called **Special Economic Zones (SEZs)**. SEZs have world class facilities: electricity, water, roads, transport, storage, recreational and educational facilities.
- Companies who set-up production units in the SEZs do not have to pay taxes for an initial period of five years.
- Government has also allowed flexibility in the labour laws to attract foreign investment.
- The companies in the organised sector have to obey certain rules that aim to protect the workers' rights.
- Instead of hiring workers on a regular basis, companies hire workers **flexibly** for short periods when there is intense pressure of work. This is done to reduce the cost of labour for the company.

### Growing Competition and Uncertain Employment

Globalisation and the pressure of competition have changed the lives of workers. With growing competition, most employers these days prefer **flexible employment**[5]. This means that workers jobs are no longer secure. For example, in the garment export industry.

Indian garment exporters try to cut their own costs by reducing labour costs, as raw material costs cannot be reduced. So, they employ workers only on a temporary basis. Workers get very low wages and forced to do overtime to manage their expenses. Even in the organised sector, workers no longer get the protection and benefits that they enjoyed earlier.

# The Struggle for a Fair Globalisation

People with education, skill and wealth have made the best use of the new opportunities arised due to globalisation. To make it more 'fair', government plays a major role which is

- It ensures that policies such as labour laws are strictly followed.
- It supports and protects small producers from global competition and to improve their performance.
- It negotiates with the WTO to ensure fair rules and concessions for developing countries.
- The government can also use trade and investment barriers to protect the interest of domestic produce.
- Government can also align with other developing countries with similar interests to fight against the authority of developed countries in the WTO.

4 **Call Centre** A centralised office used for the purpose of receiving or transmitting large volume of requests by telephone.

5 **Flexible Employment** Employment on a temporary basis, i.e. only as and when required. This is in contrast with permanent employment, which means employment throughout the year along with provident fund, provision for leave etc.

# Chapter Practice

## PART 1 Objective Questions

### • Multiple Choice Questions

**1.** What is the major benefit to the local company of a joint production with MNC? Identify the correct option.

(a) Domestic labour gets high wages.
(b) MNC's can provide money for additional investments.
(c) It helps to reduce production.
(d) Domestic companies started following labour laws.

***Ans.*** (b) The benefit to the local company of such joint production is two-fold. First, MNCs can provide money for additional investments, like buying new machines for faster production. Second, MNCs might bring with them the latest technology for production.

**2.** What do you mean by investment? Choose the correct option.

(a) Money spent on buying assets such as land, building, machines and other equipments.
(b) Money used by owners for luxuries.
(c) Money used for maintaining the factory.
(d) None of the above

***Ans.*** (a) Investment is the money spent on buying assets such as land, building, machines and other equipments.

**3.** Globalisation does not involve which one of the following?

(a) Rapid integration among the countries.
(b) More goods and services moving between countries.
(c) Increased taxes on imports.
(d) Movement of people between countries for jobs, education, etc.

***Ans.*** (c) Increased taxes on imports is not involved in globalisation.

**4.** Which among the following example given in the options has the least possibility of globalization?

(a) Selection of labour force (b) Increase in infrastructure
(c) To manage resources for investment
(d) Location of capital works

***Ans.*** (d) Location of capital works has the least possibility of globalisation.

**5.** Fill in the blank with suitable option.

Globalisation leads to ……… .

(a) lesser competition among the producers.
(b) greater competition among the producers.
(c) no change in the level of competition among the producers.
(d) None of the above

***Ans.*** (b) Globalisation leads to greater competition among the producers. Markets where globalisation is particularly common include financial markets, such as capital markets, money and credit markets, and insurance markets, commodity markets, etc.

**6.** 35 year old Sunil works from 8 am to 8 pm all seven days of the week in a garment exporter firm. He works as a contract labour. His employer does not give him any other facility. He knows that he is employed just for few months of the year but he continues to work as he has no other option. Analyse the information, considering one of the following correct option.

(a) Ill effects of globalisation
(b) MNC's creating job opportunities
(c) Workers jobs are no longer secure
(d) People are denied fair share of benefits

***Ans.*** (a) The given case reflects the ill effects of globalisation.

**7.** The Indian government has been following the policy of liberalisation, globalisation and privatisation since ………… .

(a) 1990 (b) 1991 (c) 1992 (d) 1993

***Ans.*** (b) The Indian government has been following the policy of liberalisation, globalisation and privatisation since 1991.

**8.** India's maximum foreign exchange is spent on which of the following?

(a) Import of food grains
(b) Import of Petroleum Products
(c) Import of Iron and Steel
(d) Import of Technical know how

***Ans.*** (b) India spends nearly 75% of its export earnings in import of petrolum products.

**9.** What is the benefit of using containers in transportation of goods? Identify.
(a) Reduction in delays
(b) Reduction in damaged goods
(c) Reduction in port handling costs
(d) All of the above

*Ans.* (d) All the given statements are correct.

**10.** World Trade Organisation (WTO) is an organisation whose aim is to liberalise
(a) Internal trade (b) External trade
(c) National trade (d) International trade

*Ans.* (d) WTO aim to liberalise international trade. It deals with the global rules of trade between nations. It was set up to ensure trade flows smoothly and freely between nations.

**11.** Identify the terminology with the help of the following features.
- Through this, businesses are allowed to make decisions freely about import or export.
- It helps to remove restrictions on foreign trade.

Select the appropriate option from the following.
(a) Quotas (b) Liberalisation
(c) Globalisation (d) Privatisation

*Ans.* (b) The given information is about liberalisation.

**12.** Match the following.

| List-I | List-II |
|---|---|
| (a) Quotas and taxes on imports are used to regulate trade. | 1. Automobiles |
| (b) Indian companies who have invested abroad. | 2. Call centers |
| (c) IT has helped in spreading of the production of services. | 3. TATA motors, Infosys, Ranbaxy |
| (d) Several MNC's have invested in setting up factories in India for production. | 4. Trade barriers |

**Codes**

| | A | B | C | D | | A | B | C | D |
|---|---|---|---|---|---|---|---|---|---|
| (a) | 2 | 4 | 3 | 1 | (b) | 3 | 1 | 2 | 4 |
| (c) | 4 | 3 | 2 | 1 | (d) | 1 | 4 | 3 | 2 |

*Ans.* (c)

## • Assertion-Reason MCQs

**Directions** (Q. Nos. 13-17) *Each of these questions contains two statements, **Assertion** (A) and **Reason** (R). Each of these questions also has four alternative choices, any one of which is the correct answer. You have to select one of the codes (a), (b), (c) and (d) given below.*

**Codes**
(a) Both A and R are true and R is the correct explanation of A
(b) Both A and R are true, but R is not the correct explanation of A
(c) A is true, but R is false
(d) A is false, but R is true

**13.** **Assertion** (A) Local businesses may set up joint production process with MNC's and can earn higher profits.

**Reason** (R) MNC's can provide money for additional investments, like buying new machines for faster production.

*Ans.* (a) At times, MNC's set up production jointly with some of the local companies of the host countries. The benefit to the local company from such joint production is that MNC's can provide for additional investments and can bring in newer technology of production that result in fast paced production. Hence, both Assertion and Reason are true and Reason is the correct explanation of Assertion.

**14.** **Assertion** (A) MNC's can exert a strong influence on production at distant locations.

**Reason** (R) MNC's can set up partnerships with local companies, use local companies for supplies, compete with the local companies or buy them up.

*Ans.* (a) By setting up partnerships with local companies, using the local companies for supplies and closely competing with the local companies or buying them up, MNC's are exerting a strong influence on production at distant locations. As a result, production is widely dispersed locations in getting interlinked. Hence, both Assertion and Reason are true and Reason is the correct explanation of Assertion.

**15.** **Assertion** (A) Foreign trade creates an opportunity for the producers to reach beyond the domestic markets.

**Reason** (R) Foreign Trade expands the choice of goods beyond what is domestically produced.

*Ans.* (a) Foreign trade creates an opportunity for the producers to reach beyond the domestic markets and thus, expands the choices available for consumers.

**16.** **Assertion** (A) Trade barrier is a restriction on the free international exchange of goods or services.

**Reason** (R) Quotas are a way of restriction on volume or quantity of goods to be imported or exported.

*Ans.* (b) Trade barrier is a restriction on the free international exchange of goods or services. It is called a barrier because some restriction has been set up by the governments to regulate foreign trade. On the other hand, Quotas are used as a way of restriction on volume or quantity of goods to be imported or exported. Hence, both Assertion and Reason are true, but Reason is not the correct explanation of Assertion.

**17. Assertion** (A) Globalisation leads to increased competition in international and domestic markets.

**Reason** (R) Globalisation makes the consumers better off as they have a wider variety of goods to choose from at lower prices.

**Ans.** (b) Globalisation leads to increased competition in international and domestic markets as there is free movement of goods, services, labour and funds across countries. Also, consumers are better off as they get better quality and increased variety of goods at lower prices. Hence, both Assertion and Reason are true and Reason is the correct explanation of Assertion.

## • Case Based MCQs

**18.** Read the case/source given and answer the questions that follow by choosing the correct option.

Let us see the effect of Foreign trade through the example of Chinese toys in the Indian markets. Chinese manufacturers learn of an opportunity to export toys to India, where toys are sold at a high price.

They start exporting plastic toys to India. Buyers in India now have the option of choosing between Indian and the Chinese toys. Because of the cheaper prices and new designs, Chinese toys become more popular in the Indian markets. Within a year, 70 to 80 per cent of the toy shops have replaced Indian toys with Chinese toys. Toys are now cheaper in the Indian markets than earlier. What is happening here?

As a result of trade, Chinese toys come into the Indian markets. In the competition between Indian and Chinese; toys, Chinese toys prove better. Indian buyers have a greater choice of toys and at lower prices. For the Chinese toy makers, this provides an opportunity to expand business. The opposite is true for Indian toy makers. They face losses, as their toys are selling much less.

(i) The Chinese toys have made a global presence in Indian markets too. If India bans Chinese products in their market then what will it imply?

(a) It will decrease the competion in the Indian markets.
(b) It will be an unhealthy business practice.
(c) It will impact economic as well as political relations between the two nations.
(d) Both (b) and (c)

**Ans.** (d) If Chinese products are banned within the Indian markets then it will promote an unhealthy business practice and it will impact economic as well as political relations between the two nations.

(ii) What is the basic function of foreign trade with reference to the given case? Identify the best suitable option from the following:

(a) It connects markets of different countries.
(b) It creates opportunities for only the buyer to approach foreign goods.
(c) It connects markets of two countries only.
(d) Foreign trade connects developed countries only.

**Ans.** (a) The basic function of foreign trade is to connect markets of different countries.

(iii) What will happen if tax is imposed on Chinese toys? Choose the correct option.

(a) Chinese toymakers will benefit.
(b) Indian toymakers will prosper.
(c) Chinese toys will remain cheap
(d) Indian consumers will buy more Chinese toys.

**Ans.** (b) If tax is imposed on Chinese toys then Indian toy-makers will prosper.

(iv) How have markets been transformed in recent years? Infer the correct option with reference to the above context.

(a) Goods become cheaper and have many choices to the user.
(b) Lower job opportunities for people.
(c) High competition among the makers of goods and services
(d) Both (a) and (c)

**Ans.** (d) Markets have been transformed in the recent years due to globalisation as the goods have become cheaper and provided people with many choices. It has also raised high competition among the makers of goods and services.

(v) How does foreign trade integrate the markets? With reference to the given context, infer the correct Codes

(a) Producers get an opportunity to go beyond their domestic markets.
(b) Producers can sell their produce in markets all over the world.
(c) Both (a) and (b)
(d) Foreign trade has limited the scope of enhancing trade among the countries.

**Ans.** (c) Foreign trade, has integrated the markets as the producers get an opportunity to go beyond their domestic markets and they can now sell their produce in markets all over the world.

(vi) Read the following statements and choose the incorrect statements about the impacts of Chinese goods on Indian goods market.

I. Indian goods are facing crises due to cheap products offered by China into the Indian markets.
II. Chinese goods dominate the Indian markets.
III. Indian goods are less expensive then Chinese goods.

**Codes**

(a) Both I and II
(b) Only II
(c) Only III
(d) Both II and III

**Ans.** (c) Statement III is incorrect. Indian goods are more expensive than Chinese goods.

PART 2

# Subjective Questions

## • Short Answer (SA) Type Questions

**1.** What is investment? Name the companies which make foreign investment. Write any two benefits which a local company expects from joint production with a Multinational company.

**Ans.** The money that is spent to buy assets such as land, building, machines and other equipments is called investment.

The companies which make foreign investment in India are Ford Motors, Nike, Coca-Cola, Pepsi, Honda, Nokia, Tata Motors, Infosys, Ranbaxy, Asian Paints, etc.

The benefits that a local company expects from joint production with a multinational company are

(*i*) To provide money for additional investments, like buying new machines for faster production.

(*ii*) To bring with them the latest technology for production.

**2.** How are local companies benefitted by collaborating with multinational companies? Explain with examples. **(CBSE 2013)**

**Ans.** The local companies are benefitted by collaborating with multinational companies in the following ways

(i) MNC's can finance the additional investments for the local companies like buying new machinery for faster production.

(ii) MNC's may provide the companies with latest technology for efficient production as MNC's have an international outreach.

(iii) Local companies will benefit financially through a partnership with an MNC because the production and its efficiency would naturally increase.

Hence, an MNC works at an international level, while local companies have a very small outreach. Therefore, a partnership with such a large company is beneficial for both.

**3.** What are the various ways in which MNCs set up or control production in other countries? **(CBSE 2016)**

*Or* Explain by giving examples that MNCs are spreading their production in different ways. **(CBSE 2019)**

**Ans.** The way in which MNCs control or spread their production are

- **By Buying Local Companies** Large MNCs buy companies that are operating locally. By doing this, they get a good customer base and the local company gets latest technology. For example, Cargill Foods (MNC) merged with Parakh Foods (local).
- **By Joint Ventures** MNCs set-up production units jointly with any company that may be operating in a country. By doing this, MNCs not only increase their production but also get a vast market. For example, Ford Motors set up automobile plant in collaboration with Mahindra and Mahindra.
- **By Placing Orders with Small Producers** MNCs place orders for their products with small producers in developing countries where the resources are cheap. Then the MNCs sell those products under their own brand. Ex Garments, footwear, jeans, footballs, etc.

**4.** List the factors that encourage the MNCs to set up their production units at a place.

*Or* Why do multinational corporations set up their offices and factories in certain areas only? **(CBSE 2019)**

**Ans.** The factors that promote the setting up of MNCs or the reason for setting up MNCs at a certain place are

- Availability of skilled and unskilled labour, e.g. India has highly skilled engineers who can understand the technical aspects of production.
- Availability of raw materials at cheap prices e.g. China provides the advantage of being a cheap manufacturing location.
- Well developed infrastructure like roads and railways
- Liberalised governmental policies.
- Closeness to markets e.g. Mexico and Eastern Europe are useful for their closeness to the markets in the US and Europe.
- Safe environment

**5.** 'Barriers on foreign trade and foreign investment were removed to a large extent in India since 1991. Justify the statement. **(CBSE 2016)**

*Or* Why did the Indian Government remove barriers to a large extent on foreign trade and foreign investment? **(CBSE 2015, 13)**

**Ans.** It is true that barriers on foreign trade and foreign investment were removed to a large extent in India since 1991 because

- In 1991, the Government of India liberalised its policy and felt that Indian producers must compete with producers around the world.
- The Government had an opinion that trade competition would improve the performance of the local producers within the country since they will be forced to improve their quality.

- Another reason was the economic crises in India in 1990-91 and support of WTO and IMF led the government to remove trade barriers.

**6.** "Information and Communication Technology (ICT) has played a major role in spreading out products and services across countries." Support this statement.

**Ans.** Information and Communication Technological (ICT) has played a major role in spreading out products and services across countries in the following ways

- Telecommunication facilities (telegraph, telephone including mobile phones, fax) are used to contact one another around the world, to access information instantly and to communicate from remote areas. This has been facilitated by satellite communication devices.
- Computers have started the amazing world of the Internet, where one can obtain and share information on almost anything. It also allows us to send instant electronic mail and (voice-mail) across the world at negligible costs which boosts trade and commerce.

**7.** How does Government attract foreign investment? Explain different ways. **(CBSE 2019)**

**Ans.** Government attracts foreign investment in the following ways

- Special Economic Zones have been set up to have world-class facilities such as cheap electricity, roads, transport, storage, etc.
- The companies setting their units in SEZs are exempted to pay tax for initial period of five years which increases their profit.
- Labour laws are made flexible in SEZs. This has attracted foreign investment.

**8.** Why had the Indian government put barriers to foreign trade and foreign investments after independence? Analyse the reason. **(CBSE 2016)**

**Ans.** Indian government put barriers to foreign trade and foreign investments after independence because

- To protect the domestic producers within the country from foreign competition in the form of imports.
- To encourage more production of goods so that more industries can be started.
- During 1950s and 1960s, Indian industries were just coming up, they were not prepared to face challenges from foreign countries.

**9.** Explain the facilities available in SEZ that are developed by Central and State governments to attract foreign Investment. **(CBSE 2019)**

**Ans.** SEZs are industrial zones set up by the government to promote the establishment of MNCs.

The facilities available in SEZ are

- SEZ are provided with world class facilities electricity, water, roads, transport, storage, recreational and educational facilities.
- Companies operating in SEZ do not have to pay taxes for five years.
- Government has allowed flexibility in the labour laws to attract MNCs.

**10.** "Globalisation has been advantageous to consumers as well as to producers." Support the statement with suitable examples. **(CBSE 2017)**

**Ans.** Globalisation has benefitted the producers and the consumers in the following ways

- Globalisation has led to an intense increase in industrial competition. As a result, producers are competing over each other to provide better and cheaper services to the consumers. This has also resulted in reduction in the prices.
- With the initiation of globalisation, producers now have relatively free access to international markets. Also, they can now avail more easily of the credit facilities forwarded in terms of capital and technology. This is illustrated by the example of the electronics goods and garments industry.
- Consumers have more choice of goods and services as compared to earlier times specially in modern digital technological equipments like cell phones, cameras etc.

**11.** Describe any four characteristics of WTO.

**Ans.** The four characteristics of WTO are

(i) World Trade Organisation (WTO) is a powerful international organisation.
(ii) It aims at liberalising international trade.
(iii) It establishes rules regarding international trade and sees that these rules are obeyed.
(iv) WTO is supposed to allow free trade for all countries. But in practice, it is seen that the developed countries have unfairly retained trade barriers.

**12.** How is stability in jobs for the workers affected due to globalisation?

**Ans.** The stability in jobs for the workers affected due to globalisation in the following ways

- There is no permanent employment, but workers are employed only when needed, i.e. they are 'flexible workers'. In the slack season, they are out of work with no compensation.
- Due to globalisation, the MNC's main objective is to lower costs. To do this, they provide temporary employment only and are given lower wages or they may have to work on per day basis.
- Workers may have to work for longer hours and be laid off from work without any compensation during the slack season.

**13.** "The impact of globalisation has not been uniform." Explain this statement.

*Or* "The impact of Globalisation has not been uniform." Explain with examples. **(CBSE 2020)**

**Ans.** The impact of globalisation has not been uniform as

- Globalisation has increased the sale of consumer goods which are demanded by only a small section of people in developing countries like cell phone, automobile, soft drinks. Large section is still deprived of basic necessities.
- Globalisation increases the concentration of economic power and leads to inequalities. It is mainly beneficial to large capitalists, industries and large companies like google. The small scale producers and workers have suffered as a result of rising competition.
- Globalisation has changed the nature of employment as now workers are hired on temporary basis and their jobs are no longer secure.

**14.** How has liberalisation of trade and investment policies helped the globalisation process?

**Ans.** Liberalisation of trade and investment policies has helped in Globalisation in the following ways

- This has helped in the import and export of goods. This means that goods can be exported and imported easily and also foreign companies could set up factories and offices here.
- Larger foreign investment and larger foreign trade have led to greater integration of production and markets across countries. As a result, more and more companies are coming closer to each other due to MNCs.
- Latest technology such as ICT is spread throughout the world due to liberalisation.

**15.** "Fair globalisation would create opportunities for all and also ensure that benefits of globalisation are shared better." Support the statement. **(CBSE 2014)**

*Or* How can the government of India play a major role to make globalisation more fair? Explain with examples. **(CBSE 2019)**

**Ans.** As fair globalisation would create opportunities for all and also ensure that benefits of globalisation are shared better, the government can play a major role in making globalisation a fair medium in the following ways

- By framing policies that protect the interests of not only the rich and powerful but also the weaker sections of the society.
- By supporting small producers so that they can compete with large manufacturers.
- By ensuring that labour laws are properly implemented and workers get their rights.
- By using trade and investment barriers and negotiating for fairer rules at the WTO.
- It can also align with other developing countries with similar interests to fight the domination of developed countries in the WTO.

## • Long Answer (LA) Type Questions

**1.** Why do Multinational Corporations (MNCs) set up their offices and factories in certain areas only? Explain any five reasons. **(CBSE 2019)**

**Ans.** Multinational Corporations set up their offices and factories in certain areas only due to the following reasons

(i) **Availability of Labour** The MNCs operate in a country to get cheap labour so they set up their factories where there is easy availability of skilled and unskilled labour.

(ii) **Availability of Raw Materials** The MNCs set up their factories where they get raw materials easily and at cheap prices.

(iii) **Well Developed Infrastructure** MNCs set up their offices and factories where there is good infrastructural facilities such as roads, railways, regular supply of electricity etc.

(iv) **Liberalised Government Policies** When the government encourages investment then it liberalises its trade policies so that MNCs could set up their offices at that place. So, MNCs set up in those areas where they get government support.

(v) **Closeness to Markets** MNCs set up their offices and industries in those places where there are good markets for selling their finished products. This reduces transportation cost also.

**2.** How has foreign trade been integrating markets of different countries ? Explain wth examples. **(CBSE 2018)**

**Ans.** Foreign trade has been integrating markets of different countries in following ways

- Since historic times foreign trade been the main channel of connecting countries, e.g. Silk route connects India and South Asia to markets both in the East and West. Foreign trade creates an opportunity for producers to reach beyond the domestic markets, i.e. markets of their own countries. Choice of goods in the markets rises. Prices of similar goods in the two markets tend to become equal. Producers in the two countries closely compete against each other even though they are separated by thousands of miles.
- With many MNCs in the market, the consumer has a wide range of products coming from different nations to choose from. Hence, it interlinks various markets across the countries. For example-Volkswagen, a German automobile company, is the biggest German automaker in the world. It came to India in 2007 and had recorded sales of 32,627 vehicles in the year 2010.

- Another example is Indian markets have a number of footwear brands available for customers. A consumer can decide what to purchase either from local footwear brands like Bata, Liberty, Red Chief or International brands like Nike, Skechers, Reebok etc as per his/her choice and need.

**3.** How have our markets been transformed in recent years? Explain with examples.

**Ans.** Our markets have been transformed in recent years due to the process of globalisation in the following ways

- As consumers in today's world, some of us have a wide choice of goods and services before us. The latest models of digital cameras, mobile phones and televisions made by the leading manufacturers of the world are within our reach.
- Every season, new models of automobiles can be seen on Indian roads. Gone are the days when Ambassador and Fiat were the only cars on Indian roads.
- Today, due to globalisation and foreign trade, Indians are buying cars produced by nearly all the top companies in the world.
- In the similar way, we can see a wide variety of brands in the market place e.g. from shirts to televisions to processed fruit juices and even chocolates and candies.

With the coming of MNCs in India, local companies are now adopting newer technology and production methods. Due to this changing pattern in production consumers in Indian markets are enjoying a much higher standard of living than ever before.

**4.** "Rapid improvement in technology has stimulated the globalisation process." Explain the statement with examples. **(CBSE 2020)**

**Ans.** Rapid improvement in technology has stimulated the globalisation process in the following ways

- There has been many improvements in transport facilities which help in export and import of goods. This increases trade relations between countries.
- Since technology improves efficiency, the process of exchange has become faster and cheaper.
- Development in information and communication technology has been the most beneficial since information can be now sent in seconds across the world.
- Development in IT also has led to the production of services through outsourcing for example, call centres, online teaching etc.
- Through internet facility, one can obtain and share information on almost anything, it allows to send e-mail and messages across the world at negligible costs.

For example, a news magazine published for London readers is to be designed and printed in Delhi. The magazine is sent through internet to the Delhi office. The designers in Delhi office get orders on how to design the magazine from the office in London using telecommunication facilities. The designing is done on a computer. After printing, the magazines are sent by air to London. Even the payment of money for designing and printing from a bank in London to a bank in Delhi is done instantly through the internet banking.

**5.** How can consumers and producers be benefited from 'foreign trade' ? Explain with examples.

**Ans.** Consumers and producers both are benefitted from 'foreign trade' in the following ways

- Foreign trade creates opportunities for the producers to sell their products not only in the domestic markets (within the country) but also all over the world. For example, Cafe Coffee Day which is an Indian MNC, exports its coffee to various countries like USA, Europe and Japan.
- Producers can also buy from the world market where raw material and labour is cheap. Similarly for the buyers, import of goods produced in another country is one way of expanding the choice of goods beyond what is domestically produced.
- Foreign trade facilitates by opening of trade goods which travel from one market to another. Choice of goods in the market rises.
- Producers in the two countries now closely compete against each other even though, they are far away to each other.
- Prices of similar goods in the two markets tend to become equal due to competition.

**6.** What is globalisation? Explain two positive and two negative impact of globalisation. **(CBSE 2016)**

**Ans.** Globalisation is the process of integration and interconnectedness between countries.

Positive impacts of Globalisation are

(i) Availability of variety of products with greater choice and quality at affordable price.

(ii) Creation of new jobs and higher standard of living.

Negative impact ofs Globalisation are

(i) Thousands of uneducated and unskilled labourers have become jobless due to closure of domestic units.

(ii) Most of the small industries like toys, tyres, plastics, dairy products are affected due to foreign competition. This results in their closure thereby reducing production.

## • Case Based Questions

**7.** Read the case given below and answer the following questions. **(CBSE 2020)**

**Source-A Globalisation and the Indian Economy**

As consumers in today's world, some of us have a wide choice of goods and services before us. The latest models of digital cameras, mobile phones and televisions made by the leading manufacturers of the world are within our reach. Every season, new models of automobiles can be seen on Indian roads.

(i) How is the impact of globalisation visible on consumers?

***Ans.*** The impact of globalisation is visible on consumers as due to globalisation there is a greater choice available before consumers who now enjoy improved quality and lower prices for several products.

**Source-B Foreign Trade and Integration of Markets**

Foreign trade creates an opportunity for the producers to reach beyond the domestic markets, i.e. markets of their own countries. Producers can sell their produce not only in markets located within the country but can also compete in markets located in other countries of the world.

Similarly, for the buyers, import of goods produced in another country is one way of expanding the choice of goods beyond what is domestically produced.

(ii) Explain the basic function of Foreign Trade.

***Ans.*** The basic functions of foreign trade is that it creates an opportunity for the producers to reach beyond the domestic markets i.e. markets of their own countries. Producers can sell their produce not only in markets located within the country but can also compete in markets located in other countries of the world.

**Source-C The Struggle for Fair Globalisation**

In the past few years, massive campaigns and representation by people's organisations have influenced important decisions relating to trade and investments at the WTO. This has demonstrated that people also can play an important role in the struggle for fair globalisation.

(iii) How do people play an important role in the struggle for fair globalisation ? Explain.

***Ans.*** People play an important role in the struggle for fair globalisation as they organise massive campaigns and protests and influence the trade and investment policies of the World Trade Organisation (WHO) and their own countries as well.

**8.** Read the cases/sources given below and answer the questions that follow.

MNC is not only selling its finished products globally, but more important, the goods and services are produced globally. As a result, production is organised in increasingly complex ways. The production process is divided into small parts and spread out across the globe. In the above example, China provides the advantage of being a cheap manufacturing location. Mexico and Eastern Europe are useful for their closeness to the markets in the US and Europe.

India has highly skilled engineers who can understand the technical aspects of production. It also has educated English speaking youth who can provide customer care services. And all this probably can mean 50-60 per cent cost savings for the MNC! The advantage of spreading out production across the borders to the multinationals can be truly immense.

(i) Why MNC's prefer India as their destination for setting business?

***Ans.*** MNC's prefer India as their destination for setting business due to the following reasons

- India has highly skilled engineers who can understand the technical aspects of production.
- India also has educated English speaking youth. It has cheap labour and resources.

(ii) What kind of criterias are looked upon by the MNC's for Investment?

***Ans.*** MNC look for various criterias before investing such as availability of skilled-unskilled labour, closeness to the markets, government policies that look after their interest, etc.

(iii) To what extent do you agree that SEZs are encouraged by the government for MNCs?

***Ans.*** Government encourage SEZs which is known from the fact that government provides world class facilities like electricity, water, roads, transport, storage, recreational and educational facilities in these industrial zones. SEZs are encouraged so that MNCs set up their factories or offices in SEZs.

# Chapter Test

## Objective Questions

**1.** Enabling producers of one country to sell their goods in other countries is known as

(a) globalisation (b) trade

(c) foreign trade (d) None of these

**2.** Which one of the following types of countries has benefitted most from globalisation?

(a) Rich countries (b) Developed countries

(c) Developing countries (d) All of these

**3.** What does fair globalisation means? Choose the correct option

(a) Fair opportunities for all (b) Fair benefits for all

(c) More support to small producers (d) All of these

**4.** Choose the incorrect option about Globalisation from the given statements.

I. Globalisation causes integration of markets as well as production centres.

II. Globalisation has increased migration of people.

III. It has facilitated new and imporved technology by which even local companies can take benefit.

IV. Globalisation has increased trade restrictions among the regions of the world.

**Codes**

(a) Only I (b) Both I and II

(c) Only III (d) Only IV

**5.** With the growing competition, most employers these days prefer to employ workers ............ .

(a) flexibly (b) selectively

(c) rationally (d) None of these

## Short Answer Type Questions

**6.** Explain any three methods of controlling production across countries by MNCs.

**7.** What is the impact of globalisation on the richer sections of society in urban India?

**8.** Explain the impact of flexible labour laws on workers.

**9.** Explain three ways in which pressure of competition due to globalisation has significantly changed the lives of Indian workers.

**10.** How do local companies get two-fold production benefits through MNCs? Explain.

## Long Answer Type Questions

**11.** Explain the good and bad effects of globalisation on Indian industry.

**12.** In what ways are MNCs different from national companies? Explain by giving three reasons.

**13.** Explain the whole process in which an MNC works.

## Answers

**1.** (c) foreign trade **2.** (b) Developed countries **3.** (d) All of these

**4.** (d) Only IV **5.** (a) flexibly

# CBSE Term II Social Science X

# Practice Papers 1-3

Social Science Class 10th (Term II)

# Practice Paper 1*
## (Solved)

*Instructions*

- **Time :** 2 Hours
- **Max. Marks :** 40

1. This question paper is divided into four sections A, B, C and D.
2. Section A has 1 question including case based multiple choice questions.
3. Section B has 5 questions including short answer questions with internal choice.
4. Section C has 3 questions including long answer questions with internal choice.
5. Section D has 1 question based on map.
6. Marks are mentioned against each question.
7. There is no negative marking.

***As exact Blue-print and Pattern for CBSE Term II exams is not released yet, so the pattern of this paper is designed by the author on the basis of trend of past CBSE Papers. Students are advised not to consider the pattern of this paper as official, it is just for practice purpose.***

## Section A

*This section consists of one case based question.*

**Case Based MCQs**

**1.** Read the given case/source and answer the questions that follow by choosing the correct option.

Emboldened with this success, Gandhiji in 1919 decided to launch a nationwide Satyagraha against the proposed Rowlatt Act (1919). This Act had been hurriedly passed through the Imperial Legislative Council despite the united opposition of the Indian members. It gave the government enormous powers to repress political activities, and allowed detention of political prisoners without trial for two years. Mahatma Gandhi wanted non-violent civil disobedience against such unjust laws, which would start with a hartal on 6 April. Rallies were organized in various cities, workers went on strike in railway workshops, and shops closed down. Alarmed by the popular upsurge, and scared that lines of communication such as the railways and telegraph would be disrupted, the British administration decided to clamp down on nationalists. Local leaders were picked up from Amritsar, and Mahatma Gandhi was barred from entering Delhi. On 10 April, the police in Amritsar fired upon a peaceful procession, provoking widespread attacks on banks, post offices and railway stations. Martial law was imposed and General Dyer took command. $(1 \times 5 = 5)$

(i) During the Indian Freedom Struggle, why did Rowlatt Act arouse popular indignation? Infer the correct option from the given information.

(a) It curbed the Trade Union Activities.
(b) It authorised the government to imprison people without trial.
(c) It imposed restrictions on Freedom of Press.
(d) It suppressed the Traditional Indian Education System.

(ii) Fill in the blanks with suitable option.

The first venture of Gandhi in all India politics was in the form of ............................... . Identify the best suitable option.

(a) Non-Cooperation Movement
(b) Dandi March
(c) Rowlatt Satyagraha
(d) Champaran Movement

(iii) Identify the reason/s behind the passing of Rowlatt Act from the given options.

(a) To curtail the national and revolutionary activities.
(b) To have a favourable balance of trade with Indian Merchants.
(c) To limit the scope of individual liberty.
(d) Both (a) and (b)

(iv) Why did Gandhiji decided to launch a nationwide Satyagraha against the Rowlatt Act? Identify the best suitable option.

(a) Because it was an undemocratic measure adopted by the British government.
(b) Because it had become an emotive political issue among the Indians.
(c) Both (a) and (b)
(d) Because common people were humiliated by the Britishers.

(v) The Martial Law imposed by General Dyer deprived the people of which of the following rights? Choose the best suitable option.

(a) Right of Assembling
(b) Right to Protest
(c) Right to Publish any Information
(d) Both (a) and (b)

## Section B

*This section consists of 5 questions of Short Answer Type.*

### Short Answer Questions

**2.** "Not all social groups were moved by the abstract concept of Swaraj." Support the statement in the light of Civil Disobedience Movement of 1930s. (3)

*Or*

Explain any three effects of the Non-Cooperation Movement on the economy of India.

**3.** What should the developing countries demand in return for liberalising their trade and investment for the developed countries? (3)

*Or*

What is WTO? How does WTO facilitate free trade for all countries? Analyse with examples.

**4.** After having which major improvements the Indian Railways has become one of the modern means of transport? (3)

*Or*

What are the major reasons due to which only air transport is much popular in the North-Eastern parts of India?

**5.** Why is there overwhelming support for the idea of democracy all over the world? Explain. (3)

**6.** Why is Barter system considered difficult to trade a commodity? Give any three reasons. (3)

## Section C

*This section consists of 3 questions of Long Answer Type.*

### Long Answer Questions

**7.** Do you think that political parties are necessary for democracy? Give reasons. (5)

*Or*

How did the growing role of money and muscle power in political party become a threat for democracy?

**8.** "Money cannot buy all the goods and services that you may need to live well." Explain the statement. (5)

*Or*

"The Reserve Bank of India supervises the functioning of formal sources of loans." Explain the statement.

**9.** How economic strength of a country is measured by the development of manufacturing industries? (5)

*Or*

"Chota Nagpur region have the maximum concentration of iron and steel industries? Analyse the statement.

# Section D

### Map Based Question

**10.** (i) On the given political map of India, two places are marked as A and B. Identify them with the help of the following informations.

A. The place where Indian National Congress was held in 1927. (1)

B. The place where the Cotton Mill Workers Satyagraha took place. (1)

(ii) On the same outline map of India, mark and locate the following.:

(a) Netaji Subhash Chandra Bose International Airport (1)

(b) Kochi Sea Port (1)

(c) Kakrapara Nuclear Power Plant (1)

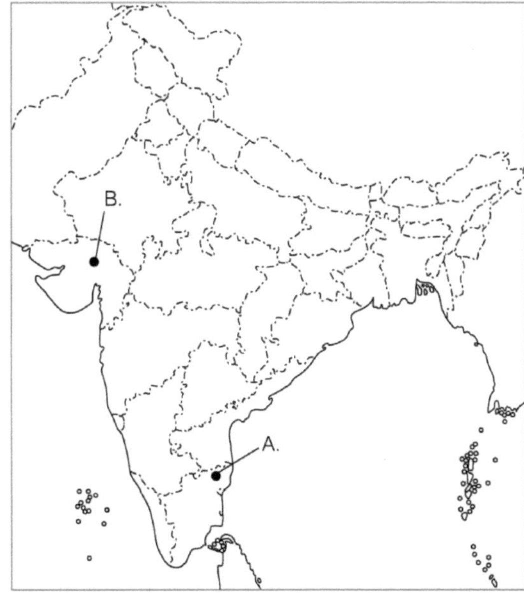

# Answers

1. (i) (b) During the Indian Freedom struggle, the Rowlatt Act arouses popular indignation because it authorised the government to imprison people without trial.

   (ii) (c) The First venture of Gandhiji in all India Politics was in the form of Rowlatt Satyagraha.

   (iii) (a) The reason behind the passing of Rowlatt Act was to curtail the national and revolutionary activities against the British Rule.

   (iv) (c) Gandhiji decided to launch a nationwide Satyagraha against the Rowlatt Act because it was an undemocratic measure adopted by the British government as well as this issue had become an emotive political issue among the Indians.

   (v) (d) The Martial Law was imposed by General Dyer which deprived the people with Right to Protest and Right of Assembling at one place.

2. In April 1930, Gandhiji launched the Civil Disobedience Movement but all social groups were not moved by the abstract concept of Swaraj or full independence. One such social group was the 'dalit'.

   Dalit or oppressed were the 'untouchable' class of our society. Many dalit leaders, specially Dr. BR Ambedkar were keen on a different political solution to the problems of the community. They believed political empowerment would only resolve the problems of their social disability. They demanded reserved seats in educational institutions and separate electorate in the Legislative councils. Thus, Dalit participation in the Civil Disobedience Movement was limited particularly in Maharashtra and Nagpur region, where the organisation of dalit was quite strong.

   *Or*

   The effects of Non-Cooperation Movement on the economic front were

   (*i*) Foreign goods were boycotted, liquor shops picketed and foreign clothes were burnt hugely.

   (*ii*) The import of foreign clothes halved between 1921 and 1922, its value dropping from 102 crore to 57 crore rupees. In many areas, traders and merchants refused to trade in foreign goods and sometimes even they refused to finance foreign trade.

   (*iii*) As the boycott movement spread, people used only Indian clothes and began to discard foreign clothes. As a result, production of Indian textile mills and handloom went up largely.

3. The demands of developing countries in return for liberalising their trade and investment for the developed countries are

   - The developing countries should demand foreign aid from them.
   - They should strongly demand for the removal of trade barriers in developed countries so that they can export to these countries.
   - They should demand for advanced technology at low prices.
   - They should also demand for long-term credit, so that they can open many production units and give jobs.

   *Or*

   The World Trade Organisation (WTO) is an international organisation dealing with the global rules of trade between nations. WTO was started at the initiative of the developed countries. Its objective is to liberalise international trade and ensure that its members obey its rules.

   The World Trade Organisation does the following functions to facilitate free trade for all countries

   - It implement rules and provisions related to trade policy review mechanism.
   - It provide a platform to member countries to decide future strategies related to trade and tariff.
   - It provide facilities for implementation, administration and operation of multilateral and bilateral agreements of the world trade.
   - It administer the rules and processes related to dispute settlement.

4. After having the following improvements, the Indian Railways has become one of the modern means of transport

   - Electrification of railway lines to reduce burden on fossil fuels and to increase speed.
   - Introduction of computerised reservation system for convenience of passengers. Conversion of metre gauge lines to broad gauge to ensure higher speed and carrying capacity.
   - Construction of new railway lines to improve the connectivity in the country. Replacing steam engines, which cause heavy pollution, by diesel and electric engines.

   *Or*

   Major reasons due to which only air transport is much popular in the North-Eastern parts of India are

   - Big and wide rivers are present there, due to which rails or road bridges over them are difficult and costly to construct. These rivers also get flooded frequently, due to which surface communication links are damaged.
   - This area has dissected relief features, preventing durable construction of rail and road links.
   - Dense forests in this region create many difficulties in construction of railway lines and roads.

**5.** There is an overwhelming support for the idea of democracy all over the world because we generally think that democracy can address all socio-economic and political problems. However, our expectations from democracy are not always fulfilled. Sometimes it may work slowly, less efficiently, having a poor response or not working cleanly.

But, in democracy, regular and free elections are held. Also, there is always scope for open public debate. The government is the people's own government as it has been elected by them. People wish to be ruled by the people they have elected. They also feel that this form of government is best for their country, thus, giving it overwhelming support.

**6.** Three reasons for the Barter system being considered difficult to trade a commodity are

(i) There are many products which cannot be divided or subdivided. For example, if the price of a cow is equal to 100 shirts, then a person having one shirt cannot exchange it for a part of the cow, as it is not possible to divide the cow into small pieces without destroying its utility.

(ii) Deciding the value of goods is difficult. For example, one can offer 1 kg rice for a pair of shoes whereas the shoe owner can demand 2 kg rice for the same shoes.

(iii) Double coincidence of wants is necessary. It means that both parties have to agree to sell and buy each other's commodities. Thus, if a farmer wants to sell his rice in exchange for a pair of shoes, then he has to find a shoe owner who wants to exchange a pair of shoes for rice.

**7.** Yes, political parties are necessary for democracy because

- If every elected representative is independent, which means he or she is not attached with a political party, then he/she will not make promise for any major policy changes. The government may be formed but its utility will remain uncertain. Non-party based Panchayat election also face the same problem.
- The rise of political parties is directly linked to the emergence of representative democracies.
- As society became larger and complicated, they also need some agency to gather different views on various issues and to present these to the government.
- Political parties inform the people about the working of the ruling party. They talk about the problems of the state, the working and failure of the government and give suggestion for the upliftment of masses. Thus, Political Party acts as a link between government and masses.

*Or*

In India, there is a growing role of money and muscle power in political parties during elections in the following ways

- Political parties are focused on winning the elections only due to which, they tend to cluster around rich people, big companies and ignore other candidates. In this way, the rich and influential people who may not be able and just, get the favour of political parties, while the able and honest candidates lag behind.
- Political parties tend to nominate those candidates who have or can raise lots of money. Rich people and companies who give funds to the parties, tend to have influence on the policies and decisions of the parties, when it is in power.
- Sometimes, parties support criminals who can win elections with their muscle power. Criminals use various illegal activities such as booth capturing, threatening and bribing the voters in order to take votes.

In this way, the increasing role of money and muscle power in political parties has become a threat for democracy.

**8.** It is true that money cannot buy all the goods and services that we may need to live well as

- Money can buy things that can be one factor on which our life depends like food, house, car, clothes etc. But the quality of non-material things like freedom, security and respect cannot be bought with money.
- Money is not all for a person to live a life adequately.
- Income is the source of material of services and goods that a person use in his daily life.
- Money is not a source of happy life because there are many rich people who are not happy even they have enough money to purchase goods and services.
- We cannot buy pollution free environment, unadulterated medicines and peace with money unless we can afford to shift to a community that already has all these non- material things.
- Money may also not be able to protect us from infectious diseases, unless the whole of our community takes some preventive steps.

*Or*

The Reserve Bank of India supervises the functioning of formal sources of loans in India in the following ways

- The Reserve Bank of India monitors that the banks actually maintain the cash balance and do not give all the deposits as loans.
- The Reserve Bank of India ensures that the banks give loans not just to profit-making businesses and rich traders, but also to small cultivators, small scale industries, small borrowers, etc.
- Periodically, banks have to submit information to the Reserve Bank of India on how much they are lending, to whom, etc.
- The rate of interest charged on loans given by the banks is decided by the Reserve bank.
- The RBI keeps a check on all the activities of banks and checks the flow of credit also.

9. The economic strength of a country is measured by the development of manufacturing industries in the following ways
   - Manufacturing industries help in modernising agriculture, which forms the backbone of our economy.
   - Manufacturing also reduces the heavy dependence of people on agricultural income by providing them jobs in secondary and tertiary sectors.
   - Industrial development helps in removal of unemployment and poverty. It also aims at bringing down regional differences by establishing industries in backward areas.
   - Export of manufactured goods expands trade and commerce and brings in foreign exchange. During the last 20 years, the share of the manufacturing sector has stayed at 17 % of GDP. This is much lower than some East Asian economies, where it is 25-35 %. The desired growth rate over the next decade is 12 per cent which has been around only 7 per cent in the last decade. To develop the sector of manufacturing industries, government has set-up the National Manufacturing Competitiveness Council (NMCC).

*Or*

Chota Nagpur region have the maximum concentration of iron and steel industries because
   - **Low Cost of Iron Ore** Iron mines are located in the nearby areas. It helps to reduce the transportation cost of iron ore to the industries.
   - **High Grade Raw Materials in Proximity** Bulky raw materials like coking coal, limestone are also available in proximity in this region.
   - **Availability of Cheap Labour** From the adjoining areas of Bihar, Jharkhand and Odisha cheap labour is available in abundance.
   - **Dense** Transport Network This region is well connected with roadways and railways that help in the swift movement of raw materials and finished goods to the industry and market areas, respectively.
   - **Port Facilities** Kolkata is a well developed port that is near to this area.

10. 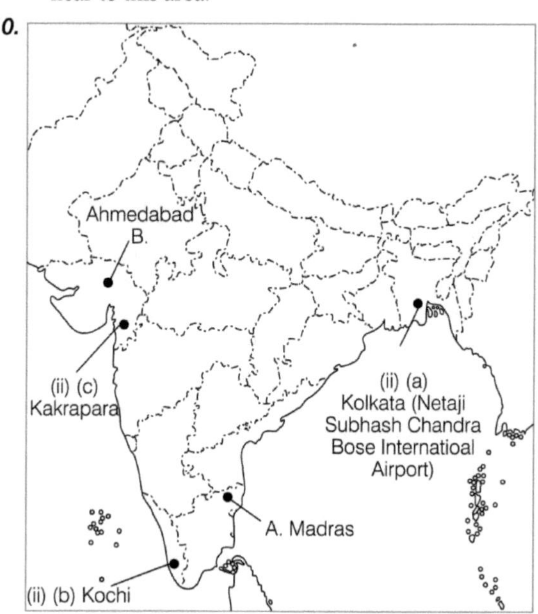

Social Science Class 10th (Term II)

# Practice Paper 2*

## (Unsolved)

*Instructions*

- **Time :** 2 Hours
- **Max. Marks :** 40

1. This question paper is divided into four sections A, B, C and D.
2. Section A has 1 question including case based multiple choice questions.
3. Section B has 5 questions including short answer questions with internal choice.
4. Section C has 3 questions including long answer questions with internal choice.
5. Section D has 1 question based on map.
6. Marks are mentioned against each question.
7. There is no negative marking.

***As exact Blue-print and Pattern for CBSE Term II exams is not released yet, so the pattern of this paper is designed by the author on the basis of trend of past CBSE Papers. Students are advised not to consider the pattern of this paper as official, it is just for practice purpose.***

## Section A

*This section consists of one case based question.*

**Case Based MCQs**

**1.** Read the given source and answer the following questions.

Democracies that follow a federal system all over the world tend to have two kinds of political parties: parties that are present in only one of the federal units and parties that are present in several or all units of the federation. This is the case in India as well. There are some countrywide parties, which are called 'National parties'. These parties have their units in various states. But by and large, all these units follow the same policies, programmes and strategy that is decided at the national level.

Every party in the country has to register with the Election Commission. While the Commission treats all parties equally, it offers some special facilities to large and established parties. These parties are given a unique symbol- only the official candidates of that party can use that election symbol. Parties that get this privilege and some other special facilities are 'recognised' by the Election Commission for this purpose. That is why these parties are called, 'recognised political parties'. $(1 \times 5 = 5)$

(i) Political parties are the most visible institutions in a democracy. Identify the incorrect statement from the given options regarding political parties.

I. They are a necessary condition for a democracy.
II. They help the government to make policies.
III. Most people in a democracy are not critical of Political Parties.

**Codes**

(a) Only I
(b) Both I and II
(c) Only III
(d) Both II and III

(ii) Which of the following Political Parties is an example of National Parties? Identify the correct option.
(a) Bharatiya Janata Party
(b) Samajwadi Party
(c) Rashtriya Lok Dal
(d) Shiromani Akali Dal

(iii) Which of the following options is a correct meaning of a 'Recognised Party'?
(a) A party that is present in one of the federal units.
(b) A party that is provided with all the privileges and facilities by the Election Commission.
(c) A party that is based on regional and communal diversities.
(d) A party that is present in several units of the federation.

(iv) Which among the following facilities is offered by the Election Commission to a recognised political party?
(a) Manifesto
(b) Election Funds
(c) Members of the Party
(d) Election Symbols

(v) What is the main purpose behind the Election symbols allotted to political parties? Identify the correct option.
(a) As symbols are used for campaigning before the elections.
(b) To facilitate voting by illiterate people.
(c) As it attracts only educated voters.
(d) None of the above

## Section B

*This section consists of 5 questions of Short Answer Type.*

### Short Answer Questions

**2.** How does democracy produce an accountable government? (3)

*Or*

Which values make democracy better than any other form of government? Explain.

**3.** Why do we need to expand formal sources of credit in India? Explain. (3)

*Or*

"Banks are efficient medium of exchange." Support the statement with arguments.

**4.** Describe any three features of Indian Tourism as a trade. (3)

*Or*

Explain the significance of Mass Communication in India.

**5.** "Nationalism spreads when people begin to believe that they are all part of the same nation." Justify the statement. (3)

**6.** Explain the functions and importance of World Trade Organisation (WTO). (3)

## Section C

*This section consists of 3 questions of Long Answer Type.*

### Long Answer Questions

**7.** Globalisation and MNC's have a great impact on the lives of workers. Analyse the statement. (5)

*Or*

Explain in what ways has competition affected workers, Indian exporters and foreign MNC's in the garment industry.

**8.** "Railways are the lifelines of the country." Comment. (5)

*Or*

In India roads are classified in different classes according to their capacity. State different types of roads in brief.

**9.** How the Salt March was an effective symbol of resistance against colonialism? Explain. (5)

*Or*

"Various classes and groups of Indians participated in the Civil Disobedience with different objectives." Justify the statement.

## Section D

### Map Based Question

**10.** (i) On the given political map of India, two places are marked as A and B. Identify them with the help of given information.

A. The place where Jallianwala Bagh incident took place. (1)

B. The place where Non-Cooperation Movement was called off. (1)

(ii) On the same outline map of India, mark and locate the following:

(a) Tarapur Nuclear Power Plant (1)

(b) Namrup Thermal Plant (1)

(c) Durgapur Iron and Steel Plant (1)

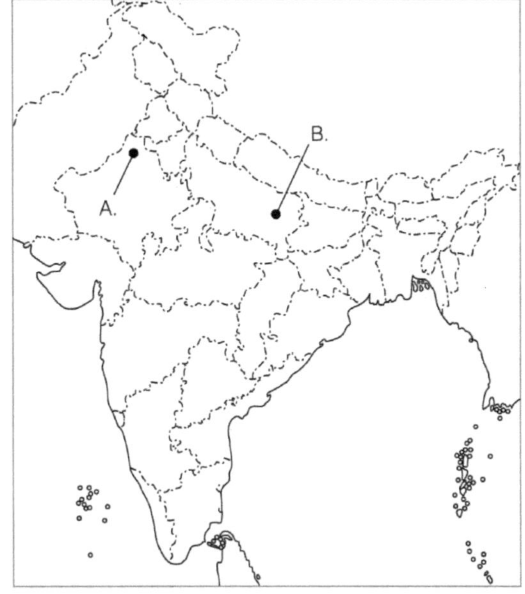


# Answers

*1. (i) (c) (ii) (a) (iii) (b) (iv) (d) (v) (b)*

*10. (i)* A. Amritsar
B. Chauri Chaura

Social Science Class 10th (Term II)

# Practice Paper 3*

## (Unsolved)

***Instructions***

- **Time** : 2 Hours
- **Max. Marks** : 40

1. This question paper is divided into four sections A, B, C and D.
2. Section A has 1 question including case based multiple choice questions.
3. Section B has 5 questions including short answer questions with internal choice.
4. Section C has 3 questions including long answer questions with internal choice.
5. Section D has 1 question based on map.
6. Marks are mentioned against each question.
7. There is no negative marking.

**** As exact Blue-print and Pattern for CBSE Term II exams is not released yet, so the pattern of this paper is designed by the author on the basis of trend of past CBSE Papers. Students are advised not to consider the pattern of this paper as official, it is just for practice purpose.***

## Section A

*This section consists of one case based question.*

**Case Based MCQs**

**1.** Read the given source and answer the following questions.

The exchange of goods among people, states and countries is referred to as trade. The market is the place where such exchanges take place. Trade between two countries is called international trade. It may take place through sea, air or land routes. While local trade is carried in cities, towns and villages, state level trade is carried between two or more states. Advancement of international trade of a country is an index to its economic prosperity. It is, therefore, considered the economic barometer for a country.

As the resources are space bound, no country can survive without international trade. Export and import are the components of trade. The balance of trade of a country is the difference between its export and import. When the value of export exceeds the value of imports, it is called a favourable balance of trade. On the contrary, if the value of imports exceeds the value of exports, it is termed as unfavorable balance of trade. India has trade relations with all the major trading blocks and all geographical regions of the world. The commodities exported from India to other countries include gems and jewellery, chemicals and related products, agriculture and allied products, etc. $(1 \times 5 = 5)$

(i) How International trade maximises world output? Choose the best suitable option:

(a) Through countries specialising in production of goods they are best suited for.
(b) Through competition between countries and other special regions.
(c) Through countries reducing various imposed taxes.
(d) All of the above

(ii) Why no country can survive without International Trade? Infer the correct option with reference to the given context.
(a) Because it helps in bringing economic prosperity.
(b) Because it helps in exchange of surplus goods with those of deficit countries.
(c) Because it helps to increase Foreign Exchange Reserves.
(d) All of the above

(iii) **Assertion** (A) Trade is economically important for a country.

**Reason** (R) Trading helps largely in developing countries like India. Advancement of trade is an index to its economic prosperity.

**Codes**
(a) Both A and R are true and R is the correct explanation of A
(b) Both A and R are true, but R is not the correct explanation of A
(c) A is true, but R is false
(d) A is false, but R is true

(iv) Which factors can influence a country's Balance of Trade? Identify the correct option.
(a) Trade Policies (b) Foreign exchange rates (c) Both (a) and (b) (d) High Import duty

(v) Fill in the blank with suitable option.

In order to make favourable balance of trade, the government should ............ .
(a) impose taxes on local producers (b) give priorities to local producers
(c) excel in the areas of production (d) impose trade barriers

## Section B

*This section consists of 5 questions of Short Answer Type.*

### Short Answer Questions

**2.** "History and fiction, folklore and songs, popular prints and symbols all played a part in making of nationalism in India." Support the statement. (3)

*Or*

Who formed the Swaraj Party? Why was the party formed?

**3.** How credit has its own unique role for development? State any three reasons. (3)

*Or*

"Banks and cooperative societies are required to increase their lending facilities in rural ares." Give reasons to explain the statement.

**4.** Pipelines transportation network is a new arrival on the transportation map of India. Analyse its merits and demerits. (3)

*Or*

"Road transport in India is not competitive but complementary to railways." Justify the statement by giving three points.

**5.** Why political parties are called the government in disguise? Give three arguments in this regard. (3)

**6.** "A public expression of dissatisfaction with democracy shows the success of democratic project." Justify the statement. (3)

## Section C

*This section consists of 3 questions of Long Answer Type.*

### Long Answer Questions

**7.** How the Civil Disobedience Movement came into force in various parts of the country and united different groups in the country? (5)

*Or*

How the Non-Cooperation Movement came into force and united the country?

**8.** Explain five political outcomes of democracy. (5)

*Or*

In actual life democracies do not appear to be very successful in reducing economic inequalities. Explain the statement.

**9.** Write down the advantages of Foreign Trade. (5)

*Or*

What are the merits and demerits of globalisation in a developing country such as India?

## Section D

### Map Based Question

**10.** (i) On the given political map of India two places are marked as A and B. Identify them with the help of given information.

A. The place where the movement of Indigo Planters took place. (1)

B. The place where Congress session took place in December 1920. (1)

(ii) On the same outline map of India, locate and label the following.

(a) Meenam Bakkam International Airport (1)

(b) Marmagao Port (1)

(c) Indore Cotton Textile Industry (1)

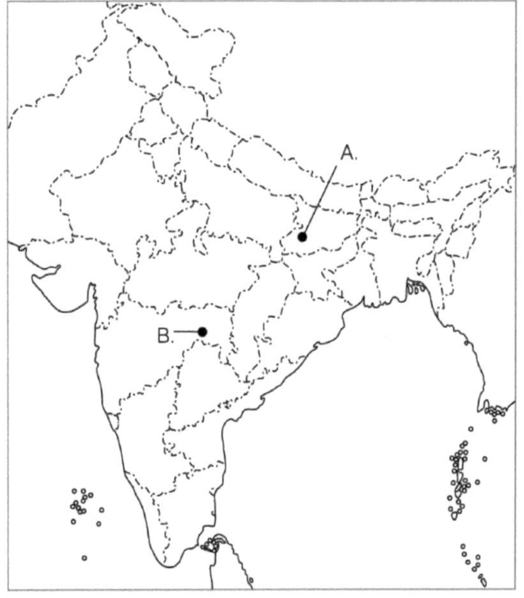


## Answers

*1. (i) (a) (ii) (d) (iii) (a) (iv) (c) (v) (a)*

*10. (i)* A. Champaran

B. Nagpur

Printed by Libri Plureos GmbH in Hamburg,
Germany